Hieroglyphics and Other Essays

ARTHUR MACHEN

Hieroglyphics and Other Essays

Edited by S. T. Joshi

Hippocampus Press

New York

Published by Hippocampus Press
P.O. Box 641, New York, NY 10156.
www.hippocampuspress.com

Hippocampus Press logo designed by Anastasia Damianakos.
Cover art and design by Dan Sauer, dansauerdesign.com

1 3 5 7 9 8 6 4 2

ISBN 978-1-61498-359-0 (paperback)
ISBN 978-1-61498-363-7 (ebook)

Contents

Introduction **7**

I. Hieroglyphics: A Note upon Ecstasy in Literature **11**

II. Philosophy: First Principles **117**

God's Beasts 119

True Comfort 124

Preface to *Afterglow* 128

Man, the Mad Mammal 133

Farewell to Materialism 137

Can We Trust Tradition? 150

III. Literary Criticism: First Principles **155**

Aristotle and Art 157

The "Inhumanity" of Art 161

The Paradox of Literature 166

Realism and Symbol 170

Science and Art 175

A Vision 180

The Wonder from Wales 183

Romance and Reality: An Introduction 189

IV. Books and Authors **193**

American Letter 195

The Matter of Romance 199

A New War Poet 206

Books of To-day 209

Jack London the Man 213

Le Morte Darthur 217

Poet and—Cockney 221
Introduction to *A Handy Dickens* 224

V. Fantasy, Horror, and the Occult 235
Review of *The War of the Worlds* by H. G. Wells 237
Science and the Ghost Story 241
Folklore and Legends of the North 248
The Literature of Occultism 256
Mr. Algernon Blackwood: Some Brilliant Short Stories 261
Poe the Enchanter 263
The Black Art 267
Has Spiritualism Come to Stay? 271
An Ancient Mystery 275
Detective Stories and Real Life 278
The Line of Terror 282
The Other Side 286
The Fair Folk 290
Magic Still Flourishes 293
Introduction to *Witches and Warlocks* 297

Bibliography 303

Introduction

What is not realised by many readers who delight in the superb horror fiction of Arthur Machen (1863–1947) is the extent to which his nonfiction—largely in the form of journalism or literary essays—quantitatively dwarfs his stories to insignificance. Machen published in many of the leading British magazines of the period, and from the 1890s to the 1930s he was a much sought-after writer of what were called "leading articles" for such literary weeklies and monthlies as *Literature, T.P.'s Weekly*, the *Bookman*, the *Academy*, and many others. The core of Machen's philosophy—metaphysics, ethics, aesthetics, even politics—is to be found here. It is remarkable that Machen himself gathered so few of these pieces into volumes during his lifetime; such books as *Dog and Duck* (1924), *Dreads and Drolls* (1926), and *The Glitter of the Brook* (1932) collect only a fraction of this body of work.

This volume reprints a series of essays that provide key insights into Machen's philosophical and literary temperament, and should thereby facilitate the appreciation of his fiction. *Hieroglyphics* is his most sustained treatise on aesthetics; and although its basic premise may be flawed—he sees such writers as Cervantes, Dickens, and others as embodying the all-important quality of "ecstasy," whereas such realists as Jane Austen or George Eliot do not because, in Machen's opinion, their work lacks this quality and they seek only to reproduce daily life with the mechanical faithfulness of a camera—it is a valuable guide to Machen's own literary preferences, and could perhaps form the basis for an aesthetic justification of the entire genre of weird fiction.

Machen has long been known as a mystic, and the comment that opens "The Black Art" (1911) could stand as a summation for his entire outlook on life: "There is deeply implanted in every sane human heart the love of mystery, the desire of wonder." Let us bypass the sarcastic emphasis on "sane"—a ploy Machen would use to condemn scientists, businessmen, and other purportedly unimaginative types as creatures scarcely belonging to the human race. Machen continues to speak in this essay of a "consciousness of a hidden, awful, and transcendent reality latent in the whole process of the material universe," and it is exactly this that he sought to illuminate in his own tales and novels.

Unfortunately, Machen—as both a mystic and an Anglo-Catholic—felt the need to wage a vicious and, it must be admitted, sadly inept polemic against science, which he felt was depriving the world of the "wonder" that he saw everywhere. He could scarcely have understood H. P. Lovecraft's comment (expressed in connexion with the advances of astrophysics in the 1930s): "The more we learn about the cosmos, the more bewildering does it appear." Interestingly, however, Machen had nothing but scorn for conventional occultism and spiritualism. He knew that most such purported manifestations were hokum and humbug, and he was too canny to be taken in by them. He himself was the victim of a bizarre incident whereby his invented "Angels of Mons"—who, in "The Bowmen" (1914), came to rescue a beleaguered English battalion during the first world war—were taken as an "actual" supernatural incident, and as late as "Has Spiritualism Come to Stay?" (1919) he is still complaining about the trouble it has caused him. But Machen in a sense wants to have his cake and eat it too: while scoffing at most occultist phenomena, he believes that perhaps a slim residue may perhaps reflect some actual strangeness in the world.

"Folklore and Legends of the North" (1898) is of direct relevance to Machen's fiction in focusing on the "little people," who make such a baleful intrusion in some of his best tales, including "Novel of the Black Seal" and "The Shining Pyramid." Here Machen says—decades before Margaret A. Murray gave a momentary scholarly imprimatur to the theory in *The Witch-Cult in Western Europe* (1921)—that there is "abundant proof" of the existence of a squat, non-Aryan race that once dwelt on the underside of civilisation, so that in a sense his use of the "little people" was a kind of science fiction!

Machen's astuteness as a critic of weird fiction is displayed in several places. It is not surprising that, in "The Literature of Occultism" (1899) and other essays, he finds fiction based on occultist conceptions far more satisfying than the dreary treatises that deal with the subject. His prejudice against science, however, prevents him from appreciating H. G. Wells's *War of the Worlds*, since he is convinced that "the things of the mind, of the soul" are "alone really wonderful." In later essays he finds M. R. James wanting (James's stories are merely "academic exercises in ghostly things"), but expresses great approbation of fellow-mystic Algernon Blackwood and also Walter de la Mare.

Machen tended to repeat himself in many of his essays, so that a relatively small number of them will convey quite adequately the range of his philosophical conceptions. In a recent review Steven J. Mariconda has mentioned that "Machen strikes us as the most unhappy of mystics"; and although this view may perhaps be partially contrasted with such essays as "God's Beasts" (1912) and "True Comfort" (1912), there is a fundamental truth to the remark. Machen waged unending war against the forces—science, materialism, the "business mentality"—that he felt were destroying civilization, and perhaps toward the end of his life he felt that the battle was lost. But that he left behind a small body of imperishable weird fiction, along with a handful of superbly crafted essays, is perhaps the only triumph he could have achieved; and it was a noble triumph indeed.

A Note on This Edition

My text of *Hieroglyphics* is a somewhat eclectic one, deriving largely from the first edition (London: Grant Richards, 1902) but taking into consideration some apparently deliberate revisions that Machen made in later editions (London: Martin Secker, 1910, 1912, 1923, and 1926 [New Adelphi Library]). The Knopf edition (1923) seems to me to have been edited without Machen's authorization. The texts of the other essays in the book derive from their original appearances in newspapers, magazines, or books. I have systematized Machen's use of book titles (all italics, except Latin and Greek titles, which—in conformity with the traditions of the time—were printed without italics or quotation marks); I have also used italics for magazines and long poems, and quotation marks (without italics) for short poems and articles. Throughout, I have enforced the stylistic and punctuational preferences that I have outlined in the introduction to my edition of Machen's *Collected Fiction* (Hippocampus Press, 2019).

I. Hieroglyphics:
A Note upon Ecstasy in Literature

Hieroglyphics: A Note upon Ecstasy in Literature

NOTE

It was my privilege, many years ago, to make the acquaintance of the obscure literary hermit, whose talk I have tried to reproduce in the pages that follow. Our first meeting was one of those chance affairs that now and then mitigate the loneliness of the London streets, and a second hazard led to the discovery that we had many interests in common. I think that the Hermit (as I shall call him) had begun to find the perpetual solitude of his years a growing terror, and he was not sorry to have a listener; at first, indeed, he talked almost with the joy of a child, or rather of a prisoner who has escaped from the house of silence, but as he chose subjects which have always interested me intensely, he gave as much pleasure as he received, and I became an assiduous visitor of his cell.

He had found an odd retreat. He avoided personalities, and had a happy knack of forgetting any that I vouchsafed on my side (he forgot my name three times on the first evening that we spent together, and succeeded in repeating this feat over and over again since then), and I never gathered much of his past history. But I believe that "something had happened" many years before, in the prehistoric age of the 'seventies. There had been a break of some sort in the man's life when he was quite young; and so he had left the world and gone to Barnsbury, an almost mythical region lying between Pentonville and the Caledonian Road. Here, in the most retired street of that retired quarter, he occupied two rooms on the ground floor of a big, mouldy house, standing apart from the street and sheltered by gaunt grown trees and ancient shrubs; and just beside the dim and dusty window of the sitting-room a laburnum had cast a green stain on the decaying wall. The laburnum had grown wild, like all the trees and shrubs, and some of its black, straggling boughs brushed the pane, and of dark, windy nights while we sat together and talked of art and life we would be startled by the sudden violence with which those branches beat angrily upon the glass.

The room seemed always dark. I suppose that the house had been built in the early eighteenth century, and had been altered and added to at various periods, with a final "doing up" for the comparative luxury of someone in the 'tens or 'twenties; there were, I think, twenty rooms in it, and my friend used to declare that when a new servant came she spent many months in finding her way in the complicated maze of stairs and passages, and that the landlady even was now and then at fault. But the room in which we sat was hung with flock paper, of a deep and heavy crimson colour, and even on bright summer evenings the crimson looked almost black, and seemed to cast a shadow into the room. Often we sat there till the veritable darkness came, and each could scarcely see the white of the other's face, and then my friend would light two lonely candles on the mantelpiece, or if he wished to read he set one on a table beside him; and when the candles were lighted I thought that the gloom grew more intense, and looking through the uncurtained window one could not see even the friendly twinkle of the gas-lamp in the street, but only the vague growth of the laburnum, and the tangle of boughs beyond.

It was a large room and gave me always a sense of empty space. Against one wall stood a heavy bookcase, with glass doors, solid and of dark mahogany, but made in the intermediate period that came between Chippendale and the modern school of machine-turned rubbish. In the duskiest corner of the room there was a secretaire of better workmanship, and two small tables and three gaunt chairs made up the furnishing. The Hermit would sometimes pace up and down in the void centre of the room as he talked, and if I chanced to be sitting by the window, his shape would almost disappear as he neared the secretaire on his march, and I heard the voice, and used to wonder for a moment whether the man had not vanished for ever, having been resolved into the shadows about him.

I have spent many evenings in that old mouldering room, where, when we were silent for an instant, the inanimate matter about us found a voice, and the decaying beams murmured together, and a vague sound might come from the cellars underneath. And it always seemed to me as if the crypt-like odour of the cellar rose also into the room, mingling with a faint suggestion of incense, though I am sure that my friend never burned it. Here then, with such surroundings as I have indicated, we held our sessions and talked freely and with enjoyment of many curious things, which, as the Hermit would say, had the huge merit of interesting no one but ourselves.

He would sometimes, whimsically, compare himself to Coleridge, and I think that he often deliberately talked in S. T. C.'s manner with delight in the joke. For, I need hardly say that the comparison was not in any way a serious one; he had a veneration for Coleridge's achievement, with a still greater veneration for that which Coleridge might have achieved, which would have caused him to regard any such comparison, seriously entertained, as unspeakably ludicrous. Still, he liked to regard himself as a very humble disciple in Coleridge's school; he was fond, as I have said, of imitating his master's manner as well as he could, and I think that he cherished, in the fashion of S. T. C., the notion that he had a "system", an esoteric philosophy of things. He sought for a key that would open, and a lamp that would enlighten all the dark treasure-houses of the Universe, and sometimes he believed that he held both the Key and the Lamp in his hands.

It is a confession of mysticism, but I incline to think that he was right in this belief. I recall the presence of that hollow, echoing room, the atmosphere with its subtle suggestion of incense sweetening the dank odours of the cellar, and the tone of the voice speaking to me, and I believe that once or twice we both saw visions, and some glimpse at least of certain eternal, ineffable Shapes. But these matters, the more esoteric doctrines of "the system", have entered hardly or not at all into the very imperfect and fragmentary notes that I have made of his conversations on literature.

I should scarcely be justified in calling him a literary monomaniac. But it is true that Art in general and the art of literature in particular had for him a very high significance and interest; and he was always ready to defend the thesis that, all the arts being glorious, the literary art was the most glorious and wonderful of all. He reverenced music, but he was firm in maintaining that in perfect lyrical poetry there is the subtlest and most beautiful melody in the world.

I can scarcely say whether he wrote much himself. He would speak of stories on which he was engaged, but I have never seen his name on publishers' lists, and I do not think that he had adopted a pseudonym. One evening, I remember, I came in a little before my accustomed time, and in the shadowy corner of the room a drawer in the secretaire was open, and I thought that it looked full of neat manuscripts. But I never spoke to him about his literary work; and I noticed that he did not much care to talk of literature from the commercial standpoint.

It is perhaps needless to say that I consulted my friend before publishing these notes of his conversations. I had been forced to leave London for some months, and I wrote to him from the country, requesting his permission to give to the world (if the world would have them) those judgments on books which I had listened to in Barnsbury. His reply allowed me to take my own way, "with all my heart, so long as you make me sufficiently apocryphal. I am not going to compete with 'real' critics whose names are printed in the papers; but if you can maintain the *incognito* and allow your readers (supposing their existence) to believe that I am a mere figment of your brain, you can print my *obiter dicta* 'with ease of body and rest of reins'. Here is a suggestion for a title: what do you say to 'Boswell in Barnsbury'? But I really had no notion that you were taking notes all the time. Remember: keep the secret, *and the secrets.*"

I regarded this as a very liberal license, and I have tried to set in the best order I could compass the "system" so far as it relates to letters. I do not pretend that I am a *verbatim* reporter, for I had to trust to my memory, and though I tried to arrange my notes at the time, I fear I have fallen here and there into confusion. Still, I think that the six chapters which follow will seem fairly consecutive in their argument and arrangement, and the "Appendix"—a confession of failure—is, in reality, the result of the "cyclical mode of discoursing", in which the Hermit jocularly professed to follow Coleridge.

Perhaps indeed Coleridge was deceived, and my dear friend with him, in the hope of real essential knowledge; but even so, these fragments which I propose are evidence that the latter earnestly desired the truth and sought it.

A. M.

I

Do you know that just before you came in I found something highly significant in the evening paper? I am afraid from your expression that you rather undervalue the influence of the press; indeed, I remember one day when we were out together you swore at an inoffensive boy who tried to allure us with news of all the winners. I think I pointed out at the time that even horse-racing and an interest in "events" are preferable to stagnation, and that there is something august in the universal human passion for gambling. And, after all, the office-boy who "puts on" half-a-crown is really only an example of the love of man for the unknown; the half-crown is a venture into mystery, with that due flavour of commercialism which we in England add to most of our interests. But you see, don't you? that gambling, even under its most sordid aspects, is not altogether sordid; it's the mystery, the uncertainty, the hours of "strange surmise" that the smallest bet gives to the bettor that make the real delight of betting. When the office-boy wins and gets ten shillings for the risk of his two-and-six, his delight is not by any means pure love of gain, it is distinguished by a very marked line from the constantly repeated joys of the grocer, who is always buying delicious tea at ninepence and selling it at one-and-six. Here you have commercialism in its simplest form; but our office-boy, though he likes the money well enough, stands on a much higher plane. For the moment he is the man who has succeeded in solving the enigma of the Sphinx, in discovering the unknown continent, in reading the cypher, in guessing at the song the Sirens sang, in unveiling the hidden treasure that the buccaneers buried on the lonely shore; he has ventured successfully into the dim region of surmises. And when he loses, there are always consolations; the Indies have not been discovered on this voyage, certainly, but there have been wonders on the way, he has enjoyed many hours of delicious expectation. The proof that he likes the sport, even when he loses, is that he invariably takes the first opportunity of venturing again in the same manner. And, by the way, perhaps I was a little severe just now on trade, and especially on the grocer's sugary and soapy enterprise. Perhaps if we were to look with a rather finer vision into the commercial spirit, we might find that it is not wholly commercial, not altogether sordid. Of course if the grocer opens his shop with a certainty, mathematical or almost mathematical, that the public will buy his wares, he is a wicked fellow; he is gambling with loaded dice, betting against a horse that he knows is to be made "all right", playing cards with honours up his sleeve, and I am sure that if this be his enterprise, it will always meet with our sternest disapproval. Casanova died towards the close of the last century, and since then cardsharping has become impossible to a man of taste. But seriously, I suspect that a good deal of the allurement that trade possesses for so many of us is the risk which it almost always implies, and risk means uncertainty, and uncertainty connotes the unknown. So you see our despised grocer turns out, after all, to be of the kin of Columbus, of the treasure-seekers, and mystery-mongers, and delvers after hidden things spiritual and material. I suppose we have here the real explanation of the human trading passion, and the solution of a problem that has often puzzled me. The problem I mean is this: how does it happen that the English are both the greatest poets and the greatest tradesmen of the modern world? Superficially, it seems that keeping shops and making poetry are incompatibles, and Wordsworth and Coleridge, Keats and Shelley, Tennyson and Poe, should have come from Provence or Sicily, from the "unpractical", uncommercial Latin races. But if we trace back the trading instinct to that love of a risk—or in other words to the desire for the unknown—the antinomy disappears, and it will become perfectly natural that the race which has gone to the world's end with its merchandise, has penetrated so gloriously into the further regions of poetry.

But that reminds me of what I was saying just after you had lit your pipe. I think I remarked that I had seen something of very high significance in the evening paper, and the glare of disgust with which you greeted my observation constituted an interruption, and an interruption that had to be dealt with. Now again you seem to hint at doubt with your eyebrows; you would say, perhaps, that I have not made out a very convincing case for journalism? But you must remember that my mental process resembles that of Coleridge; you called on the Seer at eleven o'clock in the morning, and (if young and imprudent) asked him a question. And at the waning of the light Coleridge was still diligently engaged in answering your question for you, having talked without intermission all the summer day. A "cyclical mode of discoursing" the pious Henry Nelson Coleridge called it, and he deals faithfully with certain persons who complained "that they could get no answer to a question from Coleridge". And you will please to remember this when you think that I am "wandering"—a vice of which Coleridge also was accused. To-night, for example, on the evening paper being mentioned, your face expressed disgust and contempt, which I diagnosed (and rightly, I believe?) as a tribute to the enormous interest taken by the editors of these agreeable journals in the very latest sporting news; an interest which allows but little space for the discussion of pure literature. Hence my remarks on the gambling-spirit; and now I hope you will at least assume a thrill of interest when the boy bawls in your ear "All the winners and S. P." It is possible you may be thinking of Ulysses or of Keats at the moment, and the interruption may annoy you, but it will do so no longer when you reflect that a burning anxiety as to the running of Bolter is for many thousands the symbol—and the only possible symbol—of the Doom of Troy and the wandering fields of foam, and the Isle of Calypso, and the "wild surmise" of Pizarro and all his men.

But here is the evening paper in question. Yes, the colour is, perhaps, a little sickly. A kind of pinky-green, it seems, doesn't it? But it forced itself on my notice in the most extraordinary manner, and I expect you will have to admit, when you have heard the story, that some Powers were at work. Well, I was walking up and down the room, just as it was getting dusk, and every now and then I stopped and looked out of the window. Yes, I was making phrases as usual, and thinking of a new story in the middle of the old one: hence the quarter-deck exercise. I daresay you have remarked that I do not keep my window in a very brilliant condition, and the air this evening, you will remember, was rather misty—October, I always think, wears a peculiar dim grace in Barnsbury—so I hope you will not find my impressions too incredible. I was staring, then, out of the window, when to my vast astonishment a great pale bird seemed suddenly to shoot up into the air from the road, and to flutter into the garden, where it became entangled in that sapless old laburnum that weeps green tears upon the wall. I saw, as I thought, the beating and fluttering of wings, and I ran out, imagining that I was to secure a strange companion for my solitude. It was the evening paper, not a bird, and I saw at once that it would be impious to let it flutter there unread, so I secured it and brought it in, meditating the adventure, and wondering what strange message was thus borne to my eyes. So I went through its columns patiently, even to the leaderettes, and I will do myself the justice to say that I at once recognised the communication that was addressed to me in this singular and even I may say Arabian fashion. It was a short comment upon some agitation that is now appealing rather strongly to Progressive leaders; but the subject-matter is of no consequence, since the significance lies in the last sentence. Here it is: "We are glad to hear that extensive arrangements have been made for the dissemination of literature."

You don't see the immense importance of that? You surprise me. Let us go into it, then. I told you I was not very precise as to the exact scope of the agitation alluded to—it may be a question of a heavy tax on persons who will say "lady" instead of "lydy", it may be an affair of restricting the franchise to citizens thoroughly ignorant of history; it doesn't matter—but here are men who wish some political change to be effected, and these men are issuing printed matter, the purpose of which is to convince others of the righteousness of this particular "program". And this printed matter is called "literature". You know the sort of thing indicated. It may be a series of arguments, simple and fallacious, it may be in dialogue, it may be in story form, it may assume the guise of parody, it may be a brief history. And now what I want to know is this: here we have a vast body of thought, clothed in words, ranging from the agreeable leaflets that we have been speaking of up to—let us say—the Odyssey, and all this mass is known as literature: what is to be our criterion, our means of distinguishing between the two extremes I have mentioned and all the innumerable links between them? Is the whole mass literature in the true sense of the word? If not, with what instrument, by what rule are we to divide the true from the false, to judge exactly in the case of any particular book whether it is literature or not? Of course you may say that the question is rather verbal than real; that "literature" is a general term conveniently applied to anything in print, and that in practice everybody knows the difference between a political pamphlet and the Odyssey. I very much doubt whether people do understand precisely the distinction between the two, but for the avoidance of verbal confusion I suggest that when we mean literature in its highest sense we shall say (for the present at all events), "fine literature"; and the question will be, then: what is it that differentiates fine literature from a number of grammatical, or partly grammatical, sentences arranged in a more or less logical order? Why is the Odyssey to come in, why is the "literature" of our evening paper to be kept out? And again, to put the question in a more subtle form: to which class do the works of Jane Austen belong? Is *Pride and Prejudice* to stand on the Odyssey shelf, or to lie in the pamphlet drawer? Where is Pope's place? Is he to be set in the class of Keats? If not, for what reason? What is the rank of Dickens, of Thackeray, of George Eliot, of Hawthorne; and, in a word, how are we to sort out, as it were, this huge multitude of names, giving to each one his proper rank and station?

I am glad it strikes you as a big question: to me it seems *the* question, the question which covers the final dogma of literary criticism. Of course after we have answered this prerogative riddle, there will be other questions, almost without end, classes, and sub-classes of infinite analysis. But this will be detail; while the question I have propounded is the question of first principles; it marks the parting of two ways, and in a manner, it asks itself not only of literature, but of life, but of philosophy, but of religion. What is the line, then; the mark of division which is to separate spoken, or written, or printed thought into two great genera?

Well, as you may have guessed, I have my solution, and I like it none the less because the word of the enigma seems to me actually but a single word. Yes, for me the answer comes with the one word, *Ecstasy*. If ecstasy be present, then I say there is fine literature, if it be absent, then, in spite of all the cleverness, all the talents, all the workmanship and observation and dexterity you may shew me, then, I think, we have a product (possibly a very interesting one) which is not fine literature.

Of course you will allow me to contradict myself, or rather, to amplify myself before we begin to discuss the matter fully. I said my answer was the word, ecstasy; I still say so, but I may remark that I have chosen this word as the representative of many. Substitute, if you like, rapture, beauty, adoration, wonder, awe, mystery, sense of the unknown, desire for the unknown. All and each will convey what I mean; for some particular case one term may be more appropriate than another, but in every case there will be that withdrawal from the common life and the common consciousness which justifies my choice of "ecstasy" as the best symbol of my meaning. I claim, then, that here we have the touchstone which will infallibly separate the higher from the lower in literature, which will range the innumerable multitude of books in two great divisions, which can be applied with equal justice to a Greek drama, an eighteenth-century novelist, and a modern poet, to an epic in twelve books, and to a lyric in twelve lines. I will convince you of my belief in my own nostrum by a bold experiment: here is *Pickwick* and here is *Vanity Fair;* the one regarded as a popular "comic" book, the other as a serious masterpiece, shewing vast insight into human character; and applying my test, I set *Pickwick* beside the Odyssey, and *Vanity Fair* on top of the political pamphlet.

I will not argue the matter at the moment; I would merely caution you against supposing that I imply any equality of merit in the books that I have thus summarily "bracketed". You mustn't suppose that I think Dickens's book as good as Homer's, or that I have any doubts as to the vast superiority of *Vanity Fair* over all the pamphlets in the world. "Here is a temple, here is a tub," we may suppose a child to say, learning from a picture-alphabet; but the temple may be a miserably designed structure, in ruinous condition, and the tub is, perhaps, a miracle of excellent workmanship. But one means worship and the other means washing, and that is *the* distinction. Or, to take a better example; the bottom boy in the sixth form may be a miserable dunce compared with the top boy in the fifth; still, the dunce is in the sixth form, and the genius is in the fifth. Or, to take a third instance (I want you to understand what I'm driving at), the fact that an English orator is fluent, brilliant, profound, convincing, while a Greek orator is stuttering, stupid, shallow, illogical, does not hinder that the former, though he may speak ever so well, still speaks English, while the latter, however badly he may speak, speaks in Greek for all that. Analogies, as you know, are never perfect, and must not be pressed too far; they suggest rather than prove; but I hope you understand me though you may not agree with me.

But before we argue the merits of my own literary solvent, we might very well see what we can do with other tests. I daresay you can suggest a good many. We won't go into the question of printed and not printed, written or not written, because it is obvious that the visible symbols by which literature is recorded have nothing to do with literature itself. In the beginning all literature was a matter of improvisation or recitation and memory, and hieroglyphics, writing, printing are mere conveniences. Indeed the point is only worth mentioning because there are, I believe, simple souls who think that the invention of printing has some sort of mysterious connection with the birth of literature, and that the abolition of the paper duty was its coming of age. But I don't think we need trouble ourselves much about a view of literary art which regards the cheap press as its father and the school board as its nursing mother. Many people think, on the other hand, that literature is to be estimated by its effect on the emotions, by the shock which it gives to the system. You may say that a book which interests you so intensely that you cannot put it down, that affects you so acutely that you weep, that amuses you so immensely that you roar with laughter, must be very good. I don't object to "very good", but, from my point of view, "very good" and "fine literature" are two different things. You see I believe that the difference between interesting, exciting, tear-compelling, laughter-moving reading-matter and fine art is not specific but generic: who would blaspheme against good bitter beer, who would say that *because* it is good, it is *therefore* Burgundy?

I am not quite sure that I am not muddling up two things which are in reality distinct. I mean I am in doubt whether the faculty of making the reader cry ought not to be distinguished from the faculty of interesting him intensely. On the whole I think that it would be well to draw a line between the two, especially as "interesting" is somewhat ambiguous.

And you think it a paradox, then, to maintain that the power of exciting the emotions to a high degree is not a mark of fine literature? But just think it over. Suppose that a few yards from this room—in the next house, in the next street—a woman is waiting for the return of her husband and son. A ring comes at the bell, there's a reddish brown envelope, and inside it the message: "Railway accident—father killed." Well, you can imagine the effect that these four words will have on the woman's emotions; she will either faint away or burst into an agony of tears; she may even die of the shock, and you can't have a more striking emotional result than death, can you? Very well; but is the telegram fine art? Is it art? Is it even artifice? It isn't art because it is true! But if I invented such a telegram and sent it to a woman whose husband and son were away, would it thereby become art? You must see perfectly well that it would be nothing of the kind; and I must ask you to explain how a book which is, virtually, a long succession of such telegrams can rise higher than its origin and source? You must see, I think, that the question of truth and falsity can make no real difference to our (no doubt pompous) high æsthetic standpoint; and if you admit that four words which produce an emotional result are not necessarily art, then it follows that four hundred or four hundred thousand words woven together on the same principle are in no better position. An increased quantity means no doubt an increased artifice, but artifice and art are very different things. We may agree then that it is impossible to measure the artistic merit of a book by the emotional shock that it may give to its readers. I have never read the *Sorrows of Werther;* but if you have read it and it has made you sorrowful you are hereby warned against deducing from this effect any conclusion as to its æsthetic value.

I confess all this seems A B C to me, though I see you are still inclined to think me a little paradoxical—not to say sophistical—but it grows more difficult when one gets to the question of the "interesting" or "absorbing" book. As I said "interesting" seems such an ambiguous word. It may stand for that æsthetic emotion produced, say, by the Œdipus; it may denote the wide-eyed attention of the butcher's wife listening to the story of my landlady as to the love-affairs of the grocer's daughter—and there are many books which are, virtually, *Tales of My Landlady* printed and bound. We must really then omit "interesting" in our account of the possible criteria of fine art; the word as it were cancels itself out, because it may mean on the one hand the possession of the highest artistic value, or on the other it may serve as epithet for a book which gratifies the lowest curiosity. You know there are books which the French have kindly named *romans à clef;* and I suppose there is no more miserable form of book-making. The recipe is easy enough. The grocer's daughter, to whose amours I alluded just now, is really named Miss Buggins, and the gentleman is Mr. Tibb. Well, suppose that my landlady, relating their lyric to the butcher's wife, should, with a knowing wink, profess to tell the story of Miss Ruggins and Mr. Ribb—she would simply be composing a *roman à clef* without knowing it. You might say that it is hardly worth while to labour the point, that such "interest" as this is wholly and lamentably inartistic—that it is the very contrary to all true art—but it is not long since a person of some literary note, in criticising the *Heptameron,* stated that its chief value lay in the fact that one could identify the persons who tell the stories and those also of whom they were told!

But there is another interest of a much higher kind, and that is the sensational. We have done some excellent books of this sort in England, and perhaps you will understand the class I mean when I say that a novel of this description is hard to lay down, and harder still to take up again when you have once found out the secret. This is not high art; you are always at liberty to put down "Lycidas", but then you are compelled to take it up again and again, and the secret of "Lycidas" is always a secret, and one never fails to experience the joy of an artistic surprise. Still, the books I mean sometimes shew very high artifice, and in itself, perhaps, the quality that I am talking about, the power of exciting a vivid curiosity, an earnest desire to know what is to come next, is not, like the vulgar *roman à clef* curiosity, in actual discord from the purpose of art. Indeed I imagine that this trick of stimulating the curiosity may be made subservient to purely æsthetic ends, it may become a handmaid to lead one towards that desire of the unknown which I think was one of the synonyms I gave you for the master word—Ecstasy. Still, though the trick is a good one, it will not, by itself, make fine art. You may discover so much by reading *The Moonstone,* that monument of ingenuity and absurdity. On the face of it all detective stories come under this heading: formally, no doubt, they must all be reckoned as tricks, and they may vary from the infinitely ingenious to the infinitely imbecile, and so far as I remember, the famous French tales of detection verge towards the lower rather than the higher ground. But I am inclined, not very logically, perhaps, to make an exception in favour of Poe's Dupin, and to place him almost in the sphere of pure literature. Logically, he is a detective, but I almost think that in his case the detective is a symbol of the mystagogue. As I say, I should be pressed hard if I were asked to make out my case in terms and syllogisms, but if you require me to do so, I would say first of all that the atmosphere of Dupin—and you must remember that in literature everything counts; it is not alone the plot or the style that we have to consider—has to me hints of that presence which I have called ecstasy. Listen to this:

"It was a freak of fancy in my friend (for what else shall I call it?) to be enamoured of the Night for her own sake; and into this *bizarrerie,* as into all his others, I quietly fell; giving myself up to his wild whims with a perfect *abandon.* The sable divinity would not herself dwell with us always; but we could counterfeit her presence. At the first dawn of the morning we closed all the massive shutters of our old building; lighting a couple of tapers which, strongly perfumed, threw out only the ghastliest and feeblest of rays. By the aid of these we then buried our souls in dreams—reading, writing, or conversing, until warned by the clock of the advent of the true Darkness. Then we sallied forth into the streets, arm in arm, continuing the topics of the day, or roaming far and wide until a late hour, seeking amid the wild lights and shadows of the populous city, that infinity of mental excitement which quiet observation can afford."

And again; in the stories themselves, in the conduct of M. Dupin's detective processes, I find a faint suggestion of the under-consciousness or other-consciousness of man, a mere hint, not, I think, expressed in so many words, rather latent than patent, that if you would thoroughly understand the rational man you must have sounded the irrational man, the mysterious companion that walks beside each one of us on the earthly journey. Of course the artifice in the Dupin stories is of the very highest kind, but for the reasons I have given I am inclined to think that there is more than artifice, and the shadow, at all events, of art itself.

But this exceptional case of Poe's detective tales only leads us back to the main proposition—that the power of exciting a very high sensational interest does not, in itself, mark out a book as being fine literature. I think I proved the proposition by my instance of *The Moonstone,* but if that does not convince you, we might demonstrate this theorem in the same way as we demonstrated the other one about the "literature" that produces its effect on the emotions. We have only to send out a series of telegrams, or we may even glance at the newspaper, and follow a case in the Central Criminal Court. Or we may affirm, more generally, that life often offers many highly absorbing and highly interesting spectacles, but that life is not art, and therefore, that literature which fails to rise above the level of life, or rather, to penetrate beneath the surface of life, is not fine literature in our sense of that term. A gold nugget may be as pure and fine as you like, but it is not a sovereign; it lacks the stamp; and it is the business of art to give its stamp and imprint to the matter of life.

I really think then that we have disposed of perhaps the most generally received of artistic fallacies—that books are to be judged by their power of reproducing in the reader those feelings of grief, interest, curiosity, and so forth which he experiences or may experience in his everyday life, which he really does experience in greater or less degree every time he talks to a friend, takes up a newspaper, or receives a telegram. It comes to this again and again, doesn't it, that Art and Life are two different spheres, and that the Artist with a capital A is not a clever photographer who understands selection in a greater or less degree.

But before we go on with our work and see what can be done with other literary "solvents" I want to make a digression. I should have made it before, if you had pulled me up at the proper cue, and that was when I spoke of "interest" as a highly ambiguous term, the fruitful parent of "undistributed middles". You see how the unscrupulous sophist would bend this word to his dark work, don't you? It would be, I suppose, something like this:

> A very high degree of interest [of the artistic kind] is the mark of fine literature.
>
> But, *The Moonstone* excites a very high degree of interest [of the sensational kind].
>
> *Therefore, The Moonstone* has the mark of fine literature.

You note the "paltering" with the word, its use now in one sense, and now in another; and if that sort of thing were allowed we should have Wilkie Collins placed among the Immortals before we knew where we were. But hasn't it occurred to you that nearly all the terms we are using are patient of the same vile uses? You remember that we began with "literature" itself, as a monstrous example of ambiguity, sheltering as it did both the publications of the Anti-Everything Society and the Song of Ulysses' Wandering; even now we are trying to track the monster to his den in spite of his manifold turnings and disguises. In the meanwhile, for the sake of clearness, we agreed to prefix the epithet "fine" to the word when we meant the Odyssey class, though if we say "fine" so often I am afraid we run the risk of being thought superfine. However one must run all risks in the cause of making oneself understood; and so I say you ought to have pulled me up when I talked about "art" and "books that appealed to the emotions". My "art" may not be the same as your "art", and "emotions" are still more dangerous in the same way.

I think I made some attempt to deal with "art" as I was talking. I contrasted it with "artifice", and my phrase "Artist with a big A" was another hint to you that the word must be handled cautiously. You know that in ordinary conversation we say that bees have "the art" or "an art" of making hexagonal cells of wax, that wasps have an art of making a sort of paper for their nests, that there is an art of logic, an art of cookery, an art in making a gravel path. Now in each of these instances the word really speaks of the adaptation of means to ends. In the case of the bees and wasps there is a slightly different *nuance* of meaning, because they make their cells and their paper just as a bird builds its nest, through the influence of forces which to us are occult, which we conveniently sum up under the word instinct. In the arts of cookery and pathmaking there is a conscious employment of certain means towards the securing of certain ends; and it is at least possible that the swallow, gathering its materials and shaping them, has at the moment nothing but a blind impulse, similar to that of hunger—we all know when we are hungry and we all know what to do in such a case, but we do not all know the physiology of the stomach and the gastric juices, and perhaps not one of us knows the whole secret of inanition and nutrition. We simply eat because we want to eat, not because we wish to supply ourselves with a certain quantity of peptones; and so perhaps the swallow gathers her nest and shapes it, without the consciousness of the eggs and the little birds that are to follow. But I need not remind you that there are plenty of well-authenticated instances of animals who have consciously used means to secure ends, and thus "art" in its common significance is not even an exclusively human faculty. When, for example, the bees find themselves in danger of being left queenless, they administer what has been called "royal food" to a common grub, and that which would have been a worker becomes a queen; and in this case the bees are as much "artists" as the cook who puts a particular ingredient into a dish with the view of obtaining a particular flavour.

Now, then, let us apply all this to our matter. I daresay you have often heard a book praised for its "great art", and if you have read it you will have discovered that its "art" is simply contrivance, the very adaptation of means to ends that we have been discussing. "The art with which the mystery is carefully kept in the background", "the art by which the two characters are contrasted throughout the volume", "the highly artistic manner in which Fernando and the heroine are brought together on the last page"—these, you see clearly, are contrivances, artifices, in no way differing in degree from the contrivances of the man who makes the garden path, of the cook who "dusts in" just a suspicion of lemon-rind, of the bee who administers the "royal food". This "art" then is a totally different thing from our Art with the capital letter, with the epithet "fine" or "high" before it; and in future when I mean "adaptation of means to ends", I shall always say "artifice", while "art" will be retained and set apart for higher uses.

And now as to "emotion". Here, I think, you ought to have been down on me. You might have said: "You declare that the appeal to the emotions is not a test of fine literature. But to what then does Homer appeal? What is the Œdipus but an appeal to the emotions? What is all exquisite lyric poetry but the cry of the emotions, set to music?" I suppose that, as a matter of fact, you understood my real meaning by the instance I gave; the anguish of a wife at the loss of a husband; you saw that what I wanted to say was this: that fine literature does not content itself with repeating, or mimicking, the emotions of private, personal, everyday life. Still, I should have gone into the matter more fully then, and as I did not do so we had better see what can be done now. And do you know that I believe that the best approach we can make to a rather subtle question will be a somewhat indirect one? Just now I was talking about Poe's Dupin stories, and I tried, rather vaguely, to justify my tentative inclusion of them in the higher class of letters, by pointing out that Poe seemed to hint at the "other-consciousness" of man, and to suggest, at least, the presence of that shadowy, unknown, or half-known Companion who walks beside each one of us all our days. I tried to realise the image of a man, followed or rather attended by a spiritual fellow, treading a path parallel with but different from his own; and now I want you to carry out this image into the sphere of words. Already you must have a hint of it. One might draw a figure; something like this:

Fine Literature.	"Literature."
Art.	Artifice.
Emotion.	Feelings.

And before I go into the special question, let me extend the list; it will explain itself.

Romance, romantic.	A "Romantic" Affair in the West End.
Tragedy, tragic.	"Tragedy" in Soho.
Drama, dramatic.	Le "drame" de la Rue Cochon: "Dramatic" Elopement in Peckham.
Interest, interesting [of *Hamlet*].	An "interesting" number of *Snippets*.
Lyric.	The "Lyric" Theatre.
Inebriated.	In an "inebriated" condition.

That almost gives my secret away, doesn't it? Of course you see the place that the words in the right-hand column take in the scheme. The "Romantic" Affair in the West End really concerned the life of a draper's assistant, who robbed his master's till, in order that he might make presents to Miss Claire Tilbury, one of the "Sisters Tilbury" now performing at the "Lucifer". An unmentionable person cut his throat in some alley off Greek Street; hence the "Tragedy" in Soho. Two peculiarly squalid servants, who beat out their master's brains, under singularly uninteresting circumstances, acted the "Drama" of the Rue Cochon, and it was a dissolute barmaid who eloped "dramatically" from Peckham in the dog-cart of her employer. The two varying uses of the word "lyric" need not be underlined for you, who know the Elizabethans and the Cavaliers; but perhaps I may say that he who tastes *calix meus inebrians* will not be in an "inebriated" condition. It would be possible to extend these parallel columns almost to infinity; but I think the list is long enough for our purpose, and *Trench on Words* is a well-known handbook. But you see my right-hand column word, parallel with "Emotion"? You see I have written "Feelings", and I suggest that it will be convenient to speak of feelings when we mean the things of life, of society, of personal and private relationship, while we may reserve emotion for the influence produced in man by fine art. Thus it will be with emotion that we witness the fall of Œdipus, the madness of Lear, while we feel for our friends and ourselves in misfortune. That seems to make it plain enough, doesn't it; you see now, clearly, what I mean by saying that the power of producing an emotional shock cannot be a test of fine literature. Art must appeal to emotion, and sometimes, no doubt, with a shock; but it must always be to the emotion of the left-hand column, never to the "feelings" on the right hand. So you must never tell me that a book is fine art because it made you, or somebody else, cry; your tears are, emphatically, not evidence in the court of Fine Literature.

I daresay it may have struck you that the tests we have considered hitherto have been, in the main, popular tests. No doubt many persons calling themselves critics have praised the art of a book because it has drawn tears from eyes, or because it has not suffered itself to be put down, or because it contains easily recognisable portraits of well-known people, but such critics are to be spelt with a very small initial letter, and, as I said, I don't think we want to extend that list of parallels. There is another test that I had forgotten: I suppose there really are people who believe that a book is fine "because it will do good", but I don't think we'll argue with them, though I once knew a liberally-educated man who said a certain book was fine because it tended "to raise one's opinion of the clergy". So we will reckon our "popular" tests as done with, and proceed to the more technical solvents that are proposed by professed men of letters.

Three of these more literary criteria occur to me at the moment, and I believe we shall understand them and the position which they represent better if we take them, at first, at all events, in a mass. I can conceive, then, that many persons whose opinion one would respect would state their position in literary criticism somewhat as follows:—"If a book (they would say) shews keenness of observation, insight into character, with fidelity to life as the result of these capacities; if its art (we should say, artifice) in the design and 'laying out' of the plot, in the contrivance of incident is confessedly admirable, and finally if it is written in a good style: then you have fine literature. Fine art, in short, is a clear mirror, and the artist's skill consists in arranging and selecting such parts of life as he thinks best for his purpose of reflection."

Well, now, as to the first point: fidelity to life, clearness of reflection, the selection being taken for granted, as no one out of an asylum would maintain that a book must mirror the whole of life, or even the millionth part of one particular man's life. Come, let us apply the test in question to one or two of the acknowledged excellences—to the Odyssey, for instance, to the *Morte d'Arthur,* to *Don Quixote.* Is the story of Ulysses, in any accepted sense of the phrase, "faithful" to life as we know it? Is it "faithful", that is to say, with the fidelity of Jane Austen, of Thackeray, of George Eliot, of Fielding? Is there anything in our experience answering to the episodes of the Lotus-Eaters, Calypso's Isle, the Cyclops' Cavern, the descent of the Goddess? Is the "reflection" even a reflection of Homer's own experience? Had he escaped from the cave under the belly of a ram? Had he been in the world of one-eyed giants? Were his friends in the habit of talking in hexameter verse? We may go on, of course, but is it worth while? It is surely hardly necessary to demonstrate the fact that the author of the *Morte d'Arthur* had never seen the Graal, that such a character as Don Quixote never existed in the natural order of things. We might have gone more sharply to work with this "fidelity" test: we might have said that poetry being, admittedly, fine literature at its finest, and (admittedly also) being unfaithful to life as we know it both in matter and manner, therefore the test breaks down at once. If fine literature must be faithful to life, then "Kubla Khan" is not fine literature; which, I think we may say, is highly absurd.

I daresay you think I have dealt rather crudely, in a somewhat materialistic spirit, with this criterion of "fidelity to life". I admit the charge, but you must remember that I am dealing with very bad people, who understand nothing but materialism. And when these people tell you in so many words that it is the author's business clearly and intelligently to present the life—the common, social life around him—then, believe me, the only thing to be done is to throw Odyssey and Œdipus, *Morte d'Arthur,* "Kubla Khan," and *Don Quixote* straight in their faces, and to demonstrate that these eternal books were not constructed on the proposed recipe. Of course if I were treating with the initiated, if I were commentating and not arguing, I should handle the great masterpieces in a much more reverent manner. I mean that for those who possess the secret it skills not to bring in the Cyclops (who for us is not a giant but a symbol); we have only to bow down before the great music of such a poem as the Odyssey, recognising that by the very reason of its transcendent beauty, by the very fact that it trespasses far beyond the world of our daily lives, beyond "selection" and "reflection", it is also exalted above our understanding, that because its beauty is supreme, therefore its beauty is largely beyond criticism. For ourselves we do not need to prove its transcendence of life by this or that extraordinary incident; it is the whole spirit and essence and sound and colour of the song that affect us; and we know that the Odyssey surpassed the bounds of its own age and its own land just as much as it surpasses those of our time and own country. You look as if you thought I were fighting with the vanquished, but let me tell you that great people have praised Homer because he depicted truthfully the men and manners of his time.

But as I was saying, all this would be too subtle for the enemy, for the people who maintain that fine literature is a faithful reflection of life, and think that Jane Austen touched the point of literary supremacy. With them, as I said, we must be rough; we must ask: Did Sophocles describe the ordinary life of Athens in his day? No: very well, then; since the works of Sophocles are fine literature, it follows that some fine literature does not reflect ordinary life, and therefore that fidelity to nature is not the differentia of the highest art.

I wonder whether I ought to caution you again against the ambiguity of language? We are dealing easily enough with such words as "life" and "nature", and from what you know of my system you may perhaps have seen that I have been using these words as the people use them, as those use them who would say that *Vanity Fair* is a faithful presentation of life. I thought you would understand this, but I may just mention in passing that words like "nature", "life", and "truth" or "fidelity" have also their esoteric values, that (by way of example) the truth of the scientist and the truth of the philosopher are two very different things. So it may turn out by and by that in the occult sense "fidelity to life" *is* the differentia of fine literature; that the aim of art is truth; that the artist continually mirrors nature in its eternal, essential forms; but for the present moment it is understood, is it not, that these words have been used in their common, everyday popular significance. The *Dunciad* is a study of man, and Wordsworth's "Ode on Intimations of Immortality" is a study of man, and the literary standpoint that we have been attacking is that of Pope and not that of Wordsworth.

If I remember, the next test we have to analyse is that of artifice, often and improperly called art. But I think we have already demolished this criterion. In distinguishing between art and artifice I pointed out that the latter merely signifies the adaptation of means to an end, and has no relation whatever with art properly so called; it is simply the mental instrument with which man performs every task and every work of his daily life; it consists in the rejection of that which is unfit for the particular purpose in view, and in the acceptance and use of that which is fit for the desired end and likely to bring it about. It concerns not creation but execution, and it is I need hardly say as indispensable to the author as are his pen and ink, and (I might almost say) is as little concerned as these with the essence of his art. Of course in works of the very highest genius we may declare that, in a sense, art has become all in all, that the necessary artifice has been interpenetrated with art, so that we can hardly distinguish in our minds between the idea and the realisation of it. In such cases, artifice has been lifted up and exalted into the heaven of art, and it remains artifice no longer; but in the view that we are considering it is merely the adaptation of means to an end, a clever choice of incident, the knack of putting in and leaving out. The faculty may, as I said, be glorified and transfigured by genius, but every newspaper reporter must have more or less of it, and it is clear enough I think (perhaps I may mention Wilkie Collins once more) that in itself it cannot establish the claim of any book to be fine literature.

And lastly we have to deal with style; and here again I must have recourse to my distinctions. What *is* a good style? If you mean by a "good" style, one that delivers the author's meaning in the clearest possible manner, if its purpose and effect are obviously utilitarian, if it be designed solely with the view of imparting knowledge—the knowledge of what the author intends—then I must point out that "style" in this sense is or should be amongst the accomplishments of every commercial clerk—indeed, it will be merely a synonym for plain speaking and plain writing—and in this sense it is evidently not one of the marks of art, since the object of art is not information, but a peculiar kind of æsthetic delight. But if on the other hand style is to mean such a use and choice of words and phrases and cadences that the ear and the soul through the ear receive an impression of subtle but most beautiful music, if the sense and sound and colour of the words affect us with an almost inexplicable delight, then I say that while Idea is the soul, style is the glorified body of the very highest literary art. Style, in short, is the last perfection of the very best in literature, it is the outward sign of the burning grace within. But we must keep the systematic consideration of style for some other night; it's not a subject to be dealt with by the way, and I have only said so much because it was necessary to draw the line between language as a means of imparting facts (good style in the sense of our opponents) and language as an æsthetic instrument, which is a good, or rather a beautiful style in our sense. In the latter sense it is the form of fine literature, in the former sense it is the medium of all else that is expressed in words, from a bill of exchange upwards.

It seems to me, then, that we have considered one by one the alternative tests of fine literature which have been or may be proposed, and we have come to the conclusion that each and all are impossible. It is no longer permissible, I imagine, for you or for me to say: "This book is fine literature because it makes me cry, because it was so interesting that I couldn't put it down, because it is so natural and faithful to life, because it is so well (plainly and neatly) written." We have picked these reasons to pieces one by one, and the result is that we are driven back on my "word of the enigma"—Ecstasy; the infallible instrument, as I think, by which fine literature may be discerned from reading-matter, by which art may be known from artifice, and style from intelligent expression. At any rate we have got our hypothesis, and you remember what stress Coleridge laid on the necessity of forming some hypothesis before entering on any investigation.

I believe we began to-night with the evening paper, and the strange glimpse it gives us, through a pinky-green veil, through a cloud of laborious nonsense about odds and winners and tips and all such foolery, into that ancient eternal desire of man for the unknown. And that, you remember, was one of the synonyms that I offered you for ecstasy; and so in a sense I expect that we shall have the evening paper close beside us all the way of our long voyage in quest of the lost Atlantis.

II

I think it is a horrible thing to have such a good memory as that. I recollect, now that you remind me, that I did lay down *Pickwick v. Vanity Fair* as a sort of test case of my theory of literature; but you surely do not expect me to work out the arguments in detail? Of course if I were giving a series of lectures I should "set a paper" after each one; but I expect you to content yourself with the suggestion, with the skeleton map, as it were. Besides, if we take that special case of two eminent Victorian novels as a concrete instance of the abstract argument, don't you see that we are answering the particular question all the while that we are investigating the general proposition? Surely, if you recollect all that we said about fine literature in general, you won't have much difficulty in adjudicating on the claims of Thackeray. Don't you see that he never withdraws himself from the common life and the common consciousness, that he is all the while nothing but a photographer; a showman with a set of pictures? A consummately clever photographer, certainly, a showman with a gift of amusing, interesting "patter" that is quite extraordinary, an artificer of very high merit. But where will you find Ecstasy in Thackeray? Where is his adoration? You may search, I think, from one end of his books to the other, without finding any evidence that he realised the mystery of things; he was never for a moment aware of that shadowy double, that strange companion of man, who walks, as I said, foot to foot with each one of us, and yet his paces are in an unknown world. And (unless you have got any fresh arguments) I think we decided last week that the book which lacks the sense of all this is not fine literature.

I hope you don't think I am abusing Thackeray. I am always reading him, and I chose his *Vanity Fair* because it strikes me as such a supremely clever example of its class. I suppose there is nothing more amusing than the society of a brilliant, observant man of the world. Well, Thackeray was brilliant and observant *in excelsis,* and besides that, he understood the artifice of story-telling, and he could write a terse, clean-cut English which was always sufficient for his purpose. He contrives the corporal overthrow of the Marquis of Steyne, he shews you that bald old nobleman sprawling on the floor, and the words that he uses are his brisk, willing, and capable servants. He has observation, and artifice, and "style" in that secondary sense which we distinguished from the real style; from those "melodies unheard" which I called (I think rather picturesquely) the glorified body of the highest literary art. But these qualities, we found out, are not, separately or conjointly, the differentia of fine literature as we understand the term; and consequently, with all our admiration and all our interest, we are compelled to place Thackeray in the lower form, simply because he is clearly and decisively lacking in that one essential quality of ecstasy, because he never leaves the street and the highroad to wander on the eternal hills, because he does not seem to be aware that such hills exist.

Of course I have only taken Thackeray as the representative of his class, and I chose him, as I remarked, because, for me, he is the most favourable representative of it. I am thinking, really, of the "plain man" whom we have engaged in so many forms, and of his "plain" argument which comes to this—"for me a great book is a book that amuses me greatly and that I enjoy reading". And I say that Thackeray amuses me greatly and that I enjoy reading his books immensely, but that, with due respect to "common sense", such an argument fails to prove that *Vanity Fair* is fine literature. Other people would, no doubt, have chosen other books; many would have selected Miss Austen, and I daresay they would have a good deal to say for their choice. Undoubtedly there is a severity, a self-restraint, a fineness of observation, a delicacy of irony in *Pride and Prejudice* which are unmatched of their kind (the Thackeray of the caricatures, of those queer woodblocks, comes out now and then in the books, and digression occasionally goes beyond due bounds); but I named *Vanity Fair* because, personally, I find it more amusing than *Pride and Prejudice.* In neither of these books is there art in our high sense of the word, and in preferring the one over the other I am simply saying that I prefer the company of a brilliant and witty cosmopolitan to that of a very keen and delicate, but very limited maiden lady, who lives in a remote country town and understands thoroughly the reason why the vicar bowed so low when a certain carriage rolled up the high street, and why that pretty, prim girl crossed over the way when the handsome gentleman from the Hall came out of the chymist's. Yes, the cosmopolitan at the club window certainly fails a little in his manners now and then, and the country gentlewoman's breeding is perfect of its kind, but the circles in which Pendennis moved are (to me) so infinitely the more entertaining of the two.

You see, I think that the question of liking a book or not liking it has nothing whatever to do with the consideration of fine art. Art is *there,* if I may say so, just as the Tenth Commandment is there; and if we don't like them, so much the worse for us. I may find Homer very dull reading, I may covet your ox and your ass and everything that is yours, but my limited and somewhat commonplace brains, and my envy of your prosperity, won't alter the fact that the Odyssey is fine literature and that covetousness is wicked. But when we once leave the utterances of the eternal, universal human ecstasy, which we have agreed to call art, and descend to these lower levels that we are talking of now, it seems to me that the question of liking or not liking counts for a good deal. Not for everything, of course. We must still distinguish: between plots stupid or ingenious, between observation that is close and keen and observation that is vague and inaccurate, between artifice and the want of it, between sentences that are neatly constructed and mere slipshod. All these things naturally reckon in the account, but when they have been estimated and allowed their value, you will usually find that you are influenced still more by your mere liking or disliking of the subject-matter, and it seems to me quite legitimately. For, if you look closely into the whole question, you will find that you are judging these secondary books as you judge of life, as you choose the scene of your holiday, as you read the newspaper. One man may say that he prefers to talk to artists, another, quite legitimately, may love the society of brewers; you may think Norway perfection, I am going to Constantinople; A. turns at once to the quotation for Turpentine at Savannah, B. folds down the sheet at the Police News. It is not a question of art, but of taste, that is, of individual humour and constitution; you frequent the company that suits you, you go to the place you like, you read the news that happens to be most interesting from your special standpoint. And in the same way, if I find the conversation of Miss Becky Sharp, as reported by Mr. W. M. Thackeray, more amusing than the conversation of Miss Elizabeth Bennett as reported by Miss Jane Austen; it seems to me that there is no more to be said. Elizabeth's remarks are more skilfully reported? Very likely, but, granting that, I had rather listen to the record, imperfect, if you please, of the other lady's conversation. Here is a speech on Bimetallism, given at great length, and (let us presume) with great accuracy; here is a short summary of Professor L.'s "Lecture on the Eleusinian Mysteries", very badly "sub-edited". But, you see, I happen not to care twopence about Bimetallism, so I turn away from the careful report, growling; while I cut out that wretched summary of the Lecture with the purpose of pasting it in my scrap-book, since every word about the Eleusinian Mysteries has a vivid interest for me.

It often amuses me to hear people quarrelling about the rival "artistic merit" of books which have, in most cases, no artistic merits at all. A. writes a book about greengrocers, and you, who find something singularly piquant and entertaining in the manners, speech, and habits of the class in question, pronounce A. to be a "great artist" who has written a masterpiece. I love dukes, and B's. novel of the peerage strikes me as a marvel of artistic accomplishment, while I pronounce the work that has charmed you to be as stupid and tiresome as the class it represents. Each of us is talking nonsense; there is no art in the question, which is purely a matter of individual taste. The Stock Exchange column interests one man, while the latest football news absorbs the other. That is all.

Of course, as I said, artifice counts for something: there is a pleasure in seeing the thing neatly done, and I suppose it is this pleasure that has secured Miss Austen her fervent admirers. It is a little difficult to treat this form of pleasure quite fairly; a musician perhaps would find it difficult to answer the question whether he would rather hear Palestrina badly rendered or Zingarelli executed to perfection. In the latter case there would certainly be the charm of exquisite voices in perfect order and accord, though the music were nothing or worse than nothing; still, our musician might say, on the other hand, that Palestrina martyred was better than Zingarelli triumphant. I am afraid I can imagine myself saying: "Limited country-people, as seen by Jane Austen, are so 'slow' that they rather bore me, though the author has portrayed them with wonderful skill", but I can hardly fancy myself affirming that Becky Sharp is such an interesting personage that she would still delight me, even if the author of *Ten Thousand a Year* had written her history. On the other hand I believe that the plot of *Jekyll and Hyde* would still have had some fascination, though it had been treated by the veriest dolt in letters. But that is not a good example, since *Jekyll and Hyde* is certainly in its conception, though not in its execution, a work of fine art. Let us take *The Moonstone* again as an example; I believe, then, that if the events related in it had caught our eyes in a brief newspaper paragraph they would still have interested.

It seems to me that, after all, this question of artifice, of "how the thing is done", comes under the same category as liking and disliking. I mean it is largely a matter of the personal equation, about which no very strict laws can be laid down. You might say, for example, that Becky would entertain you in any hands, however indifferent, provided that her "facts" were preserved, and I don't see that I could argue the point with you. It reminds me again of the way in which men choose their friends; one lays stress on pleasant manners, another on sterling goodness of character, a third on wit, a fourth on distinction of some kind; and argument is really voiceless. "Here is a book-case," you may say, "look how exquisitely it is made." Yes, but I don't want a book-case; whereas that table, rickety as it is, will be really useful. But if you were to say: "Look at Westminster Abbey," you can hardly imagine my answering: "Bother Westminster Abbey; I want a pig-sty." You see how, here again, we come to the generic difference between fine literature and interesting reading-matter. We read the Odyssey because we are supernatural, because we hear in it the echoes of the eternal song, because it symbolises for us certain amazing and beautiful things, because it is music; we read Miss Austen and Thackeray because we like to recognise the faces of our friends aptly reproduced, to see the external face of humanity so deftly mimicked, because we are natural. The question of our preference for one over the other is, making due allowance for analogy, the question of our preference for a table over a book-case or *vice versâ,* and the workmanship in each case is largely a matter of detail. And the great poem may be equated with the great church: each is made for beauty, the one is ecstasy in words, the other ecstasy in stone. But the church and the pig-sty, on the other hand, are not to be compared together: incidentally, no doubt, the former is rainproof or in ill repair, has good or bad acoustic properties, while the latter may be either an æsthetic pest in the back-yard, or an agreeable looking little shed enough. Still, the essence of the church is beauty, ecstasy; of the sty utility, the safe keeping of pigs. It would be absurd, you see, to say: "I prefer an abbey to a pig-sty," and it would be equally absurd to say: "I prefer the Œdipus to *Pride and Prejudice*" or "I prefer the Venus of the Louvre to the wax-figures in the exhibition." Of course these are only analogies, and you mustn't press them, but they may help to make my meaning clearer, to enforce the vast distinction between art and artifice. Please don't think that I wish to establish a proportion: as a pig-sty is to an abbey, so is Jane Austen to Sophocles. In her case you would have to substitute a neat Georgian house for "pig-sty" and then I think you would have a very fair proportion. But all that I wanted to do was to draw the line between things made for use, to occupy some definite place in relation to our common daily life; and things made by ecstasy and for ecstasy, things that are symbols, proclaiming the presence of the unknown world.

And I chose *Pickwick* as the antithesis to *Vanity Fair* deliberately. Thackeray (in my private judgment) is the chief of those who have provided interesting reading-matter; Dickens is by no means in the first rank of literary artists. I think he is golden, but he is very largely alloyed with baser stuff, with indifferent metal, which was the product of his age, of his circumstances in life, of his own uncertain taste. Just contrast the atmosphere which surrounded the young Sophocles, with that in which the young Dickens flourished. Both were men of genius, but one grew up in the City of the Violet Crown, the other in Camden Town and worse places, one was accustomed to breathe that "most pellucid air", the other inhaled the "London particular". The wonder is, not that there are faults in Dickens, but that there is genius of any kind. I am not going to analyse *Pickwick* any more than I analysed *Vanity Fair,* but of course you see that, in its conception, it is essentially one with the Odyssey. It is a book of wandering; you start from your own doorstep and you stray into the unknown; every turn of the road fills you with surmise, every little village is a discovery, a something new, a creation. You know not what may happen next; you are journeying through another world. I need not remind you how glorious all this is in the Odyssey, which of course is so much more beautiful than *Pickwick,* as that glowing Mediterranean Sea, whose bounds on every side were mystery, is more beautiful than the muddy, foggy Thames, as those rolling hexameters are more beautiful than Dickens's prose; and yet in each case the symbol is, in reality, the same; both the heroic song of the old Ionian world and the comic cockney romance of 1837 communicate that enthralling impression of the unknown, which is, at once, a whole philosophy of life, and the most exquisite of emotions. In varying degrees of intensity you will trace it all through fine literature in every age and in every nation; you will find it in Celtic voyages, in the Eastern Tale, where a door in a dull street suddenly opens into dreamland, in the mediæval stories of the wandering knights, in *Don Quixote,* and at last in our *Pickwick* where Ulysses has become a retired city man, whimsically journeying up and down the England of eighty years ago. You talk of the "grotesquerie" of *Pickwick,* but don't you see that this element is present in all the masterpieces of the kind? Remember the Cyclops, remember the grotesque shapes that decorate the *Arabian Nights,* remember the bizarre element, the almost wanton grotesquerie of many of the "Arthur" romances. In all these cases as in *Pickwick* the same result is obtained; an overpowering impression of "strangeness", of remoteness, of withdrawal from the common ways of life. *Pickwick* is, in no sense, or in no valuable sense, a portrayal, a copy, an imitation of life in the ordinary sense of "imitation" and "life"; Pickwick, and Sam, and Jingle, and the rest of them are not clever reproductions of actual people (is there any more foolish pursuit than that of disputing about the "original" of Mr. Pickwick?); the book is rather the suggestion of another life, beneath our own or beside our own, and the characters, those queer grotesque people, are queer for the same reason that the Cyclops is queer and the dwarfs and dragons of mediæval romance are queer. We are withdrawn from the common ways of life; and in that withdrawal is the beginning of ecstasy. There are sentences in *Pickwick* that give me an almost extravagant delight. You remember the lines about the Lotus-Eaters.

> τῶν δ' ὅσ τις λωτοῖο φάγοι μελιηδέα καρπὸν,
> οὐκετ' ἀπαγγεῖλαι πὰλιν ἤθελεν οὐδὲ νέεσθαι
> ἀλλ' αὐτοῦ βούλοντο μετ' ἀνδράσι Λωτοφάγοισιν
> λωτὸν ἐρεπτόμενοι μενέμεν νόστου τε λαθέσθαι.*

Well, do you know there is a brief dialogue in *Pickwick* that seems al-

---

*"But any of them who are the honey-sweet fruit of lotus was unwilling to take any message back, or to go away, but they wanted to stay there with the lotus-eating people, feeding on lotus, and forget the way home" (tr. Richmond Lattimore).

most as enchanted, to me. The scene is the manor-farm kitchen, on Christmas Eve.

"'How it snows,' said one of the men, in a low voice.

"'Snows, does it?' said Wardle.

"'Rough, cold night, sir,' replied the man, 'and there's a wind got up that drifts it across the fields, in a thick white cloud.'

"'What does Jem say?' inquired the old lady. 'There ain't anything the matter, is there?'

"'No, no, mother,' replied Wardle; 'he says there's a snow-drift, and a wind that's piercing cold.'"

You know this is the introduction to the Tale of Gabriel Grub, an admirable legend which Dickens "farsed" with an obtrusive moral. But I confess that the atmosphere (which to me seems all the wild weather and the wild legend of the north) suggested by those phrases "a thick white cloud", and "a wind that's piercing cold", is in my judgment wholly marvellous. But Dickens, of course, is full of impressions which never become expressions. You remember that chapter about the lawyer's clerks in the "Magpie and Stump"? It is always quite pathetic to me to note how Dickens *felt* the strangeness, the mystery, the haunting that are like a mist about the old Inns of Court, and how utterly unable he was to express his emotion—to find a fit symbol for his meaning. He takes refuge, as it were, behind Jack Bamber, who tells two very insignificant legends as to the mystery of the Inns. Dickens feels that these legends are insignificant, and throws in one that is pure burlesque, and then changes the subject in despair; the vague impression has refused to be put into words; probably, indeed, it had stopped short of becoming thought. But I am afraid that if I once begin to talk about the defects and faults of Dickens I shall run on for ever, and I think you will be able to find out his laches quite well for yourself. What I want to insist on is his sense of mystery, his withdrawal from common life, and, finally, his ecstasy. I have not proved my case up to the hilt by a thorough-going analysis of *Pickwick*, but I think I have suggested the "heads" of such an analysis. There is ecstasy in the main idea, in the thought of the man who wanders away from his familiar streets into unknown tracks and lanes and villages, there is ecstasy in the conception of all those queer, grotesque characters, reminders each one of the strangeness of life, there is ecstasy in the thought of the wild Christmas

Eve, of the fields and woods scourged by "a wind that's piercing cold", hidden by the thick cloud of snow, there is ecstasy in that vague impression of the old, dark Inns, of the "rotten" chambers that had been shut up for years and years. In a word: *Pickwick* is fine literature.

Well, you've got what you wanted; some sort of analysis of my case: *"Pickwick v. Vanity Fair";* but it must be clearly understood that I'm not going to "work out" every example. However, I am not sorry that I have been led to go into this particular case rather fully, because it is a typical one, and we shall not be obliged to go over the same ground again. I mean, that having witnessed the dissection of Thackeray, you will have no need to come to me for my judgment of George Eliot, or of Anthony Trollope, or—to make a very long list a very short one—of about ninety-nine per cent of our modern novels. Yes, you have mentioned a great name, and I, like you, take off my cap to the man who has gone on his way, without caring for the "public", or the "reviewers", or anything else, except his own judgment of what is right. But, frankly, if you pass from the man and come to his work, my plain opinion is this: that he has written about ordinary life, regarded from an ordinary standpoint, in a style which is extraordinary certainly, but very far from beautiful. It is not a beautiful style, since a fine style, though it may carry suggestion beyond the bourne of thought, though it may be the veil and visible body of concealed mysteries, is always plain on the surface. It may be like an ingeniously devised cryptogram, which may have an occult sense conveyed to initiated eyes in every dot and line and flourish, but is outwardly as simple and straightforward as a business letter. But in the works of the writer whom we are discussing obscurities, dubieties of all kinds are far from uncommon; and in many of his books there are passages which hardly seem to be English at all. The words are familiar—most of them—the grammatical construction often offers no very considerable difficulties—it is rarely, I mean, that one has to search very long for the nominative of the sentence—but when one has read the words and parsed them, one feels inclined to think that after all the passage is not in English but in some other language with a superficial resemblance to English. Style is not everything? Certainly not; a book may fail in style, and yet be fine, though not the finest literature. You have only to open Sir Walter Scott to have highly conclusive evidence on that point. But the writer we are considering not only fails in the body of art but even more conspicuously in the soul of it. Just think for a moment of his story of the very earnest Jew who fell in love with the baroness who was not very earnest. There was a false female friend, you remember, and social complications perturbed the hearts of the curiously assorted lovers, and finally the Jew was shot in a duel by another, less "detrimental" courtier. Can you conceive anything more trivial than this? Don't you see that from such a book as that the *idea,* the soul of fine literature, is completely lacking? Great books may always be summed up in a phrase, often in a single word, and that phrase or that word will always signify some primary and palmary idea. To me the only "idea" suggested by the plot I have outlined is unimportance; and, as in the case of Thackeray, ecstasy is entirely absent both from this and from all other of the author's books. You say that, after all, the plot in question is a plot of the love of a man for a woman, and that *that* is an idea in the highest sense of the word, and an idea which is the most of all fit for the purpose and the making of the finest literature. I agree with you in the latter clause of your sentence, but I must point out that the book is *not* the story of the love of a man for a woman, it is the story of the flirtation of a baroness with a German Jew Socialist—a very different matter. In a word, it is a tale of the accidental, of the particular, of the inessential; it is completely the play of Hamlet with the part of Hamlet omitted, and the greatest stress laid on the minor characters.

It is quite true that when an author writes a romance containing a hero and a heroine he must tell you who they are, he must give, briefly and succinctly, the necessary details—names, ages, conditions and so forth—but if he is a great author he will do this incidentally and make us feel that such details are incidental. In short, he must poise his feet on earth, but his way is to the stars. Think of *The Scarlet Letter,* open it again and see how admirably Hawthorne has omitted a world of inessential details that a lesser man would have put in. He has left out a whole encyclopædia of useless and tedious information; there is the dim, necessary background of time and place, but in reality the scene is Eternity, and the drama is the Mystery of Love and Vengeance and Hell-fire. Of course fine literature must have its gross and carnal body, we must know "who's who", for I don't think an old-fashioned recipe that I remember was ever very successful. Oh, you must have read some of the tales I mean; they used to flourish in the old *Keepsakes,* and the hero was boldly labelled "Fernando" for all distinction and description. One might surmise that Fernando was domiciled on the continent of Europe, but that was all. It was not successful, this well-meaning school of fiction, and I repeat that the finest literature must have its accidents—it cannot exist as shining substance alone. It is just the same with the art of sculpture, with the art of painting. You cannot look at a Greek Apollo without looking at that part of the body which conceals the bowels, but I imagine you don't want to treasure this thought or to insist on it? And I suppose a geologist, looking at a picture, could tell you whether those wild and terrible rocks were volcanic or carboniferous; but really one doesn't want to know. Bowels, geological formation, in sculpture and painting, the social position of the characters and all other such details in fine literature are inessential; and the great artist will, as I said, make us feel that they are inessential. If you want an instance of what I mean read a book which is very comparable with the German-Jew-Baroness tale that we were talking about. I mean *Two on a Tower* by Mr. Hardy. In that you have the contrast of social ranks: the "two" are the lady of the manor and an educated peasant, but how utterly all thought of "society" (in any sense of the word) disappears from those wonderful pages, as you advance and find that the theme is really Love. Why even the accidents are glorified and are made of the essence of the book. The old tower standing in the midst of lonely, red ploughlands far from the highway is at first only the convenient place where the young peasant studies astronomy; but as you read you feel the change coming, the tower is transmuted, glorified; every stone of it is aglow with mystic light; it is made the abode of the Lover and the Beloved, it is seen to be a symbol of Love, of an ecstasy, remote, and passionate, and eternal, dwelling far from the ways of men. Compare these two books, I say again, and you will know the chief distinction between fine literature and reading-matter. To me, I confess, the "Jew-book" has not even interest of the lower sort, not by any means the interest of Thackeray, or Jane Austen or even of poor, dreary, draggle-tailed George Eliot; but if you are amused by it, I have no objection to make. You may be amused by the plates of the "Spring and Summer Novelties" in the ladies' paper, if you please; but for heaven's sake don't come here and tell me that on the whole you prefer Botticelli's Primavera! Nay, but the fashion-plates are sometimes very nicely done, and they put in backgrounds, and they are trying to give the faces some character. Do get it into your head—firmly and fixedly—that the camera and the soul of man are two entirely different things.

You think the "photographic" comparison unfair, in this and other instances, because of the mechanical element in photography, because of that camera I have just mentioned? Well, I suppose that it *is* a little misleading. The sun and the camera between them certainly do your picture for you, and as you urge, there is more of artifice in the merest Sunday-school tale than in the best of photographs. Still, you must remember that photography too has its artifice, its choice of the right and the wrong way, and its exercise of judgment; there is a great deal in it that is not mechanical; and in its essence it is of the same class as the books I have been alluding to. The means employed are different, and a higher and finer artifice is required for making books than for taking photographs, but the end of each is the same, and that end is to portray the surface of life, to make a picture of the outside of things. It is on this ground that I defend my use of the analogy, and you must understand me to speak only of the object which is common to each, when I compare the secondary writer to a photographer. The writers, to be sure, have invention in a greater or less degree, but you will remark that the artists in literature have the power of creation, a totally different process. Invention is the finding of a thing in its more or less obscure hiding-place; creation is the making of a new thing, the invocation of Something from Nothingness. Don Quixote is a creation, the clergyman in *Pride and Prejudice* is an invention, Colonel Newcome is, in all probability, a composite portrait, while the Jew-Socialist who fell in love with the Baroness is simply a portrait of Ferdinand Lassalle.

You must remember that while the two classes—fine literature and reading-matter—differ the one from the other generically, the individuals of each class differ from each other only specifically. Thus the difference in merit between the Odyssey and *Pickwick* is enormous, but it is a specific difference. In the same way it is hard to measure with the imagination the difference between *Madame Bovary* and that famous Sunday-school story *Jackie's Holiday:* the former is immensely clever, the latter is immensely silly; but the two are, emphatically, of the same genus. In each case the effort of the author is to "describe life", the aim of Flaubert is absolutely identical with the aim of Miss Flopkins, and their results differ only as the Frenchman differs from the Englishwoman, the one being a serious and patient artificer while the other is a bungling idiot, who obtrudes her very empty personality and her very trashy ethics instead of studiously concealing them. Still: a photograph taken in the most famous studio in London is still a photograph equally with the spotted and misty effort of the amateur, and no amount of "touching-up" or "finishing", however patient it may be, will turn a photograph into a work of art. And, in like manner, no labour, no care, no polishing of the phrase, no patience in investigation, no artifice in plot or in construction will ever make "reading-matter" into fine literature.

III

I see that I shall be obliged to keep on reiterating the difference between fine literature and "literature", or in other words between art and observation expressed with artifice. I am afraid that, in your heart of hearts, you still believe that the Odyssey is fine literature, and that *Pride and Prejudice* is fine literature, though the Odyssey is "better" than *Pride and Prejudice.* It is that "better" that I want to get out of your head, that monstrous fallacy of comparing Westminster Abbey with the charming old houses in Queen Square. You would see the absurdity of imagining that there can be any degree of comparison between two things entirely different, if I substituted for *Pride and Prejudice* some ordinary circulating-library novel of our own times. At least I hope you would see, though, as I told you a few weeks ago, I doubt very much whether many people realise the distinction between the Odyssey and a political pamphlet. The general opinion, I expect, is that both belong to the same class, though the Greek poem is much more "important" than the pamphlet. I think we succeeded in demonstrating the falsity of this idea, in shewing clearly and decisively that fine literature means the expression of the eternal human ecstasy in the medium of words, and that it means nothing else whatsoever. Words, it is true, are used for other ends than this: they are used in sending telegrams to stockbrokers, for example, but why should this double office create any confusion? A tub and a tabernacle may each be made of wood, but you don't mix the two things up on that account? The other day you gave me a most amusing account of your landlady's quarrels with her servant girls. I remember that I laughed consumedly, and at the moment that solemn preconisation of the servant Mabel to the effect that her mistress, Mrs. Stickings, was not a "lydy", was more to my taste than the recitation of the "Ode on a Grecian Urn". But you surely didn't think that you were making literature all the while? Or that the history of Mrs. Stickings and Mabel would have mysteriously become literature if you had written it down and got somebody to print it? Or that it would have been literature if some of the details had been a little exaggerated (I thought you had embroidered here and there); or if you had made the whole story up out of your own head? Exactly, you were, as you say, amusing me by the relation of facts a little altered, compressed, and embellished, and I am glad that you see that no process of writing or printing, no variation in the proportion of truth and invention, even to the total lack of all truth, could have changed an amusing presentation of the Stickings *ménage* into fine literature. But, surely, it is so very obvious. Did any cook ever think that he could change a turkey into a bird of paradise by careful attention to the *farse* and the sauce? The farmer might as well expect to breed early phœnixes for Leadenhall Market by the simple process of lighting a bonfire in the farmyard. The young ducks would jump into the blaze, and the transformation would be the work of a second! There is no more madness in *that* notion than in the other one—that one has only to print an amusing, interesting, life-like, or pathetic tale to make it into fine literature.

Yes; but what I am afraid is still lurking somewhere in your skull is this: that if only the stuffing is extremely well made, if only the sauce is an exquisite concoction, the turkey *is,* somehow or other, changed into a bird of paradise. That is, to translate the analogy, if only the plot is very ingenious, if only the construction is well carried out, if the characters are extremely life-like, if the English is admirably neat and sufficient, then reading-matter becomes fine literature. Make the bonfire high enough and your young ducks will be burned into phœnixes fast enough; let the artifice be sufficiently artificial and it will be art. Indeed, you might as well maintain that a wooden statue, if it be really well carved, is thereby made into a gold statue.

Well, I remember saying one night that you were here that ecstasy is at once the most exquisite of emotions and a whole philosophy of life. And it is to the philosophy of life that we are brought, in the last resort. You know that there are, speaking very generally, two solutions of existence; one is the materialistic or rationalistic, the other, the spiritual or mystic. If the former were true, then Keats would be a queer kind of madman, and the *Morte d'Arthur* would be an elaborate symptom of insanity; if the latter is true, then *Pride and Prejudice* is not fine literature, and the works of George Eliot are the works of a superior insect—and nothing more. You must make your choice: is the story of the Graal lunacy, or not? You think it is not: then do not talk any more of turning glass into diamonds by careful polishing and cutting. Do not say: Mr. A. spends five years over a book, and therefore what he writes is fine literature; Miss B. polishes off five novels in a year, and therefore she does not write fine literature. Do not say, Mr. Shorthouse got the name of a man who kept a private school in the time of Charles I. quite right; therefore *John Inglesant* is fine literature, while the archæological details in *Ivanhoe* are all wrong, therefore it is not fine literature. Good Lord! You might as well say: but my landlady's name is Mrs. Stickings, and the girl (who left last month) was really called Mabel; *therefore* that story of mine was fine literature. What's that about sustained effort? Can you turn a deal ladder into a golden staircase by making it of a thousand rungs? What I say three times is right, eh? and if I tell the tale of Mrs. Stickings so that it extends to "our minimum length for three-volume novels", it becomes fine literature.

Well, I really hope that we have at last settled the matter; that fine literature is simply the expression of the eternal things that are in man, that it is beauty clothed in words, that it is always ecstasy, that it always draws itself away, and goes apart into lonely places, far from the common course of life. Realise this, and you will never be misled into pronouncing mere reading-matter, however interesting, to be fine literature; and now that we clearly understand the difference between the two, I propose that we drop the "fine" and speak simply of literature.

But I assure you that, even after having established the grand distinction, it is by no means plain sailing. Everything terrestrial is so composite (except, perhaps, pure music) that one is confronted by an almost endless task of distinguishing matter from form, and body from spirit. Literature, we say, is ecstasy, but a book must be written about something and about somebody; it must be expressed in words, it must have arrangement and artifice, it must have accident as well as essence. Consider *Don Quixote* as an example; it is, I suppose, the finest prose romance in existence. Essentially, it expresses the eternal quest of the unknown, that longing, peculiar to man, which makes him reach out towards infinity; and he lifts up his eyes, and he strains his eyes, looking across the ocean, for certain fabled, happy islands, for Avalon that is beyond the setting of the sun. And he comes into life from the unknown world, from glorious places, and all his days he journeys through the world, spying about him, going on and ever on, expecting beyond every hill to find the holy city, seeing signs, and omens, and tokens by the way, reminded every hour of his everlasting citizenship. "From the great deep to the great deep he goes": it is true of King Arthur and of each one of us; and this, I take it, is the essence of *Don Quixote,* and of all his forerunners and successors. Then, in the second place, you get the eternal moral of the book, and you will understand that I am not using "moral" in the vulgar sense. The eternal moral, then, of *Don Quixote* is the strife between temporal and eternal, between the soul and the body, between things spiritual and things corporal, between ecstasy and the common life. You read the book and you see that there is a perpetual jar, you are continually confronted by the great antinomy of life. It seems a mere comic incident when the knight dreaming of enchantment is knocked about, and made ridiculous; but I tell you it is the perpetual tragedy of life itself, symbolised. I say that it is, under a figure, the picture of humanity in the world, that you will find the truth it represents repeated again and again throughout all history. You know that if one goes back resolutely to the first principles of things, one finds oneself, as it were, in a place where all lines that seemed parallel and eternally divided meet, and so it is with this tragedy symbolised by the Don Quixote. It is, you may say, the tragedy of the Unknown and the Known, of the Soul and Body, of the Idea and the Fact, of Ecstasy and Common Life; at last, I suppose, of Good and Evil. The source of it lies far beyond our understanding, but its symbol is shewn again and again in Cervantes's page.

Then, there is a third element in the book. The author intended to write a burlesque on the current romances of chivalry; and he wrote, I suppose, the best burlesque that has ever been written, or ever will be written. If you unhappily so choose, you can shut your eyes to everything serious and everything beautiful, and read merely of Amadis and Arthur "taken off", of the highest ideals turned into nonsense, of the best motives shewn to be, in effect, mischievous. You will read how the knight, in the approved manner of knights, helped the oppressed and the wretched, and how he usually worsened their condition tenfold. You may lend your ear to Sancho, grumbling and quoting "common-sense" proverbs all the road, as he rides on his ass, and if it were not for the wit and the comedy, you might fancy yourself in a suburban train bound for the city. Why, if you so please, *Don Quixote* is the institute of cynicism, the reduction of every generous impulse to absurdity.

Finally, the knight is the mouthpiece of Cervantes himself, especially towards the end of the second part, where the armour and the fantasy drop off, piece by piece, and shred by shred, on that mournful, homeward journey. At last, I say, Don Quixote is almost simply Cervantes, commenting on men and affairs in Spain, and I think that in those final chapters the art has vanished together with the armour and the ecstasy. Yes, I always dread the ending of *Don Quixote.* A star drops a line of streaming fire, down the vault of the sky, and perhaps you may have seen the ugly, shapeless thing that sinks into the earth.

But this very brief and imperfect analysis of a great masterpiece of literary art may give you some idea of the extraordinary complexity of all literature. As it is I have omitted one most important item in the account; I have said nothing of the style, because, I am sorry to say that I have no Spanish, and Cervantes speaks to me through an interpreter named Charles Jarvis. But, omitting style, you see that we have, in this particular case, five books in one; we have the utterance of pure ecstasy, the strife between ecstasy and the common life, the burlesque of chivalry, the institutes of cynicism, and the comments on affairs. Each of these different themes is managed with consummate ability, and (always excepting the last chapters of the book) each keeps its due place, so that it really rests with the reader, in a manner, to choose which book he is to read.

And then there are other elements which must be accounted for if one is to judge a book as a whole, fairly and thoroughly. I may be so charmed with the writer's rapture, with the wonder and beauty of his idea, that I may forget the fact that the artist must also be the artificer; that while the soul conceives, the understanding must formulate the conception, that while ecstasy must suggest the conduct of the story, common-sense must help to range each circumstance in order, that while an inward, mysterious delight must dictate the burning phrases and sound in the music and melody of the words, cool judgment must go through every line, reminding the author that, if literature be the language of the Shadowy Companion, it must yet be translated out of the unknown speech into the vulgar tongue. Here then we have the elements of a book. Firstly the Idea or Conception, the thing of exquisite beauty which dwells in the author's soul, not yet clothed in words, nor even in thought, but a pure emotion. Secondly, when this emotion has taken definite form, is made incarnate as it were, in the shape of a story, which can be roughly jotted down on paper, we may speak of the Plot. Thirdly, the plot has to be systematised, to be drawn to scale, to be carried out to its legitimate conclusions, to be displayed by means of Incident; and here we have Construction. Fourthly, the story is to be written down, and Style is the invention of beautiful words which shall affect the reader by their meaning, by their sound, by their mysterious suggestion.

This, then, is the fourfold work of literature, and if you want to be perfect you must be perfect in each part. Art must inspire and shape each and all, but only the first, the Idea, is pure art; with Plot, and Construction, and Style there is an alloy of artifice. If then any given book can be shewn to proceed from an Idea, it is to be placed in the class of literature, in the shelf of the Odyssey as I think I once expressed it. It may be placed very high in the class; the more it have of rapture in its every part, the higher it will be: or, it may be placed very low, because, for example, having once admired the Conception, the dream that came to the author from the other world, we are forced to admit that the Story or Plot was feebly imagined, that the Construction was clumsily carried out, that the Style is, æsthetically, non-existent. You will notice that I am never afraid of blaming my favourites, of finding fault with the books which I most adore. I can do so freely and without fear of consequences, since having once applied my test, and having found that *Pickwick,* for example, is literature, I am not in the least afraid that I shall be compelled to eat my words if flaws in plot and style and construction are afterwards made apparent. The statue is gold; we have settled that much, and we need not fear that it will turn into lead, if we find that the graving and carving is poor enough. Once be sure that your temple *is* a temple, and I will warrant you against it being suddenly transmuted into a tub, through the discovery of scamped workmanship.

Well, suppose we begin to apply our analysis. Let us take the strange case of R. L. Stevenson, and especially his *Jekyll and Hyde,* which, in some ways, is his most characteristic and most effective book. Now I suppose that instructed opinion (granting its existence) was about equally divided as to the class in which this most skilful and striking story was to be placed. Many, I have no doubt, gave it a very high place in the ranks of imaginative literature, or (as we should now say) in the ranks of literature; while many other judges set it down as an extremely clever piece of sensationalism, and nothing more. Well, I think both these opinions are wrong; and I should be inclined to say that *Jekyll and Hyde* just scrapes by the skin of its teeth, as it were, into the shelves of literature, and no more. On the surface it would seem to be merely sensationalism; I expect that when you read it, you did so with breathless absorption, hurrying over the pages in your eagerness to find out the secret, and this secret once discovered, I imagine that *Jekyll and Hyde* retired to your shelf—and stays there, rather dusty. You have never opened it again? Exactly. I *have* read it for a second time, and I was astonished to find how it had, if I may say so, evaporated. At the first reading one was enthralled by mere curiosity, but when once this curiosity had been satisfied, what remained? If I may speak from my own experience, simply a rather languid admiration of the ingenuity of the plot with its construction, combined with a slight feeling of impatience, such as one might experience if one were asked to solve a puzzle for the second time. You see that the secret once disclosed all the steps which lead to the disclosure become, *ipso facto,* insignificant, or rather they become nothing at all, since their only significance and their only existence lay in the secret, and when the secret has ceased to be a secret, the signs and cyphers of it fall also into the world of non-entity. You may be amazed, and perplexed, and entranced by a cryptogram, while you are solving it, but the solution once attained, your cryptogram is either nothing or perilously near to nothingness.

Well, all this points, doesn't it, towards mere sensationalism, very cleverly done? But, as I said, I think *Jekyll and Hyde* just scrapes over the border-line and takes its place, very low down, among books that are literature. And I base my verdict solely on the Idea, on the Conception that lies, buried rather deeply, beneath the plot. The plot, in itself, strikes me as mechanical—this actual physical transformation, produced by a drug, linked certainly with a theory of ethical change, but not linked at all with the really mysterious, the really psychical—all this affects me, I say, as ingenious mechanism and nothing more; while I have shewn how the construction is ingenious artifice, and the style is affected by the same plague of laboured ingenuity. Throughout it is a thoroughly conscious style, and in literature all the highest things are unconsciously, or at least, subconsciously produced. It has music, but it has no under-music, and there are no phrases in it that seem veils of dreams, echoes of the "inexpressive song". It is on the conception, then, alone, that I justify my inclusion of *Jekyll* amongst works of art; for it seems to me that, lurking behind the plot, we divine the presence of an Idea, of an inspiration. "Man is not truly one, but truly two," or, perhaps, a polity with many inhabitants, Dr. Jekyll writes in his confession, and I think that I see here a trace that Mr. Stevenson had received a vision of the mystery of human nature, compounded of the dust and of the stars, of a dim vast city, splendid and ruinous as drowned Atlantis deep beneath the waves, of a haunted quire where a flickering light burns before the Veil. This, I believe, was the vision that came to the artist, but the admirable artificer seized hold of it at once and made it all his own, omitting what he did not understand, translating roughly from the unknown tongue, materialising, coarsening, hardening. Don't you see how thoroughly *physical* the actual plot is, and if one escapes for a moment from the atmosphere of the laboratory it is only to be confronted by the most obvious vein of moral allegory; and from this latter light *Jekyll and Hyde* seems almost the vivid metaphor of a clever preacher. You mustn't imagine, you know, that I condemn the powder business as bad in itself, for (let us revert for a moment to philosophy) man is a sacrament, soul manifested under the form of body, and art has to deal with each and both and to shew their interaction and interdependence. The most perfect form of literature is, no doubt, lyrical poetry which is, one might say, almost pure Idea, art with scarcely an alloy of artifice, expressed in magic words, in the voice of music. In a word, a perfect lyric, such as Keats's "Belle Dame sans Mercy" is *almost* pure soul, a spirit with the luminous body of melody. But (in our age, at all events) a prose romance must put on a grosser and more material envelope than this, it must have incident, corporeity, relation to material things, and all these will occupy a considerable part of the whole. To a certain extent, then, the Idea must be materialised, but still it must always shine through the fleshly vestment; the body must never be mere body but always the body of the spirit, existing to conceal and yet to manifest the spirit; and here it seems to me that Mr. Stevenson's story breaks down. The transformation of

Jekyll into Hyde is solely material as you read it, without artistic significance; it is simply an astounding incident, and not an outward sign of an inward mystery. As for the possible allegory I have too much respect for Mr. Stevenson as an artificer to think that he would regard this element as anything but a very grave defect. Allegory, as Poe so well observed, is always a literary vice, and we are only able to enjoy *The Pilgrim's Progress* by forgetting that the allegory exists. Yes, that seems to me the *vitium* of *Jekyll and Hyde:* the conception has been badly realised, and by badly I do not mean clumsily, because from the logical, literal standpoint, the plot and the construction are marvels of cleverness; but I mean inartistically: ecstasy, which as we have settled is the synonym of art, gave birth to the idea, but immediately abandoned it to artifice, and to artifice only, instead of presiding over and inspiring every further step in plot, in construction, and in style. All this may seem to you very fine-drawn and over-subtle, but I am convinced that it is the true account of the matter, and perhaps you may realise my theory better if I draw out that analogy of "translation" which I suggested, I think, a few minutes ago. I was passing along New Oxford Street the other day, and I happened to look into a shop which displays Bibles in all languages, and I glanced at the French version, open at the seventh chapter of the Book of Proverbs. I saw the words "un jeune homme dépourvu de bon sens", and then, lower down, "comme un bœuf à la boucherie", and it was some considerable time before I realised that these phrases "translated", "a young man void of understanding", and "as an ox goeth to the slaughter". Now you notice that these are in every way commonplace examples; there is nothing extraordinarily poetical in either phrase as it stands in the Authorised Version. I might have made the contrast much more violent by choosing a passage from the Song of Songs or Ecclesiastes; and I wonder how "Therefore with Angels and Archangels" would go into French. But isn't the gulf astounding between "void of understanding" and "dépourvu de bon sens"? Yet the meaning of the French is really the same as the meaning of the English; logically, I should think, the two phrases are exactly equivalent. And yet . . . well, we know perfectly well that "dépourvu de bon sens" in no way renders that noble and austere simplicity that we reverence in the English text.

Now, I think, you ought to see what I have been trying to express about the gulf that may open always between the conception and the plot, or story, that does divide the conception from the plot of *Jekyll and Hyde.* Of course the analogy is not perfect, because the *magnum chaos* that yawns between the unformulated idea and the formulated plot, between pure ecstasy and ecstasy *plus* artifice, is much vaster than the distinction between English and French, indeed between the two former there is almost or altogether the difference of the infinite and the finite, of soul and body; still, you see how a book is a rendering, a translation of an Idea, and how a very fine idea may be embodied in a very mechanical plot.

You remember the "Socialist and Baroness" novel that we were talking about the other night. We placed it outside of literature firstly and chiefly because it was not based on ecstasy, on an idea of any kind, and secondly, and by way of consequence, because in its execution and detail it was so thoroughly insignificant, because it played Hamlet with the part of the Prince omitted. Now I think that it is strong evidence of the soundness of my literary theory that we are enabled by it to take two books so utterly dissimilar in manner and method, in story and treatment, and to judge them both by the same scale. For this is what it really comes to: we say that *The Tragic Comedians* is not literature because it simply tells of facts without their significance, because it deals with the outward show and not with the inward spirit, because it is accidental and not essential. And in just the same way we say that *Jekyll and Hyde* (its conception apart) is not literature inasmuch as it too has the body of a story without the soul of a story, the incident, the fact, without the inward thing of which the fact is a symbol. For if you will consider the matter you will see that a fact *qua* fact has no existence in art at all. It is not the painter's business to make us a likeness of a tree or a rock; it is his business to communicate to us an emotion—an ecstasy, if you please—and that he may do so he uses a tree or a rock as a symbol, a word in his language of colour and form. It is not the business of the sculptor to chisel likenesses of men in marble; the human form is to him also a symbol which stands for an idea. In the same manner it is not the business of the literary artist to describe facts—real or imaginary—in words: he is possessed with an idea which he symbolises by incident, by a story of men and women and things. He is possessed, let us say, by the idea of Love: then he must write a story of lovers, but he must never forget that A. and B., his actual lovers in the tale, with their social positions, their whims and fancies, their sayings and doings, are only of consequence in the degree that they symbolise the universal human passion, which in its turn is a copy of certain eternal and ineffable things. If A. and B. do *not* do this then they are nothing, and worse than nothing, so far as art is concerned. "But my tree is like a tree," says the dull painter, and "my anatomy is faultless," says the bad sculptor, and "my characters are life-like," says the novelist.

And one can apply exactly the same reasoning to Mr. Stevenson's ingenious story. I do not know whether there is, or has been, or will be a salt in existence which can turn a man into another person; that is of not the slightest consequence to the argument. The result of the powder, as it is described in the book, is an incident, and it makes no difference to the critical judgment whether the incident is true or false, probable or improbable. The only point, absolutely the only point is this: is the incident significant or insignificant, is it related for its own sake, or is it posited because it is a sign, a symbol, a word which veils and reveals the artist's ecstasy and inspiration? The socialist fell in love with the baroness: it is true, you say, it really happened so in Germany some fifty years ago. But in the book it is insignificant. The doctor took the powder and became another man; it is probably untrue. But it is also insignificant; and to the critic of art in literature the one incident stands precisely on the same footing as the other.

And, do you know, I am glad I have made this comparison between *Jekyll and Hyde* and *The Tragic Comedians,* because it has struck me that what I have been saying about the essential element of all literature might be open to very grave misunderstanding. I have been insisting, with reiteration that must have tired you, that there is only one test by which literature may be distinguished from mere reading-matter, and that that test is summed up in the word, ecstasy. And then we admitted a whole string of synonyms—desire of the unknown, sense of the unknown, rapture, adoration, mystery, wonder, withdrawal from the common life—and I daresay I have used many other phrases in the same sense without giving you any special warning that it was our old friend again in a new guise. But it has just occurred to me that with all this wealth of synonyms, I may not have made my meaning perfectly clear. For example, while I was laying down the law about Dr. Jekyll's powder and its effects, you might have interrupted me with the remark: "But I thought you said the sense of wonder was characteristic of literature; and surely the change from Jekyll into Hyde is extremely wonderful." Or again, when I was belauding the Odyssey, dwelling on the voyage of Ulysses amongst strange peoples, you might have put in some modern tale of strange adventure, and requested me to distinguish between the two, to justify my praise of the old, and rejection of the new. And we have mentioned Sunday-school books, always, I think, with a certain *nuance* of contempt; but Sunday-school books usually deal with religion, and religion and adoration are almost synonymous. And so one could go on with the list, making out, on our premisses, with our own test, a plausible case for books which we know very well are neither literature nor anything remotely approaching it. And that would look rather like the collapse of our literary case, wouldn't it?

Well, the solution of the difficulty seems to me to be sought for in the remarks I was making just now about "facts" in art. I said, you remember, that in art, facts as facts have no existence at all. Facts, incidents, plots, simply form the artistic speech—its mode of expression, or medium—and if there is no idea behind the facts, then you have no longer language but gibberish. Just as language is made up of the letters of the alphabet, arranged in significant words and sentences, so is the artistic language made up of plots, incidents, sentences which are informed with significance. If I heap up letters of the alphabet, and arrange them in an arbitrary collocation, without meaning, I am forming gibberish, and not a language; and so if I pepper my pages with extraordinary incidents, without attaching to them any significance, I am writing, it may be, an exciting, absorbing, interesting book, but I am not making literature. Indeed, some of the books that might be mentioned in this connection remind me of a man swearing: he uses the holiest names but he does so in such a manner that he excites not reverence and awe but disgust and repulsion. Tell the bare "plot" of the Odyssey to one of these writers, and hint that it might be made into a "successful Christmas book for boys", and he will produce you a book which will contain the Lotus-Eaters, and Calypso, and the Cyclops, but which will have just the same relation to literature as blasphemy bears to the Liturgy. That seems to me the explanation; one must say again that mere incident is nothing, that it only becomes something when it is a symbol of an interior meaning. And, turning this maxim inside out, as it were, we shall sometimes find that a book which seems on the surface to be "reading-matter" is really literature, and incidents, apparently insignificant, may turn out, on a closer examination, to be significant and symbolic in a very high degree. So I don't think our literary criterion is in any way invalidated by the occurrence of surprising incidents in very worthless books. Look at *Mr. Isaacs* for example. In a sense it is a "wonderful" book, inasmuch as it contains incidents which are far removed from common experience; but you have only to read it to discover that the author had not been visited by any inspiration of the unseen. One may trace some acquaintance with theosophical "literature", but not even the dimmest vision of "the other things". The "other things"? Ah, that is another synonym, but who can furnish a precise definition of the indefinable? They are sometimes in the song of a bird, sometimes in the scent of a flower, sometimes in the whirl of a London street, sometimes hidden under a great lonely hill. Some of us seek them with most hope and the fullest assurance in the sacring of the Mass, others receive tidings through the sound of music, in the colour of a picture, in the shining form of a statue, in the meditation of eternal truth. Do you know that I can never hear a jangling piano-organ contending with the roar of traffic without the tears—not of feeling but of emotion—coming to my eyes?

And that instance—it is grotesque enough—reminds me that I think I have an explanation of another puzzle that has often perplexed me, and I daresay has perplexed you. Do you remember the books that you read when you were a boy? I can think of stories that I read long ago (I have forgotten the very names of them) that filled me with emotions that I recognised, afterwards, as purely artistic. The sorriest pirate, the most wretchedly concealed treasure, poor Captain Mayne Reid at his boldest gave me then the sensations that I now search for in the Odyssey or in the thought of it; and I looked into some of these shabby old tales years afterwards, and wondered how on earth I had managed to penetrate into "faëry lands forlorn" through such miserable stucco portals. And you, you say, extracted, somehow or other, from Harrison Ainsworth's *Lancashire Witches,* that essence of the unknown that you now find in Poe, and I expect that everybody who loves literature could gather similar recollections.

Well, it would be easy enough to solve the problem by saying that the emotions of children are of no consequence and don't count, but then I don't think that proposition is true. I think, on the contrary, that children, especially young children before they have been defiled by the horrors of "education", possess the artistic emotion in remarkable purity, that they reproduce, in a measure, the primitive man before he was defiled, artistically, by the horrors of civilisation. The ecstasy of the artist is but a recollection, a remnant from the childish vision, and the child undoubtedly looks at the world through "magic casements". But you see all this is unconscious or subconscious (to a less degree it is so in later life, and artists are rare simply because it is their almost impossible task to translate the emotion of the sub-consciousness into the speech of consciousness), and as you may sometimes see children uttering their conceptions in words that are nonsense, or next door to it, so nonsense or at any rate very poor stuff suffices with them to summon up the vision from the depths of the soul. Suppose we could catch a genius at the age of nine or ten and request him to utter what he felt; the boy would speak or write rubbish, and in the same way you would find that he read rubbish, and that it excited in him an ineffable joy and ecstasy. Coleridge was a Bluecoat boy when he read the "poems" of William Lisle Bowles, and admired them to enthusiasm, and I am quite sure that at some early period Poe had been enraptured by Mrs. Radcliffe, and we know how Burns founded himself on Fergusson. When men are young, the inward ecstasy, the "red powder of projection" is of such efficacy and virtue that the grossest and vilest matter is transmuted for them into pure gold, glistering and glorious as the sun. The child (and with him you may link all primitive and childlike people) approaches books and pictures just as he approaches nature itself and life; and a wonderful vision appears where many of us can only see the common and insignificant.

But all this has been a digression; it has come by the way in a talk about worthless and insignificant books. But I think that we should by this time have brought our testing apparatus into working order; we should be able to criticise any given book on some ground or principle, not on the rule of thumb of "It sent me to sleep," or "It kept me awake." And I think that what I have already remarked about the subconscious element in literature should have answered that question about "books with a purpose". As a matter of fact I believe that they are mostly trash, but it is not a case for *à priori* reasoning; you must test each book by itself. Mr. Stevenson was, I believe, an artist at heart, but we have seen how the artificer overcame the artist in *Jekyll and Hyde,* and in like manner there have been cases of people who were artificers, and even preachers, at heart, who were forced to succumb to the concealed, subconscious artist, when pen touched paper. For example; first logically analyse "Lycidas"; you will be disgusted just as Dr. Johnson, who had no analysis but the logical, was disgusted. Forget your logic, your common-sense, and read it again as poetry; you will acknowledge the presence of an amazing masterpiece. An unimportant lament over an unimportant personage, constructed on an affected pseudo-pastoral plan, full of acrid, Puritanical declamation and abuse, wantonly absurd with its mixture of nymphs and St. Peter; it is not only wretched in plan but clumsy in construction, the artifice is atrocious. And it is also perfect beauty! It is the very soul set to music; its austere and exquisite rapture thrills one so that I could almost say: he who understands the mystery and the beauty of "Lycidas" understands also the final and eternal secret of art and life and man.

IV

Do you know that when we last talked *belles lettres* the whole evening went by (or at least I think so) without my saying anything about *Pickwick?* I hope you noted the omission in your diary, if you keep one, because I find it difficult to talk much about literature, without drawing some illustration from that very notable, and curious, and unappreciated book. Yes, I maintain the justice of the last epithet in spite of circulation, in spite of popularity, and in spite of "Pickwick 'literature'". You may like a book very much and read it three times a year without appreciating it, and if a great book is really popular it is sure to owe its popularity to entirely wrong reasons. There are people, you know, who study Homer every day, because he throws so much light on the manners and customs of the ancients, and if a book of our own time is both great and popular, you may be sure that it is loved for its most peccant parts, just as nine people out of ten will recall "The Raven" and "The Bells" if the poetry of Edgar Allan Poe is mentioned.

After all, I needn't have excused myself for my constant references to Dickens's masterpiece, since I have already informed you that, like Coleridge, I love a "cyclical" mode of discoursing; and I honestly think that if you want to understand something about the Mysteries or the Fine Arts (which are the expression of the mysteries) it is the only way. A proposition in Euclid is demonstrated and done with, since nothing can be added to a mathematical proof; but literature is different. It is many-sided and many-coloured, and variable always; you can consider it in half-a-dozen ways, from half-a-dozen standpoints, and from half-a-dozen judgments, each of which will be true and perfect in itself, and yet each will supplement the other. Two or three weeks ago I think I tried to shew you what a complex organism any given book reveals, if one examines it with a little attention, and if one specimen be so curiously and intricately fashioned, you may imagine the complexity of the whole subject.

But I have a more particular reason for turning once more to *The Posthumous Papers.* We have noted that that which at first sight seems significant, may turn out to be insignificant, and I think that in passing I hinted that the reverse was sometimes the case. Very good; and the especial instance that is in my mind is the enormous capacity for strong drink exhibited by Mr. Pickwick and all his friends and associates. Of course you've noticed it; perhaps you have thought it a nuisance and a blemish from the artistic standpoint, just as many "good people" have found it a nuisance and a blemish from the temperance or teetotal standpoint. You may have felt quite certain that a set of men who were always drinking brandy and water, and strong ale, and milk-punch, and madeira, who constantly drank a great deal too much of each and all of these things, would be extremely unpleasant companions in private life; I daresay you have been thankful that you never knew Mr. Pickwick or any of his followers. You know, I expect, by personal experience, that a man whose daily life is a pilgrimage from one whiskey bar to another is, in most cases, an extremely tedious and unprofitable companion; and it is undeniable that the "Pickwickians" rather made opportunities for brandy and water than avoided them. And in an indirect manner, you feel that all this makes you like the book less.

But (I can no more miss an opportunity of digression than Mr. Pickwick could keep on the coach if there were a chance of drinking his favourite beverage) do you know that there are really people who make their liking or disliking of the characters the criterion of literature—of romances, I mean? We touched on this some time ago, and I remember saying that in the case of such secondary books as Jane Austen's and Thackeray's, it was permissible enough to go where one was best amused, that one had a right to say, "Yes, the artifice may be the better here, but the characters are much more amusing there, and I had rather talk to the cosmopolitan whose manners are now and then a little to seek, than to the maiden lady in the village, whose decorum is so unexceptionable." But I confess that at the time it had not dawned upon me that there are people who try to judge fine art—the true literature—on the same grounds. I believe, however, that such is the case; I believe, indeed, that the egregious M. Voltaire was dimly moved by some such feeling when he wrote his famous "criticism" of the prophet Habakkuk. What (he must have said to himself) would they think in the *salons* of a man who talked like this:—

> And the everlasting mountains were scattered,
> The perpetual hills did bow:
> His ways are everlasting?

Evidently Habakkuk could never hope for a second invitation; and *therefore* he wrote rubbish. And I believe, as I said, that there are many people who more or less unconsciously judge literature by this measure, by asking, "Would these people be pleasant to meet? would one like to hear this kind of thing in one's drawing-room?" And this is well enough with secondary books, since they contain nothing but "characters", and "incidents", and "scenes", and "facts"; but it is by no means well in literature, in which, as we found out, all these things are symbols, words of a language, used, not for themselves, but because they are significant. Remember our old definition—ecstasy, the withdrawal, the standing apart from common life—and you will see that we may almost reverse this popular method of judgment, and turn it into another test, or rather another way of putting the test, of art. For, if literature be a kind of withdrawal from the common atmosphere of life, we shall naturally expect to find its utterance, both in matter and manner, wholly unsuitable for the drawing-room or the street, and its "characters" persons whom we cannot imagine ourselves associating with on pleasant or comfortable terms. Neither you nor I would be very happy on Ulysses's boat, we should soon become irritated with Don Quixote, we should hardly feel at home with Sir Galahad. It is true that all the good there is in men is this—that at rare intervals, in certain lonely moments of exaltation they do feel for the time a faint stirring of the beautiful within them, and *then* they would adventure on the Quest of the Graal; but as you know few of us are saints, fewer, perhaps, are men of genius; we are sunk for the most part of our days in the common life, and our care is for the body and for the things of the body, for the street and the drawing-room, and not for the perpetual, solitary hills. So you see that if you read a book and can say of the characters in it: "I wish I knew them," there is very strong reason to suspect that the book in question is not literature, though it may well be a pleasant picture of pleasant people.

Yes, I was expecting that question. I should have been sorry if your sense of humour had *not* prompted you to ask whether the drinking of too much milk-punch constituted a withdrawal from the common life, a profound and lonely ecstasy. But don't you remember that when we were discussing *Pickwick* before, and comparing it with the Odyssey, I suddenly deserted Homer, and brought in Sophocles? I think I contrasted, very briefly, the education of the dramatist with the education of the romance writer, the London of the 'twenties and 'thirties with the city of the Violet Crown, the fate of him

> ἀεὶ διὰ λαμπροτάτου
> βαίνοντος ἁβρῶς ἀιθέρος*

with that of the other who tried to find the way through the evil and hideous London fog.

Well, you might have been inclined to ask, why Sophocles? But do you remember for whose festivals, in whose honour the Greek wrote his dramas and his choral songs? It was the god of wine who was worshipped and invoked at the Dionysiaca, in the praise of Dionysus the chorus sang and danced about the altar, and all the drama arose from the celebration of the Bacchic mysteries. So you get, I think, a pretty fair proportion: as the Athens of Sophocles is to the Cockneydom of Dickens, so is the cult of Dionysus to the cult of cold punch and brandy and water. The interior meaning is in each case the same; the artistic expression has lamentably deteriorated, in the degree that the artistic atmosphere on the banks of Fleet Ditch, the "mother of dead dogs", was inferior to the artistic atmosphere on the banks of the Ilissus.

I expect you have gathered from all this talk the point I want to make: that the brandy and water and punch business in *Pickwick,* which at first sight seems trivial and insignificant and even disgusting, is, in fact, full of the highest significance. Don't you notice the insistence with which the writer dwells on drinking, the unction and enthusiasm with which he describes it? We have admitted the poverty of the "materials" with which Dickens works, and of course it would be as idle to expect him to write a choral song in honour of Dionysus as it would be to expect him to write in Greek. He expressed himself as best he could, in the "language" (that is with the incidents and in the atmosphere) that he knew, but there can be no possible doubt as to his meaning. In a word, I absolutely identify the "brandy and water scenes" with the Bacchic cultus and all that it implies.

This is "a little too much for you", is it? Well, let us take another

---

*". . . always stepping gracefully through the bright air." From Euripides, *Medea* 824-25.

well-known book, the *Gargantua* and *Pantagruel.* You know it well, and I have only to remind you of the name to remind you that as *Pickwick* has been said to "reek with brandy and water", so does Rabelais assuredly reek of wine. The history begins:—

> "Grandgousier estoit bon raillard en son temps, aimant à boire net,"

it ends with the Oracle of the Holy Bottle, with the word

> "*Terrinch* . . . un mot panomphée, celebré et entendu de toutes nations, et nous signifie, *beuvez;*"

and I refer you to the allocution of Bacbuc, the priestess of the Bottle, at large. "By wine," she says, "is man made divine," and I may say that if you have not got the key to these Rabelaisian riddles much of the value—the highest value—of the book is lost to you. You know how they drink, those strange figures, the giants and their followers, you know the aroma of the vintage, the odour of the wine vat that fills all those marvellous and enigmatic pages, and I tell you that here again I recognise the same signs as in *Pickwick,* the same music as that of the dithyrambic choruses in honour of Dionysus, which were eventually amplified into that magnificent literary product, the Greek drama. And if we wish to penetrate the secret we must not forget the Hebrew psalmist, with his *calix meus inebrians quam præclarus est.* And remember, too, if you feel inclined to shudder at the milk-punch, that the words which I have just quoted might be rendered, "how splendid is this cup of wine that makes me drunk!" and we may say that, in a manner, poor Dickens did so render them, since, as I have reminded you, he belonged, after the flesh, to the Camden Town of the 'twenties, and was forced to use its unbeautiful dialect because he knew no other.

And after all, then, what does this Bacchic cultus mean? We have seen that under various disguises the one spirit appeared in Greece, in the France of the Renaissance, and in Victorian England, and that in each instance there is an apparent glorification of drunkenness. The Greeks, indeed, a sober people by necessity, as all Southerners are, impersonated the genius of intoxication, and made excessive drinking, as it would seem, an elaborate religion, with rites and festivals and mysteries. The Tourainian, whose personal habit was that not of a drunkard, but of a learned physician and restorer of ancient letters, who probably drank very much in the manner of the good curé I once knew ("My God!" he said to me, after the third small glass of small white wine, "'tis a veritable debauch!"), has, on the face of it, dedicated all his enormous book to the same cause, so that to read Pantagruel is like walking through a French village in the vintage season, when the whole world, as Zola unpleasantly and nastily expresses it, "pue le raisin". Thirdly, Dickens, who loved to talk of concocting gin-punch, and left it, when concocted, to be drunk by his guests, shews us Mr. Pickwick "dead drunk" in the wheelbarrow. And, for a final touch of apparent absurdity, you remember that the Dionysus myth represents wine as a civilising influence! You may well think of the public-house at the corner, and ask yourself how strong drink can contribute to civilisation.

Well, that is, in very brief outline, the problem and the puzzle; and I may say at once that to the literalist, the rationalist, the materialist critic, the problem is quite insoluble. But to you and me, who do not end in any kind of *ist,* the enigma will not be quite so hopeless. Let us get back to our maxim that, in literature, facts and incidents are not present for their own sake but as symbols, as words of the language of art; it will follow, then, that the incidents of the Dionysus myth, the incidents of *Pantagruel* and *Pickwick* are not to be taken literally, but symbolically. We are not to conclude that the Greeks were a race of drunkards, or that Rabelais and Dickens preached habitual excess in drink as the highest virtue; we are to conclude that both the ancient people and the modern writers recognised Ecstasy as the supreme gift and state of man, and that they chose the Vine and the juice of the Vine as the most beautiful and significant symbol of that Power which withdraws a man from the common life and the common consciousness, and taking him from the dust of the earth, sets him in high places, in the eternal world of ideas. And, after all, I cannot do better than quote at length the sermon of Bacbuc, priestess of the Dive Bouteille.

"Et icy maintenons que non rire, ains boire, est le propre de l'homme: je ne dis boire simplement et absolument, car aussi bien boivent les bestes: je dis boire vin ban et frais. Notez, amis, que de vin, divin on devient: et n'y a argument tant seur, ni art de divination moins fallace. Vos academiques l'afferment, rendans l'etymologie de vin lequel ils disent en Grec ΟΙΝΟΣ, estre comme *vis,* force, puissance.

Car pouvoir il a d'emplir l'ame de toute verité, tout savoir et philosophie. Si vous avez noté ce qui est en lettres Ioniques escrit dessus la porte du temple, vous avez peu entendre qu'en vin est verité cachée."

You see how that passage lights up the whole book, and you see what Rabelais meant in the Prologue to the first book by that reference to "certain little boxes such as we see nowadays in apothecaries' shops, the which boxes are painted on the outside with joyous and fantastic figures . . . but within they hold rare drugs, as balm, ambergris, ammonium, musk, civet, certain stones of high virtue, and all manner of precious things." I do not know whether you have read any of our English commentators on Rabelais, if not, I would not advise you to do so, unless you take pleasure in futility. For instance they take the passage from the prologue, and seeing the hint that something is concealed, try by some complicated chain of argument to shew that Rabelais veiled his attacks on the Church under a mask of "wild buffoonery". Of course the attacks on the Church (the "secondary" and comparatively unimportant element in the book, fairly answering to the attacks on books of chivalry in the *Don Quixote*) are as open as any attack can well be, and anyone who finds a veil drawn between Rabelais' dislike for the clergy and his expression of it must have a very singular notion of what constitutes concealment, and a still more singular misapprehension of the motive-forces which make and shape great books. Art, you may feel quite assured, proceeds always from love and rapture, never from hatred and disdain, and satire of every kind *qua* satire is eternally condemned to that Gehenna where the pamphlets, the "literature of the subject", and the "life-like" books lie all together. In *Don Quixote* one perceives that Cervantes loved the romances he condemns, and the satire is therefore good-humoured, and, one may say, does his book little harm or none at all; but Rabelais had been harshly treated by the friars, and his consequent ill-humour, his very violent abuse *are* in disaccord with the eternal melodies which may be discerned in *Pantagruel,* noted there under strange symbols. Yes, the satire in Rabelais is an "accident", which one has to accept and to make the best of; some of it is amusing enough, "joyous and fantastic", like the "apes and owls and antiques" that adorn the little boxes of the apothecaries, some of it is a little acrid, as I said; but let us never forget that the essence of the book is its splendid celebration of ecstasy, under the figure of the vine.

You know I have not opened the door; I have only put the key into your hands, in this as in other instances. There are things which, strange to say, are better left unsaid, and this, no doubt, Rabelais perceived when he devised his symbolism and set many traps in the paths of the shallow commentator. It was not from dread of the consequences of attacking the clergy that he devised curious veils and concealments, since, as I have noted, his hatred of the church is quite open and unconcealed. He chose the method of symbolism, firstly because he was an artist, and symbolism is the speech of art; and secondly because the high truth that he prophesied was not, and is not, fit for vulgar ears. The secret places of the human nature are not heedlessly to be exposed to the uninitiated, who would merely profane this occult knowledge if they had it. By consequence the *Complete Works of Rabelais* are obtainable in Holywell Street, and many, seeking the libidinous, have found merely the tiresome, and have cursed their bargain.

No, I will positively say no more. The key is in your hands, and with it you may open what chambers you can. There is only this to be mentioned: that, if I were you, I would not be "afraid with any amazement" should Mr. Pickwick's overdose of milk-punch prove, ultimately, a clue to the labyrinth of mystic theology.

There are, however, one or two minor points in Rabelais that may be worth notice. I might, you know, analyse it as I attempted to analyse *Don Quixote*. There is in *Gargantua* and *Pantagruel* that same complexity of thought and construction: you may note, first of all, the great essence which is common to these masterpieces as to all literature—ecstasy, expressed in the one case under the similitude of knight-errantry, in the other by the symbol of the vine. Then, in Rabelais you have another symbolism of ecstasy—the shape of *gauloiserie,* of gross, exuberant gaiety, expressing itself by outrageous tales, outrageous words, by a very cataract of obscenity, if you please, if only you will notice how the obscenity of Rabelais transcends the obscenity of common life; how grossness is poured out in a sort of mad torrent, in a frenzy, a very passion of the unspeakable. Then, thirdly, there is the impression one collects from the book: a transfigured picture of that wonderful age: there is the note of the vast, interminable argument of the schools, and for a respond, the clear, enchanted voice of Plato;

there is the vision, there is the mystery of the vast, far-lifted Gothic quire; and those fair, ornate, and smiling *châteaux* rise smiling from the rich banks of the Loire and the Vienne. The old tales told in farmhouse kitchens in the Chinonnais, the exultation of the new learning, of lost beauty recovered, the joy of the vintage, the old legends, the ancient turns of speech, the new style and manner of speaking: so to the old world answers the new. Then one has the satire of clergy and lawyers—the criticism of life—analogous, as I said, with much that is in Cervantes, and so from divers elements you see how a literary masterpiece is made into a whole.

But now, do you know, I am going to make a confession. You have heard me say more than once that in art, in literature properly so called, liking and disliking count for nothing. We have understood, I think, that when once amusing reading-matter has been put out of court, the question of how often, with what absorption one reads a work of art, matters nothing. Well, I want to contradict, or rather to modify that axiom; we have been speaking of three great books, each of which I believe firmly to be true literature—*Pickwick, Don Quixote,* and *Pantagruel.* Here is my confession. I read *Pickwick,* say, once a year, *Don Quixote,* once every three years, while I read Rabelais in fragments perhaps once in six years. You might suppose that I have indicated the order of merit? Well, I have, but you must reverse the order, since I firmly believe that *Pantagruel* is the finest of the three. We will leave Dickens out of account, since we are agreed that though the message was that of angels, the accent and the speech were of Camden Town; he, that is to say, approaches most nearly to the common life, to the common passages in which we live, and hence he, naturally, pleases us the most in our ordinary and common humours. But, of the other two, I confess that Cervantes pleases me much the more; the vulgarity of Dickens is absent, or rather it is concentrated in Sancho in a much milder form than that of *Pickwick,* for a Spanish peasant of the sixteenth century, with all his "common-sense", and practical reason, is less remote from beauty than the retired "business man" of the early nineteenth century; just as poor Mr. Pickwick, an honest, kindly creature, is vastly superior to the blatant, pretentious, diamond-bedecked swindlers who represent the city in our day. But Cervantes, who lacks, as I say, the "commonness" of Dickens, has something of the urbanity, the cosmopolitanism of Thackeray, he is, to a certain degree, a Colonel Newcome of his time, but he has seen the world more sagaciously than Colonel Newcome ever could. So while Rabelais appals me with his extravagance, his torrents of obscene words, I am charmed with the good-humoured and observant companionship of Cervantes.

And hence I conclude that *Pantagruel* is the finer book. It may sound paradoxical to say so, but don't you see that the very *grotesquerie* of Rabelais shews a further remove from the daily round, a purer metal, less tinged with the personal, material interest than *Don Quixote.* Mind you, I find greater deftness, a finer artifice in Cervantes, who I think expressed his conception the more perfectly, but I think that the conception of Rabelais is the higher, precisely because it is the more remote. Look at the *Pantagruel;* consider those "lists", that more than frankness, that ebullition of grossness, plainly intentional, designed: it is either the merest lunacy, or else it is sublime. Don't you remember the trite saying "extremes meet", don't you perceive that when a certain depth has been passed you begin to ascend into the heights? The Persian poet expresses the most transcendental secrets of the Divine Love by the grossest phrases of the carnal love; so Rabelais soars above the common life, above the streets and the gutter by going far lower than the streets and the gutter: he brings before you the highest by positing that which is lower than the lowest, and if you have the prepared, initiated mind, a Rabelaisian "list" is the best preface to the angelic song. All this may strike you as extreme paradox, but it has the disadvantage of being true, and perhaps you may assure yourself of its truth by recollecting the converse proposition—that it is when one is absorbed in the highest emotions that the most degrading images will intrude themselves. No; you are right: this is not the psychology of the "scientific" persons who write hand-books on the subject, it is not the psychology of the "serious" novelists, of those who write the annals of the "engaged"; but it happens to be the psychology of man.

I don't know that very much can be made of the signification of the characters in *Pantagruel,* as I hardly think that Rabelais was anxious to be systematic or consistent in delineating them. I believe that there are two reasons for the gigantic stature of Pantagruel, or perhaps three. The form of the whole story came from popular legends about a giant named Gargantua, and that is the first and least important reason. Secondly the "giant" conception does something to remove the book from common experience; it is a sign-post, warning you *not* to expect a faithful picture of life, but rather a withdrawal from life and from common experience, and you are in a position to appreciate the value of that motive, since I have never ceased from telling you that it is the principal motive of all literature. And, thirdly, I hesitate and doubt, but nothing more, whether the giant Pantagruel, he who is "all thirst" and ever athirst, may not be a hint of the stature of the perfect man, of the ideal man, freed from the bonds of the common life, and common appetites, having only the eternal thirst for the eternal vine. Candidly, I am inclined to favour this view, but only as a private interpretation; it may be all nonsense, and I shall not be offended or surprised if you can prove to me that it is nonsense. But have you noticed how Pantagruel is at once the most important and the least important figure in the book? He is the most important personage; he is the hero, the leader, the son of the king, the giant, wiser than any or all of his followers: formally, he is to Rabelais that which Don Quixote is to Cervantes. And yet, actually, he is little more than a vague, tremendous shadow; the living, speaking, impressive personages are Frère Jean and Panurge, who occupy the stage and capture our attention. Doesn't this rather suggest to you the part played by the "real" man in life itself; a subordinate, unobtrusive part usually, hidden very often by an exterior which bears little resemblance to the true man within. You know Coleridge says that:—

"Pantagruel is the Reason; Panurge the Understanding—the pollarded man, the man with every faculty except the reason. I scarcely know an example more illustrative of the distinction between the two. Rabelais had no mode of speaking the truth in those days but in such form as this; as it was, he was indebted to the king's protection for his life."

I must cavil at the last sentence, in which Coleridge seems to hint that Rabelais was in danger because he had hinted the distinction between the Reason and the Understanding. With all respect to Coleridge, Rabelais might have gone to the limits of psychology and metaphysics without incurring any danger; he was threatened on account of his very open satire of the church and the clergy, which, as I have pointed out, is as plain spoken as satire well can be. Still, I think that Coleridge, using the technical language of German philosophy, had a glimpse of the truth, and Mr. Besant's remark that Panurge is a careful portrait of a man without a soul is virtually the same definition in another terminology. As I have already said, I don't think that Rabelais kept his characters within the strict limits of consistence—they are only significant, perhaps, now and then—and I want to say, again, that I speak under correction in this matter, not feeling at all sure of my ground. But I am inclined to think that Pantagruel, Panurge, and the Monk are not so much three different characters, as the representative of man in his three persons. Frère Jean is, perhaps, the natural man, the "healthy animal", Panurge is the rational man, and Pantagruel, as I said, is the spiritual, or perfect man, who looms, gigantic, in the background, almost invisible, and yet all-important, and the three are, in reality, One. If I may apply the case to our own subject, I may say that while Pantagruel conceives the idea, Panurge writes the book, and Brother John has the courage to take it to the publishers. The first is the artist, the second the artificer, and the third the social being, ready to battle for his place in the material world. The giant is always calm, since his head is high above earth—*vidit nubes et sidera*—but the other two have to face the compromises of life, and suffer its defeats. All this may be purely fantastical; and at any rate I am sure that anyone who knows his Rabelais could pick many holes in my interpretation. For example, I said that the monk was the "healthy animal", and Panurge the rational man; but there are occasions when Panurge assumes the character of the unhealthy beast, the hairy-legged, hybrid creature of the Greek myth, who uses the superior human artifice for ends that are wholly bestial or worse than bestial. Still; is this a valid objection? Are there not such men in life itself? Is it not, perhaps, the peculiar and terrible privilege of humanity that it may, if it pleases, prostitute its most holy and most blessed gifts to the worst and most horrible uses? And does not each one of us feel that, potentially, at all events, there is such a being within him, not yielded to, perhaps, for a moment, yet always present, always ready to assume the command? The greatest saints, we are told, have suffered the most fiery temptations; in other words—Pantagruel is always attended by *Panurge diabolicus.* I have talked once or twice of the Shadowy Companion, but one must not forget that there is the Muddy Companion also; a being often of exquisite wit and deep understanding, but given to evil ways if one do not hold him in check.

But, in any case, I think I have shewn that the *Pantagruel* is one of the most extraordinary efforts of the human mind, full of "Pantagruelism"; and that word stands for many concealed and wonderful mysteries.

It is not in the least a "pleasant," or a "life-like," or even an "interesting" book; I think that when one knows of the key—or rather of the keys—one opens the pages almost with a sensation of dread. So it is a book that one consults at long intervals, because it is only at rare moments that a man can bear the spectacle of his own naked soul, and a vision that is splendid, certainly, but awful also, in its constant apposition of the eternal heights and the eternal depths.

V

I have been waiting for that question for a very long time, and I only wonder that you have been able to restrain yourself so well—through such a series of what I know you believe to be paradoxes, though I have assured you that I deal merely in the plainest truth. But, after all, your question is quite a legitimate one, and I remember when I first began to think of these things I went astray—simply because I did not recognise the existence of the difficulty that has been bothering you, ever since that talk of ours about the *haulte sagesse Pantagruel-ine—et Pickwickienne,* and perhaps before it.

Yes, I will put the question in its plainest, crudest form, and I will make you ask, if you please, whether Charles Dickens had any consciousness of the interior significance of the milk-punch, strong ale, and brandy and water which he caused Mr. Pickwick and his friends to consume in such outrageous quantities. It sounds plain enough and simple enough, doesn't it, and yet I must tell you that to answer that question fairly you must first analyse human nature, and I needn't remind you that *that* is a task very far from simple. "Man" sounds a very simple predicate, as you utter it; you imagine that you understand its significance perfectly well, but when you begin to refine a little, and to bring in distinctions, and to carry propositions to their legitimate bounds, you find that you have undertaken the definition of that which is essentially indefinite and probably indefinable. And, after all, we need not pitch on this term or on that, there is no need to select "man" as offering any especial difficulty, for I take it that the truth is that all human knowledge is subject to the same disadvantage, the same doubts and reservations. *Omnia exeunt in mysterium* was an old scholastic maxim; and the only people who have always a plain answer for a plain question are the pseudo-scientists, the people who think that one can solve the enigma of the universe with a box of chemicals.

But all this is a caution—necessary I suppose—that you need not expect me to give you a plain, cut and dried answer to your question whether literature is a conscious production—or, in more particular form—was Dickens aware that by milk-punch he meant ecstasy? I shall "ask you another" in the approved Scotch manner. You were telling me that as you came along this evening you had to stop for five minutes at the corner of the Caledonian Road to watch the exquisite grace of two slum-girls of fourteen or fifteen, dancing to the rattling tune of a piano-organ. You spoke of the charm of their movements—*motus Ionici,* some of them, I fear—of the purely æsthetic delight there was in the sight of young girls, disguised as horrible little slatterns, leaping and dancing as young girls have always leapt and danced, I suppose, from the time of the cave-dwellers onwards. Well, but do you suppose that this charm you have remarked was conscious? Do you think that Harriet and Emily realised that they were of the kin of the ecstatic dancers of all time, that they were beautiful because they were naturally expressing by a symbol that is universal, the universal and eternal ecstasy of life? Look back in your memory for illustrations; I, as you know, am rather the enemy of facts, and it is rarely that I am able to support a theory by a systematic *catena* of instances and authorities. But, if one had the industry and energy, one might make a most curious history of the dance. Remember the Hebrew dances of religious joy, of ecstasy in its highest form, remember that strange survival of the choristers' dance before the high altar in Spain on certain solemn feasts, a survival which has persisted in spite of the strong Roman influences which make for rigid uniformity. Think of the Greek Mænads and Bacchantes, of the Dionysiac chorus in the theatre, of our old English peasants "treading the mazes", and dancing round the maypole, of dances at Breton *Pardons,* of the fairies, supposed to dance in the forest glade beneath the moon. Why, dancing is as much an expression of the human secret as literature itself, and I expect it is even more ancient; and Harriet and Emily, leaping on the pavement, to that jingling, clattering tune, were merely shewing that though they were the children of the slum, and the step-children of the School Board, they were yet human, and partakers of the universal sacrament.

But if you ask, were they conscious of all this, it will be very difficult to give a direct answer. I need hardly say that they could not have put their very real emotion into the terms I have used—nor perhaps into any terms at all—and yet they know the delight of what they do, as much as if they had been initiated in all the mysteries. If someone with the genius of Socrates for propounding searching questions could "corner" Harriet and Emily, and face and overcome that preliminary, inevitable "garn", it is possible that he might find that they were fully conscious of the reasons why they danced and delighted in dancing; just as Socrates demonstrated to the slave that he was perfectly acquainted with geometry; but failing a Socrates, and using words in their usual senses, I suppose we must say that they are not conscious. They dance and leap without calculation, as they eat and drink, and as birds sing in springtime; and very much the same answer must be given to the similar question as to literature.

I said that to answer the riddle fully and completely one would have to make an analysis of human nature; and, in truth, the problem is simply a problem of the consciousness and subconsciousness, and of the action and interaction between the two. I will not be too dogmatic. We are in misty, uncertain, and unexplored regions, and it is impossible to chart all the cities and mountains and streams, and fix with the nicety of the ordnance survey their several places on the map—but I am strangely inclined to think that all the quintessence of art is distilled from the subconscious and not from the conscious self; or, in other words, that the artificer seldom or never understands the ends and designs and spirit of the artist. Our literary architects have all, I think, builded better than they knew, and very often, I expect the draughtsman who sees the triumph and enjoys it in his manner, takes all the credit to himself, and ludicrously imagines that it is his careful drawing and amplification of the sketch, and following the scale, that have created the high and holy house of God. There is a queer instance of what I mean in Dickens's preface to the later editions of *Pickwick*—I put the book up on a high shelf the other day, and I can't be bothered getting it down and verifying the quotation—but I believe the author, after telling us that the original design was to give opportunities to the etcher Seymour, goes on to recapitulate, as it were, the achievements of the book, and his list of triumphs is much more amusing than any list in Rabelais. The law of imprisonment for debt has been altered! Fleet Prison has been pulled down! The School Board is coming! Lawyers' clerks have nicer manners! Parliamentary elections are a little better, but they might be better still! and one wonders that he does not announce that, in consequence of the publication of *Pickwick,* medical students have given up brandy for barley-water. It is evident, you see, that Dickens thought (or thought that he thought, for it is very difficult to be exact) that his masterpiece of the *picaresque,* his epitome of Pantagruelism, was written to correct abuses, and looking back, many years after its publication, he congratulates himself that most of these abuses have been corrected, and (one can almost hear him say) *ergo,* it is a very fine book. He was impelled to write this nonsense of the preface because he was, by comparison, "educated"; Harriet, the dancer, would probably tell you, if you succeeded in penetrating beyond "garn", that she danced because she liked it; but, granting that the poisoning process had been carried out more successfully in the case of Emily, she might, conceivably, reply that she danced "becos it's 'elthy, and Teacher says as 'ow it cirkilates the blood". Emily, you see, obtained the prize for Physiology, as well as for French and the Piano-Forte; she is thus enabled to give "reasons", and they are quite as valuable as the "reasons" of Dickens, explaining the merits of *Pickwick.* You know that pompous old fool Forster, who took in Dickens at times, sniffed a little at *Pickwick,* and thought the later books, with their ingenious plots, and floods of maudlin tears, and portentous "character-drawing", immense advances, and I suppose the master felt obliged to justify himself for that first enterprise—to shew that he had not really been inspired, but had written a useful tract! You remember he "explains" Stiggins; he warns you not to be under any misconceptions, not to suppose that Stiggins satirises a, b, or c, since he is only aimed at x, y, and z. Can you conceive that a mediæval artist in gurgoyles, having perfected for our eternal joy a splendid grinning creature, lurking on the parapet, and having endowed him, greatly to our oblectation, with the tail of a dragon, the body of a dog, the feet of an eagle, the head of a bull in hysterics, with a Franciscan cowl, by way of finish, should afterwards explain that no offence was intended to Father Ambrose, the prior over the way?

So it seems fairly plain, doesn't it, that in the case of Dickens, at all events, there was no very clear consciousness of what had been achieved, and I believe that you would find the rule hold good with other artists in a greater or less degree. With Dickens it holds in a very high degree, just because there was that tremendous gulf I have so often spoken about between his inward and his outward self; because, with the soul of rare genius, his intelligence lived in those dreary, dusty London streets, because the artificer, even while he carried out the artist's commands, understood very little what he was doing. But one can trace the same working in other cases. Take the case of Mr. Hardy, for instance. You remember what I said about his *Two on a Tower;* I praised it for its ecstatic passion, for that revelation of a great rapture, for its symbolism, shewing how one must withdraw from the common ways, from the dusty highroad and the swarming street, and go apart into high, lonely places, if one would perceive the high, eternal mysteries. I did not say so in so many words, but you no doubt saw that I was indicating that which is, in my opinion, valuable in Mr. Hardy's work, that which makes his books literature. And I am sure he would most decidedly and entirely disagree with me, and if you want to know why I am sure, I refer you to his later books, to his *Tess* and *Jude.* You know how the *Tess* was talked about, how it remade the author from the commercial standpoint, simply because it contained, with many beautiful things, many absurd "preachments", much pseudo-philosophy of a kind suited to the intelligence of persons who think that *Robert Elsmere* is literature. If Mr. Hardy had been a conscious artist, if he had understood, I mean, what makes the charm and the wonder of *Two on a Tower,* he could never have adulterated the tale of *Tess* with a free-thinking tract, he would never have turned *Jude* into a long pamphlet on secondary education for farm labourers, with agnostic notes. It is pathetic in the latter book amidst much weary and futile writing to come across a passage here and there that shews the artist striving for utterance, longing to sing us his incantations, in spite of the preacher, who howls him down. Think of that distant vision of Oxford from the lonely field, of all those clustering roofs and spires, wet with rain, suddenly kindling into glancing and scintillant fire, at the sunset; and then remember, with what sorrow, that this is but an oasis in a barren land of blundering argument. It is almost as if literature had become "literature"—the "literature of the subject"—and one must only rejoice that the artist still lives even if the enemy has shut him up in prison. You can trace the struggle all through the book: "Sue" was an artistic conception, a very curious but a very beautiful revelation of some strange elements in the nature and in the love of women; but how difficult it is to detect this—the real Sue—underneath the surface, which makes Sue seem the prophetess of the "Woman Question", or whatever the contemporary twaddle on the subject was called. Conceive the Odyssey so handled that it seems like a volume in a "technical series" dealing with

"Seamanship and Navigation", think what might have happened if the Rabelais who had been put in the dark cell of Fontenay-le-Comte had completely gained the upper hand, and had silenced that other Rabelais—that solitary and rapturous soul who had seen as in a glass the marvellous face of man. Well, the five books of the *Pantagruel* would have conveyed to us, no doubt with some eloquence and vigour, the highly unimportant fact that François Rabelais, runaway Franciscan friar, did not like Franciscan friars; and now that the centuries have gone by we see how (comparatively) worthless such a book as that would have been. Fortunately Pantagruel was too strong for the forces of Panurge and Frère Jean combined, and so they have been able to do little harm to the book.

And how one wishes that it might be so with Mr. Hardy! It is not as if he had no "body" for his conceptions; his studies of peasant folk do very well as backgrounds for his dramas, though, of course, his work in this way, good as it is, is not his element of real value. But it is inoffensive always, sometimes amusing, and it might well suffice him in his more material moments, when he feels the necessity of descending from the solitary heights into the pleasant, populous valleys and villages of common life. But his true work is—as it is the work of all artists—the shaping for us of ecstasy by means of symbols; and for him the symbol which he understands is, no doubt, the passion of love, and with it the symbol of red, lonely ploughlands, of deep overshadowed lanes that climb the hills and wander into lands that we know not, of dark woods that hide a secret, of strange, immemorial barrows where one may have communion with the souls of the dead. The passion of love, the passion of the hills—no artist could desire more exquisite or significant symbols than these, nor need he seek for more beautiful forms for the expression of the perfect beauty. And Mr. Hardy has chosen to be a pamphleteer, to voice for us our poor, ignorant contemporary chatter: it is as if an angel's pen were to be occupied in inditing "Society Small Talk!"

But it proves the unconsciousness of Mr. Hardy's art; and here, by the way, I am moved to revert to the case of Rabelais. How far, you may ask, was he conscious of what he was saying, and I see you remember that passage I quoted from the last book—the splendid declaration of the Priestess Bacbuc that "by wine is man made divine". That passage, and indeed many other passages in the final chapters, would seem to shew that the author had worked consciously, and I certainly think the point worth our consideration. You will remember that I stated my rule without bigotry; I rather proposed it as a pious opinion—to the effect that in literature the finest things are not designed. And I confess, that at first sight, this matter of Bacbuc and her allocution looks rather like an exception to the rule, a proof that Rabelais, at all events, understood clearly what he was doing.

Well, it may have been so; for Rabelais was, as I think I have shewn, a very exceptional man, whom it would be difficult to place in any class. But I hardly think this *is* an instance of the proverbial (and fallacious) exception that proves the rule. In the first place I believe that some French editors have grave doubts whether Rabelais wrote the fifth book at all; but I am not inclined to press this point. *My* point is that the allocution of Bacbuc and all these chapters which describe the Oracle of the Holy Bottle are the last in the book—the last words of the author; and I am in no way concerned to defend the position that an author must always remain unconscious of the work that he has done. As a matter of fact I think that always, or almost always, he is unconscious while he is writing; but I see no reason why the revelation may not come to him afterwards, especially in such a case as the *Pantagruel,* which was the affair of many years—of a lifetime, indeed. In the beginning of production, in the youth, the springtime of artistic work, the creative influence prevails, and this, it seems to me, always or almost always operates secretly; but in later years the critical spirit is apt to assert itself, and this will lead, very naturally, to the artist's understanding more plainly the nature of his accomplishment. Rabelais had a long, wonderful career; his life was full of incident, of violent breaks, and his books were produced at intervals, and it seems to me very possible that, towards the end, he may have reflected on what he had done, and have understood in part, at all events, the sense of the amazing message that he had delivered. This, I think, is the explanation of the "Holy Bottle" chapters, and you will note that, admirable as criticism, they are inferior as art to those astounding early pages where there is no hint of conscious workmanship, but rather evidence of a man for whom the world has been transformed, who has been visited by an astounding vision. He takes an old, popular story about a giant, he takes the vine that flourishes in his native Chinonnais, he takes the New Learning that seems to him like the New Wine, he takes the gross tale of the farmhouse and the tavern, the rank speech of the people, and with these elements, with these "facts", he symbolises the revelation that he has received. He writes, he writes on, he writes madly, and every line is written in a fury of delight; but, I think I may say, there is at the moment of writing, no conscious apperception of all that that torrent of words conveys and implies. *That* may well come later; one may well begin with legend: "Grandgousier was a good drinker," and end with the interpretation: "All truth and every philosophy is contained in wine"; but I believe that if Rabelais had perceived this at the beginning he would have been not an artist but a philosopher.

Well; if you are content with this comment on Bacbuc, I should like to give you a very curious instance of our own day, in which the unconscious artist has been subdued by the conscious preacher. You remember those very notable books: *Keynotes* and *Discords?* I have not seen them for some time, so I am afraid my criticism will be very loose and general, but I think that the two volumes mark very well the fatal descent from the higher to the lower ground. In the first, it seems to me, there is a somewhat slight, but very genuine, note of ecstasy; I mean that you can collect a certain distinct image of real womanhood—not the laboured, foolish, inane psychology of Mr. Meredith and those who work with him—not the analysis of the surface, of the "society" woman, belonging to a particular grade and a particular period, but of the very woman who remains really the same in all social grades and in all ages. I remember thinking when I read *Keynotes* that it was a "lonely" book; it hinted, I think, a soul apart, and afar from the secondary, tertiary problems of an organised civilisation, and though there was an undertone of "preaching" and arguing, the total impression was curiously and beautifully artistic. I found, if I remember rightly, that subordination of the accidental to the essential that I praised in *Two on a Tower,* and I am the more convinced that this is so by my own recollections. I have forgotten all about social conditions, if any such things are indicated; I only think of women and of men, of the true, inalterable human nature; and here, it seems to me, you have a very high achievement. But the next volume *Discords* took distinctly lower ground. The artifice was better, the stories, as stories, were told with more skill and more deftness than anything in *Keynotes;* but there was no more literature; there was only the "literature of the subject". The incidents were no longer symbols of an emotion; they had become the basis of an agitation, concerning which my curiosity never led me to inquire further: and there you see another proof of the unconsciousness of art. If the author of *Keynotes* had understood her achievement *Discords* would never have been written. One might continue the *catena* almost *ad infinitum:* would not Wordsworth, supposing him to have been a conscious artist, have rather cut off his right hand than have suffered such a *magisterium* as the "Ode on Intimations of Immortality" to have the companionship of the enormous mass of futility and stupidity which constitutes the greater part of the *Complete Works?*

Well, there is the evidence that must guide us in answering the question you propounded, and it shews, conclusively enough, I think, that art is not, in the ordinary acceptation of the term, a conscious product. Perhaps it would be a perilous dogmatism, on the other hand, definitely to pronounce it to be unconscious; and I expect we had better take refuge in the subconscious, that convenient name for the transcendental element in human nature. For myself, I like best my old figure of the Shadowy Companion, the invisible attendant who walks all the way beside us, though his feet are in the Other World; and I think that it is he who whispers to us his ineffable secrets, which we clumsily endeavour to set down in mortal language. I think that while the artist works he is conscious of joy and of nothing more; he works beautifully but he could give no *rationale* of the process, and when he endeavours to explain himself, we are often perplexed by this strange spectacle of a man wholly ignorant of his own creation. Consider again the grotesqueness of that preface to *Pickwick;* it is really as if a great sculptor, congratulated on his achievement, should answer that his Venus was indeed beautiful—because it tended to improve the marble industry and the general knowledge of anatomy.

And after all the conclusion does return to us from other than literary sources. You cannot conceive a builder of the fourteenth century hesitating as to the respective merits of Romanesque, Norman, First and Second Pointed; to him there was only one possible method, and he built, as he spoke, without calculation and without conscious effort, only knowing the joy of his work. So indeed we all speak and live when we are not bound by convention and acquired usages and manners, and you see that art, properly so called, takes its place in the great scheme of things; it is no studied contortion, no strange trick acquired by the late ingenuity of man, but as "natural" (and as supernatural) as the blossoming of a flower, and the singing of the nightingale. Art, indeed, is wholly natural, artifice is more or less acquired, the creature of reason, of experiment, of systematised intelligence. It is doubtful, I suppose, whether the natural, untaught man has of himself, by endowment, any artifice at all; doubtful, perhaps, whether, in the beginning, his artifice was not the product of his art; whether he did not learn to speak with artifice because he had received from nature the art of singing; certainly the child, entering the world, has not the inborn artifice of the swallow and the bee. This artifice, it seems, man has been forced to acquire by slow and painful degrees, and perhaps it only differs from the artifice of animals in that it has been aided and reinforced by imagination, that is by art, that is by the power the human soul possesses of projecting itself into the unknown, and adventuring in the realm of nothingness. Man, I mean, could never have invented the telephone, had he not first created it, had he not conceived the possibility of its existence, when as yet, it was non-existent, and so his artifice will always be progressive, and distinguished from the artifice of animals.

But art is born with man, and is of the essence, the very differentia of man. It is of his very inmost being, and therefore, I suppose, is removed from his consciousness simply because it is within and not from without. You may say that I have been vague, that I have not solved the problem I propounded, that I have not clearly explained whether the Greeks knew what they did when they worshipped Dionysus, whether Rabelais was conscious of an inner meaning in his praise of wine, whether Dickens understood the value of his punch and brandy. But if I have been vague it is because man, in the last analysis, is a tremendous mystery, because he is a complex being, because he is at once Pantagruel and Panurge and Frère Jean, because he is both Don Quixote and Sancho Panza. In some cases Pantagruel and Panurge seem to speak a common language, to be able to communicate the one with the other: if Rabelais wrote the "Dive Bouteille" chapters, he certainly understood much of that which he had expressed in symbols. Sometimes the two seem like foreigners in one home, Pantagruel dictates and Panurge the scribe writes down his words, hardly or not at all comprehending the magic symbols that he expresses. So Dickens ludicrously misinterprets his own *Pickwick*. And, doubtless, this understanding of the artificer of the artist varies in an almost infinite chain of *nuances:* there have been artists, perhaps, who have worked like men under the influence of haschish, who have opened their mouths and prophesied, and then recovering from the possession have sat up and stared, and asked where they were, and what they had been doing. Indeed, it may be that this was the condition of the working of art in the very dawn of human life, for this, no doubt, is the explanation of that old equation in which bards, magicians, seers, prophets, and madmen ranked all together as men who spoke and worked miracles, things unintelligible to the "common sense", to the understanding which regulates and arranges the affairs of the common life. All these were alike men of the mountains, men who withdrew from the camp, and went apart into high solitary places, into the lonely wilderness, into the forest, and in such retirements and cells they uttered the voices that came to them, speaking words that were unintelligible to themselves.

On the other hand there may have been artists in whom the two persons have been happily reconciled, who have not only the "gift of tongues" but also the gift of the interpretation of tongues. Even these, I think, are always "possessed", ecstatic, rapt from their common nature at the moment of inspiration, but afterwards, when the magic song is done, they awake and return and remember and understand, in a measure at least, the meaning of their prophecies. They never wholly understand, they are never able to express in rational terms the *whole* force of the message, for the good reason that the language of the soul infinitely transcends the language of the understanding; because art is, indeed, the sole channel by which the highest and purest truth can reach us. You may, perhaps, succeed in giving a Boer "some notion" of a Greek chorus through the medium of the "Taal", but it would be vain to dream of translating almost perfect beauty into that poor medium, framed for the temporary and corporal necessities of rough and illiterate farmers. And so, however well an artist or those who appreciate his work may "understand" his meaning, they do but "understand" a little; since the tongue of art has many words which have no rendering in the speech of the understanding.

Here, then, is another form of our text which enables us to separate art from artifice, literature from reading-matter. Artifice is explicable; you remember that someone has said Thackeray was simply the ordinary clubman *plus* genius and a style. We must correct his phrases: but if you substitute an "immense talent of observation" for genius, and a "great gift of expression" for style, I think the definition admirable. Thackeray, in short, is the clubman of heightened faculties; he differs not in quiddity but in quality and quantity from his neighbour at the window; he looks more closely than Tom Eaves, and he can give you the result of his inspection in better phrases and with a better system, but he looks at the same things from the same standpoint, and you and I can admire his work and be amused and delighted by it, but we have no sense of miracle, of transcendent vision and achievement. We simply see a man who does the things that we do, but does them with a far greater dexterity: you may watch an acrobat with an immense admiration, but you recognise that you, too, are potentially an acrobat, that with a little training you, too, could hang by the heels, though not with such grace, nor for so long a time.

But art is always miraculous. In its origin, in its working, in its results it is beyond and above explanation, and the artist's unconsciousness is only one phase of its infinite mysteries.

VI

I am afraid that at our last conversation I rather spoke to you "as if you were a public meeting". Not precisely in that manner, perhaps, since no public meeting that I can imagine would have stood me for a moment, but I fear that I was what is called "high-flown". And yet how can one avoid that reproach? Look here: let us suppose an examination paper, and the following questions set.

1. Explain, in rational terms, the "Quest of the Holy Graal". State whether in your opinion such a vessel ever existed, and if you think it did not, justify your pleasure in reading the account of the search for it.

2. Explain, logically, your delight in colour. State, in terms that Voltaire would have understood, the meaning of the phrase, "the beauty of line".

3. What do you mean by the word "music"? Give the rational explanation of Bach's Fugues, shewing them to be as (1) true as Biology and (2) useful as Applied Mechanics.

4. Estimate the value of Westminster Abbey in the Avoirdupois measure.

5. "The light that never was on land or sea." What light?

6. "Faery lands forlorn." Draw a map of the district in question, putting in principal towns and naming exports.

7. Shew that "heaven lies about us in our infancy" must mean "wholesome maternal influences surround us in our childhood".

You say that is all nonsense? that one cannot express art of any kind in the terms of rationalism? Well, I agree with you that it *is* nonsense; that the tables of weights and measures give no æsthetic guide to the value of Westminster Abbey; but if we agree on this I am afraid that we must be content to be called high-flown. Having once for all settled that "common sense" has nothing to do with literary art, we must be, I suppose, uncommon, and (apparently) nonsensical if we want to talk about it to any profit. That is what it comes to, after all. If literature be a kind of dignified reporting, in which the reporter is at liberty to invent some incidents and leave out others, and to arrange all in the order that pleases him best; then, let us have as much "common sense" and "rationalism" as you please, and the more the better; but if literature is a mysterious ecstasy, the withdrawal from all common and ordinary conditions—well, I suppose, we had better be mystics when we discuss the subject, and frankly confess that with its first principles logic has nothing to do. I suppose that there are only two parties in the world: the Rationalists and the Mystics, and one's vote on literature goes with one's party. One might leave the matter there, and amiably agree to differ with the other side; but I, personally, have the ferocity to insist, that my side, the mystical, is wholly right, and the other, the rationalist, wholly wrong, and moreover I shall be so indecent as to prove the truth of my position. But, I have done so, and with that "Examination Paper" I just read out to you. For if rationalism be the truth, then all literature, all that both sides agree in thinking the finest literature, is simple lunacy, and all the world of the arts must go into the region of mania. Take the lowest, the simplest instance. Here is a knife with a wooden handle, and the handle has certain curious carved designs on it, which do *not* enable it to be held better. Why is this knife better, more to be valued, than that other knife, which is not decorated at all? It does not cut better; it does not justify its existence and purpose as a knife more than the other; where is its superiority? Because I find pleasure in seeing those designs? But *why* do I find any pleasure in ornament? What is the rationalistic justification for that pleasure? By logical definition a knife is an instrument for cutting, and nothing else; the plain cuts as well as the ornate; *why* then are you sorry if you lose the one, while you don't care twopence for the loss of the other? You have at last to answer that you have a joy which you cannot in any way define in the purely decorative pattern; and with that answer the whole system of Rationalism topples over. Rationalism may say to you: Either give a definite reason for going to Mass, or leave off going. You have only to answer: Your command is based on the premiss that one should do nothing without being able to give a definite reason for it. But I can give no definite reason for liking—the Odyssey or a curiously carved knife—and yet you confess that I am right in liking these things. Then I have proved the contradictory of your premiss, as you have admitted that there are things that one may do without being able to give a definite reason for doing them: *ergo,* I shall not neglect the "parson's bell".

Of course, all this is altogether outside of my business; but I confess I am fond of carrying things to their limits. You remember how poor S. T. C. used to talk, humbly and yet proudly, of "my system", though I am afraid "my system" never emerged from the state of fragments and *disjecta membra.* And I too, though I have only broken morsels and ruinous stones to shew for the splendid outlines and indicated arches of Coleridge, still like to follow up an argument whithersoever it will lead me, regardless of consequences; and this, I am sure, should count for righteousness with our friends the rationalists. I love to start a *sorites,* something as follows: I admire that odd but beautiful little decorative scheme on the seventeenth-century chest, and therefore I think poetry, as poetry, finer than prose, as prose. Hence I approve of "Ritualism" in the service of the church, and from the same premiss I draw the conclusion that Keats was a poet and that Pope was not. Pope not being a poet, it follows that to "intone" is in every way better than to "read" the Liturgy and the Offices, and "reading" the service being wrong, you will easily infer that I dislike Mr. Frith's pictures. And after learning that I do not care for the "Derby Day", you will scarcely require my opinion as to the (theoretical) righteousness of the first Reform Bill, and from my attitude towards Lord John Russell's measure, you can, of course, guess my opinion on the respective merits of the French and English languages as literary instruments. And French being vastly inferior to English, it necessarily follows that the English Reformation was a great (though perhaps unavoidable) misfortune. Hence, you see, admiring certain lines cut in an old oaken box, I am led by the strictest logic to dislike the religious policy of Edward VI., with all the other consequences in order; and on the other hand if I saw no sense in that rude ornament I should be an Atheist, or, at the mildest, an attendant at Pleasant Sunday Afternoons, with George Eliot for my favourite reading.

Yes, I like my theories to "work through", and I confess that my belief in the truth of "my system" is very much strengthened by the fact that it does "work through", that it seems to me justified by the facts of life. I mean that the premiss which enables me to declare Keats to be a poet and Pope not to be a poet does really enable me to pronounce democracy to be a bad system in theory; and the premiss baldly stated is simply this: that logic does not cover life, or in other words, that life cannot be judged by the rules of logic, of common sense.

But yet I am using logic all the time, you say? Certainly, but I am using it in its right place, to do the work for which it is competent. If I say that a scythe is not exactly the instrument for performing a surgical operation, I am not therefore bound to have my meadow mown with a bistoury? A microscope is good and a telescope is good, but it is the microscope that one uses in bacteriology. You know, don't you, that ever since that unhappy Reformation of ours people have been talking nonsense about the Aristotelian logic, and fumbling, in the most grotesque manner, for some "new" logic. Our great false prophet Bacon (a wretch infinitely more guilty than Hobbes) began it in England with his *Novum Organum;* and if you wish really to estimate "educated" folly, to touch the bottom of the incredible depths to which a man of information may sink, read Macaulay's comparison of the "old" philosophy and the "new" philosophy. The essayist says that the "old" philosophy was no good, because it never led up to the steam-engine and the telegraph post. Isn't it almost humiliating to think that we have to acknowledge ourselves of the same genus as that "brilliant" Macaulay? But if I told you that the Greek alphabet was no good because it has never grilled a single steak you would probably get uneasy and make for the door, and if you were charitable you would tell the landlady that I ought to be "taken care of". But such a remark as that is no whit more lunatic than Macaulay's "comparison" between philosophy, properly so called, and physical science applied to utilitarian purposes. Well, all the portentous stuff that has been written about logic is nonsense of exactly the same kind. The scholastic logic, people said, won't discover the truth. That is perfectly true, but then the scholastic logic was not intended to discover truth. It will draw conclusions from truths already discovered, from premisses granted, but it won't make premisses any more than a scythe will make grass. And it is, curiously enough, the very class of people who despise the formal logic, who insist on your giving logical reasons for actions and emotions which are altogether outside the jurisdiction of logic. With one breath they say: Aristotle is useless, because the Organon could never have led men to discover the stomach-pump; and with the next breath they ask you what you mean by admiring the "Ode on a Grecian Urn" if you can't give any logical reason for your admiration. Your religion doesn't rest on a logical foundation, they say. But does anything of any consequence rest on a logical foundation? Can you reduce the *Morte d'Arthur* into valid syllogisms in *Barbara,* can you "disprove" Salisbury Cathedral by the aid of *Celarent?* What is the "rational" explanation of our wonder and joy at the vision of the hills? Are a great symphony, the swell and triumph of the organ, the voices of the choristers, to be tested by the process of the understanding? But perhaps I am misjudging the people who ask these questions. When they say that logic does not discover truth, they doubtless mean by logic that formal analysis of the ratiocinative process that is rightly so called; but I am inclined to think that when they condemn religious or artistic emotions because they are "illogical", they mean by "illogical" that which does not conduce to the ease and comfort of the digestive apparatus or the money-making faculty. They are terrible fellows, you know, some of these persons. For example, I asked, with a tone of undue triumph, I am afraid, for the "reason why" we experience awe and delight in the presence of the hills. But in certain quarters my problem would be very quickly solved. I should be told, more in sorrow than in anger, that my emotion at the sight of certain shapes of earth was due to the fact that hill air was highly ozonised, and that the human race had acquired an instinctive pleasure in breathing it, greatly to its digestive profit. And if I tried to turn the tables by declaring that I experienced an equal, though a different delight in the spectacle of a desolate, smoking marsh, where a red sun sinks from a world of shivering reeds, I suppose I should hear that some remote ancestor of mine had found in some such place "pterodactyls plentiful and strong on the wing". And if I like the woods, it was because a monkey sat at the root of my family tree, and if I love an ancient garden it is because I am "second cousin to the worm".

There: I confess it is difficult to keep one's temper with these people, but one must try to do so. Do you remember how Trunnion's marriage was delayed? The bridegroom set out bravely with his retinue for the parish church, where the bride waited a whole half hour—in vain. A messenger was sent who saw:

"The whole troop disposed in a long field, crossing the road obliquely, and headed by the bridegroom and his friend Hatchway, who finding himself hindered by a hedge from proceeding farther in the same direction, fired a pistol and stood over to the other side, making an obtuse angle with the line of his former course; and the rest of the squadron followed his example, keeping always in the rear of each other like a flight of wild geese.

"Surprised at this strange method of journeying, the messenger came up . . . and desired he would proceed with more expedition. To this message Mr. Trunnion replied, 'Hark ye, brother, don't you see we make all possible speed? Go back, and tell those who sent you that the wind has shifted since we weighed anchor, and that we are obliged to make short trips in tacking, by reason of the narrowness of the channel; and that, as we lie within six points of the wind, they must make some allowance for variation and leeway.' 'Lord, sir!' said the valet, 'what occasion have you to go zig-zag in that manner? Do but clap spurs to your horses, and ride straight forward, and I'll engage you shall be at the church porch in less than a quarter of an hour.' 'What! right in the wind's eye?' answered the commander. 'Ahey! brother, where did you learn your navigation?'"

You see Commodore Trunnion's "logic" was perfect, only it was the logic of seamanship and not of riding to church on horseback. There are a good many people at the present day who are quite unable to get to church in time, for "reasons" as valid as Trunnion's; and when I hear of "the scientific basis of literature" I am always a little reminded of those scarecrows straggling in short tacks from one side of the lane to the other on their way to the wedding. The moral is, you know, that they didn't get there.

I tackled a materialist once on very similar lines. He began by saying that time and thought devoted to religion (they never see that art and religion stand or fall together, religion being the foundation of the fine arts) were an utter waste of time, as they only diverted us from consideration of the present world, which we ought to study to the utmost; and he went on to praise some saying of Confucius on the folly of troubling about the future things. Then I went for him. He had to admit that agriculture is good, and I pointed out to him that England was changed from a savage wilderness into a pleasant garden by the monastic houses. He agreed that to found and endow hospitals and almshouses was not precisely a waste of time, and I shewed him that such institutions were begun by the religion of the past and carried on by the religion of the present. Then he allowed, in response to my Socratic question, that painting was something, and I demonstrated that all painting arose from the religious impulse, that the greatest paintings in the world were meant to adorn churches. Then he admitted the value of architecture, and he got the Parthenon, all the mediæval cathedrals, and the wonderful mound temples of Ceylon right at his head. He granted me that travel civilised, and I rubbed in the pilgrimage; he confessed that he liked to read the Latin and Greek classics—sometimes—and he received from me information as to the monastic scriptorium, and its part in the preservation of the old literature. As for the blessedness of forming one's character on the teaching of Confucius; there happened to be an article in the morning's paper on the Mandarin class! Well, my rationalist hadn't anything to say to it at all, with the exception of some vague remark that the Romans made roads, which, considering the state of England in the sixth century, was about as helpful as the somewhat similar remark of Mr. F.'s Aunt—that there are milestones on the Dover Road. I told him that the only Roman civilisation which contributed to the making of our country was that brought over by St. Austin; and he had to allow that his statement that religion was a waste of time, an elaborate form of idleness, was, to put it mildly, not proven. Then he said kindly but firmly that religion wasn't rational, and I used up most of the arguments that I have used to-night; I mean, I shewed him that it is good to paint pictures, to write poems, to devise romances, and to compose symphonies, and that it is also good to meditate and enjoy all these things. Hence, he was forced to admit that his suppressed premiss had been disproved, and that he must no longer say: "that which is not rational is absurd."

And then, I think, the fun really began. I carried the war into the very camp of the enemy; that is, into actual, observable life, into the everyday world of fact and experience. You talk about "reason", I said, and I presume you won't mind if I substitute, occasionally, "common sense" for reason, as I think that in your phraseology the two terms are very fairly equated. Very well, then, don't you think that there is a good deal of common sense in many of the actions of animals? Take the case of the small birds who mob an owl all day, in order that their enemy may be kept awake, and so unable to hunt at night. Take the case of the ants, who milk the aphides, and go slave-hunting. Take the bees, who rise to an emergency, and remedy, with singular contrivance, the threatened lack of a queen. Take the dog, who brought a wounded fellow to the hospital where he had been cured. All these are instances of common sense, aren't they, as rational as the telegram "Sell Cobras at once"? Very good; animals, then, have a plentiful supply of reason, and not of a mere mechanical reason, but of reason that can rise to the height of unforeseen cases, and remedy unexpected evils. When the experimenter tilted the bees' house to one side, so that the equilibrium was in danger, a sufficient number of bees climbed up and placed themselves on the other side so that they constituted a balance; here there was no mechanism, but a calculated and rational contrivance. Animals, then, have reason and its effect, artifice; the adaptation of means to secure ends. But, then, how about instinct? By what motion does the swallow make her nest in spring? Can the bee demonstrate the advantages of the hexagon cell? Does the fly, laying its eggs here and there, in this or in that according to its kind, in meat or in dung, or in the crevices of a wall, rationally foresee that it is providing for the future grub its only possible food? No; but then animals, even, perform "irrational" actions; though they have common sense they do things which must be troublesome to them, at some instance, which is not common sense. But if a bluebottle lays her eggs in my beef, and knows not why, perhaps I, a man, may sing the *Sanctus,* and pray that I may be joined *cum angelis et archangelis, cum thronis et dominationibus, Cumque omni militiâ cœlestis exercitus.*

And consider our own human life; the great *coups* of war, commerce, diplomacy, of all the conduct of life, are often, or usually, the result of "intuitions", that is of irrational and inexplicable mental processes, which elude all analysis. If the knowledge, the successful and triumphant knowledge of men and affairs and strategy were a "rational" product; then, indeed, Carlyle's dictum were true, and each one of us were, at choice, a man of genius in diplomacy, or business, or battle. We know that it is not so, and that no man by taking thought can make himself, say, a Stonewall Jackson. And we have all heard of the "woman's reason"—"I don't know why I am sure that x = a, but I am sure"—and this extremely irrational process often corresponds with the truth. So, I finished up, your "reason", far from being the despot of the world, turns out to be a humble, though useful, deputy-assistant councillor-general, and is by no means a prerogative force, even in affairs of common, everyday existence. Why, "reason", alone and unassisted, won't enable you to make a decent living by selling ribbons and laces, and you have been trying to make me accept its dictation in the highest affairs of the soul. You have been appealing from the King's Majesty in Council to the Magistrates of Little Pedlington in Petty Sessions assembled!

Then my rationalist made a point. You know, he said, that some men seem to have an almost miraculous skill in solving mathematical problems: would you, therefore, give up teaching the ordinary arithmetic? I was not alarmed; I pointed out that the analogy was not quite perfect. The case, I said, was this. A certain number of "problems" were, confessedly, beyond the jurisdiction of the "ordinary arithmetic" altogether, but offered no difficulties to the "lightning calculator", who obtained results that were demonstrably correct, and I therefore thought it well to trust to him in all problems of a similar character, even though the "ordinary arithmetic", confessedly incompetent, assured me that his answers were wholly unreliable—a case of a schoolboy, well on in Colenso, scouting the Binomial Theorem because one couldn't prove it by Practice or the Rule of Three. I left then, unanswered, and I suppose my friend passed the rest of the evening in shewing that Salisbury Cathedral was "opposed" to the facts of Biology, and that Sisters of Charity are to be classed with criminal lunatics.

But, you know, I was the real lunatic. You would not have "argued" with me if I *had* disparaged the Greek alphabet, because it never grilled a single steak; I hinted the course you would probably have pursued if I had chanced to make such an alarming remark. And why should I argue with the sect of Macaulay, with the tribe which utters such stuff as this:

"Assuredly if the tree which Socrates planted and Plato watered is to be judged of by its flowers and leaves, it is the noblest of trees. But if we take the homely test of Bacon—if we judge the tree by its *fruits*—our opinion of it may be less favourable. When we sum up the useful truths which we owe to that philosophy, to what do they amount. . . . But when we look for something more—for something which adds to the comfort, or alleviates the calamities of the human race—we are forced to own ourselves disappointed."

No; there is, really, nothing to be said. If the Learned Pig found voice and articulate speech and expressed his scorn of the poet's art, since it added nothing to the pleasures of the wash-tub, we might wonder but we should not argue; and it were idle to contend with a Laughing Jackass, contemptuously amused by the chanting of the cathedral choir.

And, perhaps, you are wondering what all this talk of mine has to do with our main subject—literature? But don't you see that all the while I have merely been reiterating our old conclusions in a new phraseology? I may have appeared to you to be the last of the Cavaliers, gallantly contending for the rights of Holy Church, but, in reality, I have been shewing, at every step, that Jane Austen's works are not literature. Yes, but it is so. If the science of life, if philosophy, consisted of a series of mathematical propositions, capable of rational demonstration, then *Pride and Prejudice* would be the highest pinnacle of the literary art; but if not, but oh! if we, being wondrous, journey through a wonderful world, if all our joys are from above, from the other world where the Shadowy Companion walks, then no mere making of the likeness of the external shape will be our art, no veracious document will be our truth; but to us, initiated, the Symbol will be offered, and we shall take the Sign and adore, beneath the outward and perhaps unlovely accidents, the very Presence and eternal indwelling of God.

We have tracked Ecstasy by many strange paths, in divers strange disguises, but I think that now, and only now, we have discovered its full and perfect definition. For Artifice is of Time, but Art is of Eternity.

APPENDIX

Poe was not altogether right in saying that the object of poetry was Beauty as distinguished from Truth. I don't for a moment suppose that his meaning was amiss, but I hardly like his expression of it. I should contend, on the other hand, that poetry κατ' ἐξοχήν, and literature, generally, are the sole media by which the very highest truth can be conveyed. Poe, no doubt, meant to state a proposition which is true and self-evident—that poetry has nothing to do with scientific truth, or facts, or information of any kind, and I say that that proposition is self-evident, because we have already seen that in literature, facts as facts have no existence at all. They are only "words" in the language of literary art, and are used as symbols of something else. That A. is in love with B. is a "scientific truth", a fact; but if it be not also a symbol, it has no literary existence whatever; and this of course is what Poe wished to say—literature is not a matter of information.

But I doubt, after all, whether Poe had quite grasped the theory of literature, of all the arts. You remember that he says that he yields to no man in his love of the truth; and unless he meant the highest truth the statement is almost nonsensical. No one, I should imagine, surely not Poe, would express his enthusiasm for facts as facts, would adore correct information in the abstract. You remember what Rossetti said—that he neither knew nor cared whether the sun went round the earth or the earth went round the sun—and so far as art is concerned, this is, no doubt, the expression of the true faith, which, from what we know of Poe, would be his faith also. We should therefore conclude that by truth he meant philosophical truth, the highest truth, the essential truth as distinguished from the accidental, the universal as distinguished from the particular. Yet in the next breath he contrasts this Truth with Beauty, being clearly under the impression that they were two different things. Of course he was completely mistaken. In the last analysis it is entirely true that "Beauty is Truth and Truth Beauty": they are one and the same entity seen from different points of view. You will see how this fits in with all we have been saying about literature lately: how we can if we please put our test of literature into yet another phraseology. For instance: *Vanity Fair* is information, while *Pickwick* is Truth; the one tells you a number of facts about Becky Sharp and other people, while the other symbolises certain eternal and essential elements in human nature by means of incidents. And, as I said, it is doubtful whether truth in this, its highest and its real significance, can be adequately expressed in any other way. All the profound verities which have been revealed to man have come to him under the guise of myths and symbols—such as the myth of Dionysus—and truth in the form of a mathematical demonstration or a "rational" statement is a contradiction in terms. Yet note the profound vice of language; we are obliged to use the same word to imply things which are separated by an immeasurable gulf. It is "true" that Mrs. Stickings sent away Ethelberta to-night (you imparted that interesting fact, and I rely on your testimony), and the *Don Quixote* is "true": that is, it conveys to us by means of symbols the verities of our own nature.

But Poe had not grasped the essential distinction between literature and "literature". He thought that poetry alone should be beautiful, or, as we should say, ecstatic; he did not see that the qualities which make poetry to be what it is must also be present in prose if it is to be something more than "reading-matter". Poetry of course is literature in its purest state; it is, as I think I once said, *almost* the soul without the body; at its highest it is *almost* pure art unmixed with the alloy of artifice. And to carry on the analysis, the finest form of poetry is necessarily the lyrical. Where you get the element of narrative, you are apt also to get the element of prose; there have to be passages linking the raptures together, and these will, probably or indeed necessarily, run on lower levels.

Of course primitive man had moods in which rapture seemed to embrace everything, to invest every detail of existence with its own singular and inexplicable glory. A meal by the seashore, the dry wood flaming and crackling on the sand, the roasting goat's flesh, the honey-sweet wine, dark and almost as glorious as the sea itself—a mere dinner of half-savages, one might think it, but it too seems to have its solemnity and its inner meaning. I believe this element in the early poetry has often been noticed; people have wondered at the *naïve* delight with which the writers describe the work of man's hands, and they are, I think, inclined to account for it on the ground that then everything was new. This might pass, perhaps, since as you, no doubt, perceive, "everything new" means "everything unknown" (that which is known is no longer new), but I hardly think that the explanation can stand in its present form. I am not at all up in the theories which assign this or that age to the appearance of man on the earth, but I presume that on the gentlest and most antiquated computation man must have long known the world before Homer wrote; so one scarcely sees that human skill and art, the knack of making things and the gift of adorning them, could have been novelties, or, in any sense, "things unknown". I repeat I know nothing or next to nothing about these dates in anthropology, but one has heard something about the neolithic age, and the palæolithic age, about the very early man who scratched the rude likeness of a reindeer on the brute's own bone, and so there hardly seems room for this theory of novelty. And besides, as we have seen, the rapture is universal or all but universal; it colours the whole of life, including the meal by the seashore; and there, we see, there was no possibility of invention or sense of newness. No; the theory is tempting, and it would fall in perfectly, as I daresay you see, with all that we have concluded about literature, but I really think that it must be definitely abandoned. No; it seems to me that primitive man, Homeric man, mediæval man, man, indeed, almost to our own day when the School Board (and other things) have got hold of him, had such an unconscious but all-pervading, all-influencing conviction that he was a wonderful being, descended of a wonderful ancestry, and surrounded by mysteries of all kinds, that even the smallest details of his life partook of the ruling ecstasy; he was so sure that he was miraculous that it seemed that no part of his life could escape from the miracle, so that to him every meal became a sacrament.

It is the attitude of the primitive man, of the real man, of the child, always and everywhere; it may be briefly summed up in the phrase: things are because they are wonderful. This, of course, is the atmosphere in which poets ought to live, and in which poetry should be produced. Formerly it was natural to all men or almost all; now, perhaps, it has to be regained by a conscious effort; and the difficulty of the effort, the impossibility of sustaining it for long, explain the supremacy of lyrical poetry. If you lived in a world that could regard a common meal as a sacrament, you could be supreme in narrative poetry; but, that atmosphere wanting, we have to be content for the most part with the lyric, with the simple incantation, without any description of the circumstance or occasion.

Yet prose, though it yields in much to the world, must still keep the same ideal before it as poetry. I say, distinctly, that the only essential, defining difference between the two is to be sought in the "numbering" of poetry, in the fact that art, in its intensest raptures, in its most truly "natural" moment, desires and obtains the strictest and most formal laws. It is, I suppose, immaterial what these laws are, rhyme, assonance, accents, feet, alliteration, all testify to the important and essential rule that freedom is chiefly free when it is most bound and bounded by restrictions which *we* should call artificial, which are, in truth, in the highest sense, natural. And this, I am sure, is the only possible distinction that can be established between such a book as the Odyssey and such a book as the *Morte d'Arthur.* Neither is "prosaic" in the common sense of the word; each is "poetical"; but the Greek book is poetry because it is numbered, and the English is prose because it lacks number. Of course there are difficult cases; hybrids, as there always are, whatever laws one may lay down.

That word "natural" is another of the many traps that language sets us. I think that its real meaning has become almost reversed. Take the average man to church, and ask him his opinion of the "intoning", and in nine cases out of ten he will say that it may be pretty, but that it is very unnatural. He means, of course, that speaking is natural, and that singing—"numerosity" of tone—is not natural, is, in a word, artificial. He is utterly wrong. It is artificial to speak in the ordinary manner, while the priests' chant, and every chant are purely natural. For the proof of this you have only to read a little—a very little—about primitive or "natural" peoples, or, more simply, to listen to children at play. You will always find that where convention has not cast out nature, some kind of "sing-song", some sort of chant is the entirely natural utterance of man in his most fervent, that is, his most natural moments. Listen to half-a-dozen children (children, you must remember, are all "primitives" and therefore natural) playing some game, learning their lesson at school. Their voices are pretty sure to fall into a very rude, but a distinctly measured, chant. The Greek drama was intoned, the Koran is intoned, the Welsh preacher of to-day at the impassioned height of eloquence begins to chant, the Persian passion-plays are recited in a sing-song. Nay, but think of one of our great tragic actors. Quite unconsciously, I am sure, Irving elaborated for himself a distinctly musical and measured utterance, so that a skilful musician, provided with scored paper, could have noted his delivery of many passages, as if it were music. The Chinese language, I am told, depends largely on the tonal variations which distinguish the meaning of one word from that of another; you will find the same thing in the Norwegian; and the Jewish "cantillation", which is "sing-song" in a very simple form, bears witness to the truth—that "speaking" is acquired, conventional, and artificial, while "singing" is natural. All this would be perfectly clear in itself, would require no demonstration of any kind, if it were not for the fact that we have, somehow or other, got into the way of making the very impudent assumption that man is only natural when he is doing business on the Stock Exchange or reading leading articles. It seems almost too nonsensical an assumption to put into words, but I really do believe that "at the back of our heads" there is a sort of vague, floating idea that there never were any real men at all till the period of the first Reform Bill, and I suppose that before very long Lord John Russell will be pushed back into the region of myth, and the foundation of the School Board will be the era of true humanity. I say, this sounds too ridiculous, but examine yourself and see whether you don't dimly believe that before the advent of trousers the whole world was really "play-acting", that existence in the days of laced coats was, in a way, a kind of phantasmagoria, and that a man who wore chain-mail was hardly a man. I believe it really is so, and you will find the same nonsense influencing religious opinion. Take your average Protestant, and I am much mistaken if you do not discover that he believes some grotesque preacher, in his greasy black suit, mouthing platitudes at his conventicle to be somehow more "natural" than the priest, clad in the mystical robes of his office, chanting Mass at the altar. But in literature—why this perversion of the word influences the whole of criticism. Jane Austen, we say, is natural, and Edgar Allan Poe is unnatural, or, as it is sometimes expressed, inhuman. Of course, if you wish for the truth, the proposition must be reversed, unless you are willing to believe that a company prospectus is, somehow, more natural and more human than, say, Tennyson's "Fatima". If you think that the real man is the stomach, there is, of course, an end of the discussion; but then we should have to admit that all the greatest artists of the world were maniacs. But you see clearly, don't you, that all these questions as to what we shall get for dinner, and whom shall we meet at dinner, and in what order shall we go in to dinner, and how shall we behave at dinner, are in no sense natural, since they are all so purely temporary, since they will be answered by one age in a manner that will seem wholly "unnatural" to the next. That, I think, is truly natural which is unchanging, which belongs to men always, at all times, and in all ages. In this sense, ecstasy is natural to man, and it finds expression in the arts, in poetry, in romance, in singing, in melody, in dancing, in painting, in architecture. Many animals have sufficient artifice to shelter themselves from the weather, no animal has architecture, or the art of beauty in building; many animals, or all animals, have the faculty of communicating with one another by means of signs, but man alone has the art of language.

Has it ever struck you while I have been talking of ecstasy in books, that it is nearly always a question of degree, of more or less? I think I indicated as much while I was talking about *Pickwick;* I shewed how the ecstatic conception had been alloyed with much baser matter, in other words that there was much in *Pickwick* that was by no means literature. And, I daresay, though I am not sure, that if you were to go through your Meredith you might succeed in finding some passages and sentences which are literature, and for all I know there may be hints of rapture between the lines of *Pride and Prejudice.* Still, we do not call a man poet on the strength of a single line.

But sometimes one is confronted with books which are really very difficult to judge, and this sometimes happens because the ecstasy, the true literary feeling, supposing it to be present, is present not here or there, not in a phrase or in a particular passage, but throughout, in a very weak solution, if one may borrow the phraseology of physical science. We read such books, and are puzzled, feeling that, somehow, they are literature, only we can't say why, since on the face of it they seem only to be entertaining reading. Do you know that I can conceive many people who would find something of this difficulty in Mark Twain's *Huckleberry Finn?* Here you have a tale of the rude America of fifty or sixty years ago, of a Mississippi village, full of the most ordinary people, of a boy and a negro who "run away". I don't think anyone with the slightest perception of literature could read it without experiencing extraordinary delight, but I can imagine many people would be a good deal puzzled to justify the pleasure they had received. The "stuff" of the book is so very common and commonplace, isn't it, it seems so frankly a rough bit of recollection drawn up from the author's boyish days with jottings added from the time when he was a pilot on one of the river-boats—it is all so apparently devoid of "literary" feeling that I am sure many a reader must have felt greatly ashamed of his huge enjoyment. To me *Huckleberry Finn* is not a very difficult case. That flight by night down the great unknown, rolling river, between the dim marshy lands and the high "bluffs" of the other shore, comes in my mind well under the great Odyssey class; it has, indeed, the old, unquenchable joy of wandering into the unknown in a more acute degree than *Pickwick*, which, as we have seen, is to be reckoned under the same heading. In a word it is pure romance, and you will note that the story is told by a boy, and that by this method a larger element of wonder is secured, for even in this absurd age children are allowed to be amazed at the spectacle of the world. In the mouth of a man the tale would necessarily have lost somewhat of its "strangeness", since partly from affectation, partly from vicious training, partly from the absorption of the "getting-on" process, grown-up people have largely succeeded in quenching the sense of mystery which should be their principal delight. You have only to read the average book of travels to see how this affectation (or perversion of the soul) has deprived the seeing being of his sight. Dip into a book—say a book on China—and you will probably find that Pekin streets are dusty in summer and muddy in winter, and that the author caught cold through imprudent bathing. So it is well for us that Mark Twain put his story in the mouth of an "infant", who is frankly at liberty to express his sense of the marvels of the world. Later, there is an introduction of the "literary" feeling; those chapters about Jim's "Evasion" are very Cervantic in their artifice and method, but, to my thinking, they have lost the spirit, though they preserve the body. They are most amusing reading, but they are burlesque and nothing more than burlesque; and from them one can almost imagine what *Don Quixote* would have been if it had been written by a very clever man, by an artificer who was not an artist. But the earlier chapters are wonderfully fine, and I think that it would be difficult to find a more successful rendering of the old "wandering" theme with modern language.

But there is another writer who is much more difficult to account for—I mean Miss Wilkins. I confess I find her tales delightful, and I often read them, but as you know I am not content to rest on my own pleasure in literary criticism. We are no longer talking of the great masterpieces, of the gigantic achievements of such men as Homer, Sophocles, Rabelais, Cervantes; we agreed that when we spoke of these great, enduring miracles of art, it was best to lay aside all question of liking or not liking, of reading often or reading seldom. But when one comes to modern days, to books which have yet to prove their merit by the test of their endurance, it is pardonable if one is sometimes a little confused, if one fails to discriminate at once between the merely interesting and the really artistic. I may be so delighted with a book for reasons that have nothing to do with art, that, by an unconscious trick of the mind, I persuade myself that I am reading literature while there is only reading-matter. And at one time I was inclined to think that I had "confused" Miss Wilkins in this manner. For, on the surface, you have in her books merely village tales of New Englanders, tales often sentimental, often trivial enough, and sometimes, it would seem, of scarcely more than local interest. Hardly can one conceive the possibility of any ecstasy in these pleasant stories; for they deal, ostentatiously, with the surface of things, with a breed of Englishmen whose chief pride it was to hide away and smother all those passions and emotions which are the peculiar mark of man as man.

Yet, I believe that I can justify my love of Miss Wilkins's work on a higher ground than that of mere liking. In the first place I agree with

Mr. T. P. O'Connor, who pointed out very well that the passion does come through the reserve, and occasionally in the most volcanic manner. He selects a scene from *Pembroke,* in which the young people play at some dancing game called "Copenhagen", and Mr. O'Connor shews that though the boys and girls of Pembroke knew nothing of it, they were really animated by the spirit of the Bacchanals, that the fire and glow of passion of the youthful ecstasy burst through all the hard crusts of Calvinism and New England reserve. And we have agreed that if a writer can make passion for us, if he can create the image of the eternal human ecstasy, we have agreed that in such a case the writer is an artist.

But I think that there are other things, more subtle, more delicately hinted things in Miss Wilkins's tales; or rather I should say that they are all pervaded and filled with an emotion, which I can hardly think that the writer has realised. Well, I find it difficult to express exactly what I mean, but I think that the whole impression which one receives from these tales is one of loneliness, of isolation. Compare Miss Wilkins with Jane Austen, the New England stories with *Pride and Prejudice.* You might imagine, at first, that in one case as in the other there is a sense of retirement, of separation from the world, that Miss Austen's heroines are as remote from the great streams and whirlpools of life as any "Jane Field" or Charlotte of Massachusetts. But in reality this is not so. The people in the English novels are in no sense remote; they are merely dull; they cannot be remote, indeed, since they are not human beings at all but merely the representatives of certain superficial manners and tricks of manner which were common in the rural England of a hundred years ago. "Remoteness" is an affection of the soul, and wicker-figures, dressed up in the clothes of a period, cannot have any such affections predicated of them; and consequently though Emma or Elizabeth may appear very quaint to us from the contrast between the manners of the 'tens and the 'nineties, they cannot be remote. But that does seem to me the quality of those books of Miss Wilkins's; the people appear to be very far off from the world, to live in an isolated sphere, and each one lives his own life, and dwells apart with his own soul, and in spite of all the trivial chatter and circumstance of the village one feels that each is a human being moved by eminently human affections.

It seems to me that one of the most important functions of literature is to seize the really fine flavours of life and to preserve them, as it were, in permanent form. When we were talking about *Huckleberry Finn,* for example, I remember that I spoke of it as the story of a boy who "runs away". But what a curious magic there is in these words "runs away". Doesn't it, when you come to examine the phrase, exhale the very essence and spirit of romance? Some time ago I reminded you that the essential thing is concealed under all manner of grotesque and unseemly forms, that one can detect a veritable human passion under the cry of the news-boy, shouting, "All the winners!" So I think that phrase, "run away", carries to us its meaning and significance. For, after all, what did all the heroes of romance do but "run away"? They left the region of the known, the familiar fields or the familiar shores, and adventured out in the great waste of the unexplored, into the forest or upon the sea. Here, perhaps, you have the true interpretation of the phrase "divine discontent", for surely only that is divine which revolts from the commonness of the common life, which is conscious of things beyond, of better things, of a world which transcends all daily experience. I said once, I think, that the English passion for trading goes very well with the supremacy of English poetry, since poetry and shop-keeping are but different expressions of the one idea; and here again you find confirmation of the theory in that very marked English characteristic—the desire of wandering, of "going on and on" in the manner of a knight-errant or a fairy tale hero. Of course, in practice, this really divine impulse is corrupted by all kinds of earthly, secondary motions; and just as the love of a venture which is at the root of trade often or always ends in a very vulgar wish to make money and more money and to set up a brougham and confound the Smiths, so the great joy of exploration, of running away from the mapped and charted land has for its issues the "development of markets", the "progress of civilisation", the profitable sale of poison, and all manner of base and blackguardly manœuvres. But, of course, one expects all this; it is the inevitable mixture of the lower with the higher which characterises all our human ways. Still, the higher motive dwells within us—I suspect, indeed, that if it were not for the higher the lower could hardly flourish—and so when you hear that a boy has run away to sea or elsewhere I wish you to think kindly of him as a survival of the most primitive and important human passions. Yes, I think I am right in saying that the lower things of humanity only flourish in consequence of the existence of the higher. Take the French nation, for example. It is infinitely more bent on gain for the mere sake of gain than the English; it is ready to work harder, to give more time, to live more unpleasantly, to eat less and to drink less than the English; and all in the pursuit of money. Rationally, in short, the French should be infinitely better men of business than the English; and yet we know that this is not so, that the English is, *par excellence,* the business nation. Seriously, I believe that this is so because the French are money-grubbers and nothing more, because they hate a "risk" of any kind, because they abhor any kind of mercantile venturing into the unknown. In other words, they engage in money-making simply for the sake of making money: they have no joy of the hazard, they will never deserve the title of "merchant adventurers", and, *therefore,* they remain in truth a nation of shopkeepers, and of second-rate shopkeepers. Sir, a man of acute intelligence would, in the seventeenth century, have deduced the future state of French and English commerce, of French and English colonisation from a comparison between Shakespeare and Racine. I have no doubt that the Phœnicians were shopkeepers of the French kind, and hence their extinction, their shadowy survival merely in the history of their conquerors.

You think the Roman Empire a formidable objection to my theory, because Roman literature and Roman art shew, in general, so little of the imaginative, adventurous faculty? I think the objection *is* formidable, but I believe that it can be redargued, as Dominie Sampson used to say. The Roman Empire was such a purely military settlement, wasn't it? it was, if one may say so, a garrisoning of the world, not in any way a real colonising in the Greek and the English sense. And in the second place, do you know that I have grave doubts whether we know very much of the Roman spirit from the Roman literature. How far into the English character would the works of the excellent Dr. Johnson carry us? One hardly finds Chaucer, the Elizabethans, the Cavalier poets, Keats or Wordsworth in *Rasselas* and *The Rambler*, and I have always suspected that Latin literature was in a great measure "Johnsonised", periwigged, hidden and perverted by the irresistible flood of Greek culture. It may be a paradox, but I have a very strong conviction that the Missal and the Breviary tell us more about the true Latin character than Cicero and Horace. But we must be thankful that in the sixteenth and early seventeenth centuries England stood aloof from the continent of Europe, and that when it did borrow it transformed and transmuted so that the original entirely lost its foreign character. I always think that change of Madame de Querouaille into Madam Carewell such a wonderful instance of our nationalism—our transforming force! If it had been otherwise, if we had grovelled before the literature of France or Spain or Italy, as Rome grovelled before the literature of Greece—well, perhaps, English literature would have meant "Chevy Chace" and a few old ballads, and the eighteenth century! I hate the Reformation, but perhaps it saved our literature, simply by isolating the nation.

I claimed, I think, literary merit for Miss Wilkins because her books give out an impression of loneliness. I think that is so, but I should like to point out that "loneliness" is merely another synonym for that one property which makes the difference between real literature and reading-matter. If you look into the French literature of the last two hundred years and complain of its elegant nothingness, of its wholly secondary character, I would point out that it is second-rate because it is the expression, not of the lonely human soul, like a star, dwelling apart, but of society, of the *ruelles,* of the *salon,* of polite company, of the *café* and the *boulevard.* I am not making an accusation, I am adopting the terms of the eminent M. de Brunetière, who tells us, I think, that French literature is beautiful because it is firstly sociable, and secondly because it is a kind of a long "talk to ladies". I hardly think that I need go into the merits of the question; you and I, I take it, are convinced of the vast immeasurable inferiority of Racine to Shakespeare (with these two names one sums up the whole debate), but I am quite sure that M. de Brunetière has given the true reason of the French literature being on the distinctly low level. It is always Thackeray, it is always Pope, it is always Jane Austen; it is, in our sense of the word, not literature at all, though, to be sure, its artifice is often of the most exquisite description. Of course I do not speak of the ultimate reason—that is to be sought, I presume, in the mental constitution of the nation—but when one reads M. de Brunetière's account of the formation of modern French letters, and notes his insistence on the social element as the chief factor, one may be pretty sure that this social factor is responsible for the pleasant nullities which we all know. You may feel pretty certain, I think, that real literature has always been produced by men who have preserved a certain loneliness of soul, if not of body; the masterpieces are not generated by that pleasant and witty traffic of the drawing-rooms, but by the silence of the eternal hills. Remember; we have settled that literature is the expression of the "standing out", of the withdrawal of the soul; it is the endeavour of every age to return to the first age, to an age, if you like, of savages, when a man crept away to the rocks or to the forests that he might utter, all alone, the secrets of his own soul.

So this is my plea for Miss Wilkins. I think that she has indicated this condition of "ecstasis"; she has painted a society, indeed, but a society in which each man stands apart, responsible only for himself and to himself, conscious only of himself and his God. You will note this, if you read her carefully, you will see how this doctrine of awful, individual loneliness prevails so far that it is carried into the necessary and ordinary transactions of social life, often with results that are very absurd. Many of the people in her stories are so absolutely convinced of their "loneliness", so certain that there are only two persons in the whole universe—each man and his God—that they do not shrink from transgressing and flouting all the social orders and regulations, in spite of their very strong and social instinct drawing them in the opposite direction. You remember the man who vowed that under certain circumstances he would sit on the meeting-house steps every Sunday? He kept his vow—for ten years, I think—and he kept it in spite of his profound horror of ridicule, of doing what other people didn't do, in spite of his own happiness; but he kept it because he realised his "loneliness", because he saw quite clearly that he must stand or fall by his own word and his own promise, and that the opinions of others could be of no possible importance to him. The instance is ludicrous, even to the verge of farce, and yet I call it a witness to the everlasting truth that, at last, each man must stand or fall alone, and that if he would stand, he must, to a certain extent, live alone with his own soul. It is from this mood of lonely reverie and ecstasy that literature proceeds, and I think that the sense of all this is diffused throughout Miss Wilkins's New England stories.

You ask me for a new test—or rather for a new expression of the one test—that separates literature from the mass of stuff which is not literature. I will give you a test that will startle you; literature is the expression, through the æsthetic medium of words, of the dogmas of the Catholic Church, and that which in any way is out of harmony with these dogmas is not literature. Yes, it is really so; but not exactly in the sense which you suppose. No literal compliance with Christianity is needed, no, nor even an acquaintance with the doctrines of Christianity. The Greeks, celebrating the festivals of Dionysus, Cervantes recounting the fooleries of Don Quixote, Dickens measuring Mr. Pickwick's glasses of cold punch, Rabelais with his thirsty Pantagruel were all sufficiently Catholic from our point of view, and the cultus of Aphrodite is merely a symbol misunderstood and possibly corrupted, and if you can describe an initiatory dance of savages in the proper manner, I shall call you a good Catholic. You say that *Robert Elsmere* is not literature, and you are perfectly right, but I hope you don't condemn it because it contains arguments directed against the Catholic Faith? These, from our own standpoint, are simply nothing at all, not reckoning either way. We pass them over, just as we should pass over a passage on quadratic equations pleasantly interpolated by an author into the body of his romance. The conscious opinions of a writer are simply not worth twopence in the court of literature; who cares to enquire into the theology of Keats? But when we find not only the consciousness but also the subconsciousness permeated by the impression that man is a logical, "rationalistic" creature and nothing more, when the total impression of the human being gathered from the book is of a simply demonstrating and demonstrable animal; then we may be perfectly assured that we have not to deal with literature. It is the subconsciousness, remember, alone that matters; and (to put it again theologically) you will find that books which are not literature proceed from ignorance of the Sacramental System. Thackeray was an unconscious heretic, while George Eliot was a conscious one, but each was ignorant of the meaning of Sacramentalism, and so, making allowance for the fact that the one was a clever man, while the other was a dull, industrious woman, you have from each a view of life that is substantially the same, and entirely false. Each was profoundly convinced that there *are* milestones on the Dover Road, and each, in his several way, was so intent on the truth of this proposition (and it *is* a perfectly true one) that the secret of the scenery and the secret of Canterbury Cathedral are altogether to seek in their books. Certainly the gentleman is a delightful companion, and the milestones seem few indeed while we are on the way, while with the other guide we feel like a girls' school, compelled to listen to the "Now, young ladies" and the "lessons" which every object on the road suggests. Still, the total view is much the same, the same in genus if not in species, and you may add Flaubert to your companions on the road and you will be in the same case. But read a chapter of *Don Quixote;* you will not be aware of the existence of the milestones, since your gaze is fixed on the mystery of the woods, and you are a pilgrim to the blissful shrine beyond. Don't imagine that you can improve your literary chances by subscribing the Catechism or the Decrees of the Council of Trent. No; I can give you no such short and easy plan for excelling; but I tell you that unless you have assimilated the final dogmas—the eternal truths—upon which those things rest, consciously if you please, but subconsciously of necessity, you can never write literature, however clever and amusing you may be. Think of it, and you will see that from the literary standpoint, Catholic dogma is merely the witness, under a special symbolism, of the enduring facts of human nature and the universe; it is merely the voice which tells us distinctly that man is *not* the creature of the drawing-room and the Stock Exchange, but a lonely awful soul confronted by the Source of all Souls, and you will realise that to make literature it is necessary to be, at all events subconsciously, Catholic.

Have you noticed how many of the greatest writers, so far from desiring that compliment of "fidelity to life", do their best to get away from life, to make their books, in ordinary phraseology, "unreal". I do not know whether anybody has compared the facts before or made the only possible inference from them; but you remember how Rabelais professes to derive his book from a little mouldy manuscript, found in a tomb, how Cervantes, beginning in *propria persona authoris,* breaks off and discovers the true history of *Don Quixote* in the Arabic Manuscript of Cid Hamet Benengeli, how Hawthorne prologises with the custom-house at Salem, and lights, in an old lumber-room, on the documents telling him the history of the *Scarlet Letter. Pickwick* was a transcript of the "Transactions" or "Papers" of the Pickwick Club, and Malory's *Morte d'Arthur* shelters itself, in the same way, behind the personality of an imaginary writer. There is a very profound significance in all this, and you find a trace of the same instinct in the Greek Tragedies where the final scene, the peripeteia, is not shewn on the stage, but described by a "messenger". The fact is that the true artist, so far from being the imitator of life, endures some of his severest struggles in endeavouring to get away from life, and until he can do this he knows that his labour is all in vain. It would be amusing to trace all the various devices which have been used to secure this effect of separation, of withdrawal from the common track of common things. I have just pointed out one, the hiding of the author, as it were, behind a mask, and in the Greek Play the analogous talking of what has happened in place of visibly shewing it, but there must be many more. From this instinct I imagine arises the historical novel in all its forms, you make your story remote by placing it far back in time, by the exhibition of strange dresses and unfamiliar manners. Or again you may get virtually the same effect by using the remoteness of space, by playing on the theme "far, far away" which really calls up a very similar emotion to that produced by the other theme of "long, long ago", or "once on a time", as the fairy tale has it. Briefly we may say that all "strangeness" of incident, or plot, or style makes for this one end; and of course you see that all this is only the repetition of our old text in another form. It is, perhaps, hardly necessary to give the caution that, on the principle of *corruptio optimi,* there is nothing more melancholy than the book which has the body of fine literature without the soul, which uses literary methods without understanding. You needn't ask for proofs of that proposition; our memories are aghast with recollections of futile "historical novels", of the terrific school of the "two horsemen", and every Christmas brings its huge budget of those dreadful "boys' books", which carry commonplace to the very ends of the earth, and occasionally penetrate to the stars. And in style, too, what can be more depressing than the style which is meant to be "strange" and is only flatulent? In many cases of course such books as I have alluded to are mere survivals of tradition, conventions of bookmaking which bear witness to the fact that pirates and treasure-hoards were once symbols of wonder, and the extravagances of style are probably to be accounted for in the same way. At some remote period it: may, possibly, have been effective to call the sun "the glorious orb", and even now some minds may be made to realise the strangeness of great flights of birds by the phrase "the feathered Zingari of the air"; but if one is a little sophisticated one feels the pathos and the futility of such efforts. The writer has felt and experienced the wonder of things—the beauty of the sun and the hieroglyphic mystery of the figures that the birds make in the air—and he feels, quite rightly, that to describe wonders one must suggest wonder by words. Unfortunately, he breaks down at this point, and falls back on unhappy phrases that give the very opposite impression to that which he wishes to excite. Here you have the whole history of "poetic diction". The instinct is in itself an entirely right one, and I need hardly say that the masters—those who have the secret—can use archaic forms, obsolete constructions, conventional phrases even, with miraculous effect. But the beginner would do well to be wary of these things, and to turn his face resolutely away from "flowery meads" and all the family of inversions. How is one to know when such phrases may be used? If I could give you the answer to that question I should be also giving you the secret of making literature, and from all our talks I expect you have gathered this much at all events—that the art of literature, with all the arts, is quite incommunicable. Many kinds of artifice, even, are unteachable—I could not write or be taught to write one of those George Eliot novels that I have been abusing with such hearty good will—but art is by its very definition quite without the jurisdiction of the schools and the realm of the reasoning process, since art is a miracle, superior to the laws.

II. Philosophy: First Principles

God's Beasts

Some days ago I stood and lingered in the brown hollow of a winter wood. Grey sky, still air, still boughs, all, one might say, deep in the heavy rest of winter; it seemed as if this were the very places and season of silence, till the spring returned as with the sound of singing and all woke up, and brown should be turned to green, and the wood quickened into joyful life.

But though the air was still and no breeze blew, and the grey sky hung changeless over the earth, there was no silence in the wood. From every bough, from every brown bush rang the sound of a loud exultant melody, the air was thrilling with the rapture of tiny creatures, voice answered to voice, choir to choir; and if one could have the ear to hear and the mind to perceive all the music of that wood, it would have been indeed as if a great clear chorus sang praise and adoration and ecstasy in the rising and falling and rising modulations of a faery plainsong. For to this ancient, magic chant, I think, can the bird's singing alone be compared. Each is monotonous—using the word not in its technical, but in its common sense—and each, it is to be observed, has the monotony that lovers use. The Lover speaking to the Beloved utters "My dear, my dear" again and again, and with like repeated phrases she makes answer; and yet they grow not weary, no do they feel any wish for the eloquence of Macaulay or of the leading article. But the lovers' voice is the voice of longing and rapture; and the ancient magic of the Church and the ancient music of the birds are also full of rapture and of longing. There are certain old fashions which cannot be changed with any profit. To the weary man, labouring under a hot sun, there is still no better sound than the noise of a bubbling well, no sweeter savour than that of the cold water dripping from the heart of the rock on the mountain-side.

These are the sentiments of a reactionary; for science, I feel sure, would maintain and demonstrate that a thirsty man on a burning day should either go on being thirsty or else drink boiling tea and be happy. But, to return to our real subject-matter—the song of the silly fowls who mistook their month and celebrated St. Valentines in January, misled by warm airs and heats of spring—I was reminded by them of St. Augustine, who declared that men are God's beasts. It is an odd-sounding, an odd-meaning sentence, and it has that curious quality which belongs to the thought of the Doctors of the Church; it works out. Note the contrast between this manner of thought and the stuff which now passes for thought. The modern thinker, taking him in the mass, has accepted as axiomatic the doctrines of "All men are free and equal", "Government for the people, by the people, through the people", and the formula of unlimited toleration for every possible or impossible opinion. And the result of these dogmas, combined with others of the same family, has been the Republic of the United States of America; a mass of political corruption, of flourishing crime, and of intellectual imbecility, for which there is no example in the history of the world. The theorems of modern thought strike many people—most people—as both reasonable and beautiful; but they don't work. Or rather they have worked their proper ends. If you believe that gunpowder is non-explosive, and apply a lighted candle to a barrelful of that substance—you will have your reward.

Here, then, is the difference between modernism and the antique wisdom of the holy doctors of the Church. "We are God's beasts"; so St. Augustine chanted, and so the birds in the January wood answered "Alleluya, alleluya, alleluya." To be scientific for a brief moment, the case was this: the blackbirds and thrushes, deceived by the unusual temperature of 50 deg. Fahrenheit, were endeavouring to attract the females of their species, and they did so by the means which Nature suggests to them—the word Nature meaning "something in the feminine gender which is about to produce". Here, from the scientific standpoint, is an end of the matter. The statement is quite true, and for those who can find rest for their souls in it there is no more to be said. It is true, it is scientific, and, like most of the pronouncements of science, comparatively unimportant. The really important thing about the birds' singing is this: that I, representing, *pro hac vice,* the genus homo, heard the song and was enchanted by it. More, if I had been a great man, the melody of those thrushes and blackbirds in the Amersham woods might very likely have found human expression in verse worthy to stand beside Keats' "Ode to a Nightingale". That is, all men throughout all ages would have received a permanent and priceless addition to the joy and delight and rapture of life. Nay, and not only the delight of the mind and the spirit and the imagination; even the sense might very well have profited. In the ode cited there are the lines as to the

> Magic casements, opening on the foam
> Of perilous seas, in faery lands forlorn.

These words, quoted and quoted as they have been, are a great thrill communicated to the entire universe of thought and emotion and imagination; they are, as it were, a mighty chord of the eternal music that sounds and will ever sound so long as our speech endures; they have accomplished for us far greater things than ever Columbus achieved; the region which they discover is more beautiful than the territory of the Massachusetts. So far good and more than good; but in fairness and in condescension to the fleshly tabernacle in which we now dwell for a brief season, let it be added that new and exquisite aromas have been added to the savour of good wine since Keats cried—

> O for a draught of vintage! that hath been
> Cooled a long time in the deep-delved earth,
> Tasting of Flora and the country green,
> Dance, and Provençal song, and sunburnt mirth.

He who drinks wisely of wise old wine, thinks of these lines and is glad; for they sow a new star in the depths of the rarest Bordeaux or Burgundy. So by Keats' poem all our faculties are cherished and enlarged, so from the chance singing of the amorous nightingale in the ears of a poet there has sprung a lasting bliss for the race of men.

Now, I know that there is a tribe which denies the right of existence to any being on earth, save and excepting only certified minerals and earthy salts. So far these people are content to say that men should not eat animals; that mutton is an infringement of the just rights of sheep. But, logically, it is clear that neither we nor the sheep have the right to cut short by violence the lives of cabbages and of grasses. A cabbage is meant to flower; who gave me the right to apply the gardener's knife and the torment of the boiling water, and thus abbreviate the natural life of the plant? We must go, then, and sheep must go, and the cabbage too must go, since it lives on the earth, diverting it from its Nirvana of quiescence, and without permission forming organism from the non-organic. So folly ends; but, passing it by, we revert to the old wisdom that man is the chief of things visible, and that for him they were created. "Have dominion over the fish of sea, and over the fowl of the air, and over every living thing that moveth upon the earth. And God said, Behold, I have given you every herb bearing seed which is upon the face of all the earth." Again, I say, how the ancient simple wisdom, as contrasted with the modern pompous nonsense, works out. A good Michealmas goose, with sage and onions and apple sauce, has benefited many an honest fellow, who has a palate and is not ashamed of it: and so for the higher sense of Keats the nightingale sang not vainly in the wood. He, after his human fashion, performed the Epiphany miracle of Cana in Galilee, and turned the water of Nature—good and pure and shining water—into the holy, magical wine of the imagination.

Wherefore let us in our order be faithful followers of the birds, and as they give joy on earth, so let us give joy in heaven. To a man the loves of the blackbird and the thrush are no matter of the first and last importance, and it may be that our passions and loves and desires and griefs seem but insignificant in the courts of heaven. There have not been wanting those in every age who have told us how vain a thing life is, how empty it is, how idle it is, how miserable it is, how that it is for ever by an immutable decree the state of the moth desiring the star, and finding instead a rending and a devouring flame. Man "walketh in vain shadow", "vanity of vanities" is his portion; his life is like the dream of the shadow of smoke; thus the Hebrews, and Socrates compared existence to the punishment of a prison-house to be meekly and patiently endured. Finally, the East invented Buddhism, which declares that all existence is evil and the only real evil.

It may be so; the matter of the work may be poor, sorry stuff enough, of no higher moment than the automatic loves of the birds in the wood. Let it be so; then let us take this rough, rude, ugly matter and change it into high melody; let us transmute the temporal into the eternal; let us take the world and turn it into art. Our passions and desires, our loves and our sorrows are all, as it were, the raw material of eternal beauty and of the ineffable joy of heaven; let us take the rough and jagged and ugly and shapeless thing called life, which is the rough ashlar of the masons, and from it fashion the smooth ashlar, fit to be compacted *in sublimi altari Tuo, in conspectu divinæ majestatis Tuæ.*

Let us then be God's good beasts, and though the wood be dark and obscure and wintry, it shall be filled with high immortal chanting.

True Comfort

A week or two ago, as I was taking a cup of tea with a friend, I pointed to a picture on the wall, and said: "Look; that tells you how extremely comfortable our forefathers were." The inference was not at first sight obvious, but my companion, being a man of understanding, at once understood. The picture was one of a series of reproductions of old coaching prints. It was called "Caught in a Drift", or by some such title, and shewed the coach deep to the axles in snow, three of the horses struggling ineffectively, and the fourth horse being ridden off to bring assistance through a wild, white landscape. The whole situation must have been uncomfortable enough, one would think, for the passengers; and yet my friend and I agreed at once that it promised rare delights. For eventually all that company, driver, guard, and passengers, came safely to a very ancient, goodly, and galleried inn on the Great North Road; this it was impiety to doubt. They saw the timbered gables leaning forward to meet them, dark against the white of the world; from the curtained windows the red, dancing light of great fires leapt up to welcome them. Within the old room, with the billowy floor and the dark beam across the ceiling, glowed and blazed with genial heat; the flame roared and crackled in the huge hearth. Then the solace of mighty sirloins of beef, of aromatic hams, of steaks that came spluttering hot from the gridiron in the fiery cavern of the kitchen; then, tankards of old ale, with hot punch, herald of good dreams, to end all. It was worth while to have been caught in the snowdrift; and the fierce north-easter gave savour to fire and food and drink and shelter.

There are all sorts of morals to be drawn from this text and example. Some of them I have worked out before, though, I think, not in *The Academy*. One of these morals is the intense discomfort of luxury; nobody relishes the heat in the hot-pipe halls and corridors of the Hôtel Glorieux which modern civilisation has given us. I can well imagine a sensible person finding himself in one of these splendid and dismal places going forth into the street and searching diligently till he found a man in a wigwam keeping guard over some disturbance of the roadway, and warming his hands over a glowing brazier of hot coals. This fellow would my wise man bribe, that he might occupy his seat for an hour or so, and taste real joy of warmth by the contrast of surrounding cold. Now and again he would take a hand from over the ardent coals and stretch it forth, giving it a taste of the frost or the bleak east wind, restoring it again to an intensified bliss. Then, there is another sermon to be made: This discourse would be on the futility of expecting men to be perfectly happy if you guarantee them against snowdrifts. This is a doctrine widely taught, and generally known as Liberalism. To be quite fair; a great number of snowdrifts have been removed in the last eighty years or so; but the worst of it has been that nearly all the old taverns have been razed to the ground, and the wild country on either side of the Great North Road is rapidly being converted into residential estates, garden suburbs, and municipal recreation grounds. So—to continue the parable—the coach rolls on a smooth track, in perfect security, and the passengers have nothing to fear. But their way lies through things hideous, pretentious, varnished, squalid, and altogether damnable. No highwaymen threaten them from the verge of the wood; for every tree in the dark wood has long been felled, and where the thicket of the nightingales once hung over the well, now stand Mongrelian Mansions, leading into Delaporte Avenue. And by that way there are no goodly taverns, with meat and drink of great refection; and some of the passengers are just beginning to wonder whether the way has any ending, any goal—if it be not the pit of destruction.

But I do not wish to labour these points at the present moment; I am occupied with a train of thought which is rather suggested by the snowdrift picture than deduced from it. I mean the doctrine of natural goods on which I dwelt a few weeks ago, considered in relation to an article on "God's Beasts", which also appeared in *The Academy,* to the Works of Rabelais, to a text from the New Testament, and to a petition in one of the Prayer Book collects. To take the last first: we pray that we may so pass through the things temporal that we lose not the things eternal. "Finally lose not" the reforming translator reforms the phrase, thereby altering and destroying the true meaning. The original prayer did not express a wish that we might be so good on earth that finally we should not miss heaven: it stated a subtler doctrine and a more mystic desire. In all temporal or mortal things, it would say, there is a hidden portion of immortality; there is paradise in the cold well, in the draught of wine *lætificans cor hominis,* in bread and in meat, in the flame of the fire, and in the flame of the sun. All the sensible world is enchanted; nothing in it is the devil's, nothing, that is, is common or commonplace or unclean; in a great tankard of good ale there be mysteries, if you know how to discern them. There is a great joy and a great wonderment of beauty in the dawn and the rising of the sun; and so there is to the seeing eye in the shining of a candle in a cottage. And so, the collect prays, let us discern the immortal gifts hidden beneath the mortal veils; let us not lose the mystery of a morsel of bread; rather let us confess with Paracelsus that he who partakes of a crust is made partaker also of all the stars and all the heavens. For, as the New Testament text seems to declare, this is the only way of attaining to that state called heaven; the man who does not discern the beauty of earthly love is not likely to know anything about heavenly love; the material is the way of passage to the immaterial. Johnson said that Thomson could not see two candles burning on the table save in a poetical light; and let it be remembered the "poetical" light is the real light. Reality is only to be apprehended by the imaginative faculty; and it is because this truth is not appreciated that the whole of modern education is not only useless, but poisonous and disastrous; and even from the "practical" point of view a hideous and expensive failure.

Hence the malignity and stupidity of those who hate the natural goods of the universe; their doctrine is in reality a closing of the gates of paradise, and shutting of the doors by which men can escape from earth into a world of pure joy. You see the effect of this in the work of the school in question; their books are a succession of snarls, sometimes of witty snarls, it is true. But from these books all true joy, delight, and rapture are absent and necessarily absent; since to their authors the world appears as a kind of devilish torture machine, in which everything is very evil. "O ye Winds of God": the writers in question immediately think how hard it is for a Suffragette to have her hair disordered or perhaps her hat blown off. "O ye Frost and Cold":

the Suffragette, having smashed windows, is in a cell, and suffers from catarrh; thus does the abhorrer of natural goods sing his new song, *Maledicite omnia opera.*

The old way, the wise way, was very different. In the article on "God's Beasts" I pointed out how insignificant, to our thinking, are the yearly love affairs of the birds in the hedgerows and in the wood. Yet out of these love affairs they make for us melody; they thrill our hearts, they fill our souls with rejoicing; a poet, listening to sounds temporal and losing not the sounds eternal, turns these thin, sweet pipings of repeated notes into the undying music of the spirit, transmuting the little song in the may-bush by the brook into an everlasting treasure for all men. So with the Greeks, when drinking the natural juice of natural vineyards, they quaffed the immortal shining wine of Dionysus: the god, fair, splendid and terrible, who consecrated the grape and made it into ecstasy and lyric rapture. So with Rabelais, who pretends that he is writing of heavy drinkers for the use of illustrious tosspots. "By wine is man made divine," says the Priestess of the Holy Bottle; by rapture and exaltation is man made divine.

So it is with all the natural goods, to the very simplest, if they be rightly discerned. So it was doubtless with some of those passengers rescued from the snowdrift. They were not, perhaps, technically poets; but from the wild night, from the frost and cold, the driving wind, the blazing hearth and the good meat and drink and shelter they made an antiphon without words, passing through things temporal and not missing things eternal.

A wordless antiphon; but perhaps there were words, uttered by the passenger warming his blue coat-tails at the roaring hearth: "Well, gentlemen, after what we've all gone through, I call this real comfort!" But, odd as it may seem, just as there can be no beauty without some strangeness in the proportion, so there can be no true comfort without a certain admixture of poetry entering into it.

Preface to *Afterglow*

I

All words are more or less misconstrued and misunderstood; none more grievously than the word "Paganism". Paganism is conceived generally to be that state of the ancient world, Greek and Roman, but chiefly Greek, in which men lived in a kind of Abbey of Thelema, doing what they would, satisfying the flesh according to their desires, devoid of morals altogether, using the word "morals" in its customary modern sense. Insensibly, when anyone speaks of Paganism, one thinks of garlands and dances, of the Bacchic fury, of the breasts of the nymph in the brake, of the Satyrs lurking in the grove of dark ilexes. You could do as you pleased; there was no law to restrain you, from within or from without. As for the gods, they were but pleasing fictions, invented by the poets as a kind of gilt on the gingerbread of lechery; but nobody took the gods seriously. Such, we are apt to think, was Paganism.

It was nothing of the kind; that is, in the heroic age of Greece, certainly not in the age when Socrates, about to drink the hemlock, discoursed to his disciples of immortal life in the essence of the Godhead. They were no flowery and careless voluptuaries who listened to certain rituals of predestination that have survived to our days. We can read in them still of the doom that awaits proud and insolent men, owning no master in heaven or earth; of the manner in which the sins of the fathers are visited upon the children unto the third and fourth generation; of the vengeance that lies in wait for the spiller of blood; of the remorseless decrees of destiny; and of making atonement for transgression. Such are the topics of these sermons and rituals, which are known to us as Greek Plays. Paganism, in its pure and uncorrupted state was, evidently, a good deal more than an elegant and poetic Bank

Holiday, a perpetual riot, a rosy debauch. It had its austere side; perhaps it was, in its essence, as austere as New England in the seventeenth century; though, to be sure, it wore its robes with a better grace and had somewhat a different set of taboos and commands. The descendants of the Pilgrim Fathers hanged witches; the Athenians judged the men who profaned or divulged the holy Mysteries of Eleusis to be worthy of death.

Such then was Paganism in the days of its covenant; something more than a bedecked and fleshy revel. But in the time of its dissolution, I have no doubt that it had taken on some semblance of our popular notion of it.

The Alexandria which Mr. Buck has shewn in such glowing and coloured pictures, on which the ancient and golden sunlight still shines and burns, was in a sense an Abbey of Thelema. Men did as they pleased, and all that pleased them was sensual pleasure. To be sure, they still talked of the gods. They talked of Aphrodite; but Aphrodite was only an excuse; just as, to the bad Mason, a certain very solemn and awful ceremony is only an excuse for the banquet which follows it.

II

Yet all the while there was a sense, sometimes conscious, sometimes subconscious, that it wouldn't do. In Mr. Buck's pages you will find this half-murmur of dissatisfaction, the sad murmur which finds its expression in the lines:

> *Medio de fonte Eporum*
> *Surgit amari aliquid.*

In the long run it was felt that mere pleasure failed to please. Men were evidently unable to live wholly in the body and by the body and for the body; there was some unknown element missing, and all became savourless, even deadly. Everywhere there was pleasure; nowhere was there joy. For this people had lost the old austere joys of true Paganism; they were nowise of the race of those Spartans who perished so splendidly in resisting the invasion of Greece by the Persian King; the Greek theatre had given place to the gaudy savagery of the Circus games; the old patriot city states were submerged by an orientalised cosmopolitanism. One got tired, it seemed, of wearing roses and worshipping Aphrodite; but what else was there to do? Really, it seemed, nothing; or nothing what was worth doing. One might say that Paganism was dissolving into a melancholy boredom, into that state of mind which afterwards was called *accidia* and accounted one of the deadly sins. Indeed, the sun had set. The sky was still lighted; but black clouds were gathering from all quarters of the heavens; and that red light in the west—was it not as if the roses were being changed into burning flames? Well has Mr. Buck named these pastels of his *Afterglow*.

III

One may say that the failure of this Paganism, which had become a decorated materialism, was the failure of a great experiment. The world of that day was endeavouring to live by bread alone; bread being understood to include:

"A profusion of meats and viands, oysters, lampreys, quails, roasted swans, wild boar, sauces and relishes, cakes of various grains mingled with honey, fruits and sherbets: all that the caprices of taste could suggest."

Add to this definition of bread: "Kraters of rich wine, cooled in snow brought laboriously from long distances", add even, "a group of slave girls . . . of selected beauty, nude except for their conventional girdles"—such was the bread on which the Alexandrian world tried to live. And, really, they did their best. They avoided the error of spoiling the ship for a ha'porth of tar. The Great Experiment was made completely, splendidly. The dough of this bread of theirs was of the very finest flour; it was served on a lordly dish, in a hall of great worship; it was brought to the board with all the daughters of music singing before it. I doubt whether this assay of bread can ever be conducted with such gorgeous circumstance again. And, besides, the whole thing was done without any self-consciousness. The company wore their wreaths of roses naturally, without the slightest sense of dressing-up or "making-believe"—or of making fools of themselves. In these days, the attempt at the revel is still made; but it is somewhat pathetic. We have lost the art of wearing garlands, and our attempts at revelry are more depressing that the spectacle of High School mistresses dancing the Morris. No; Alexandria did the thing in style; and yet, it seems, it was all a failure at best. Man found that he could not live on bread alone; that is, purely in the material world.

But let it not be supposed that I consider this Great Experiment as a self-evident absurdity, foredoomed to failure from the very nature of the quest. Very far from it. On the contrary, so much is the Alexandrian plan the obvious plan, that to this day many of us attempt to carry it out, in spite of its failure, in spite of the disadvantageous circumstances under which we must conduct our operations, in spite of the fact that the Kraters of rare wine cooled with snow have given place to whiskey that is dubious in England and not at all dubious in America. In spite of all, we do our best to be Alexandrians, since their way seems after all the certain way, the only way that is certain. Mr. Buck's Philosopher found the talk of the priests intolerable; and so many of us find the talk of our priests intolerable. After all, it is only the body and the things of the body which appear certain to the natural man. The philosophers may call them shadows and phantoms, but we are not philosophers. There is a legend that the great Newman was wont to regard his Cardinal's Hat and to murmur to himself: "Everything is uncertain except this: that there is a Holy Roman Catholic and Apostolic Church and that I am a Cardinal of it: for here is the hat—there is no doubt about that, at all events." The legend is, of course, a lie; but one understands the sentiment beneath it. We are quite sure of our bodies. We know that ginger is hot in the mouth. We may not know why it is hot; but as to the fact of the heat of the ginger, there is no room for argument about that. And that fact and other facts congruous therewith, the pleasant uses of wine and women, the delight of coolness afforded in summer, of a flaming hearth in winter, of a noble feast when one is hungry: these are beyond denial. And, as to all else, what do we know? "Is there a God?" asks St. Thomas Aquinas, opening his great treatise; and his answer is, "Apparently not." Mark the emphasis on "apparently"; but do not most of us live only in appearances, in phenomena, in the world wherein ginger is hot, and meat satisfies hunger, and drink quenches thirst, and women appease desire? All this we know certainly; beyond this we are in a world of conjecture, theory, dream, mystery, vague possibility. There may be a God, our bodies may be the mere veils of the spirit, the mind may be one of this spirit's instruments. All this may be so, but we do not know that it is so. We do know that when men who believe in these unseen realities, as they call them, begin to discuss matters of God, soul, mind, or spirit, they immediately begin to differ violently, to enter into endless arguments, to start debates that endure for æons and yet are never resolved. Now, we may urge, there is no argument, no quarrel, when it is a question of a hungry man eating or of a thirsty man quenching his thirst; here there are no two opinions but the undivided consent of all mankind; here, in a word, we are on sure ground. Why should we leave it for a territory which is all uncertain, misty, doubtful and, it is possible, fabulous? There are charts of the unknown ocean, it is true, but there are too many of them and no two are alike, and each pilot utterly derides and abhors the navigation of the others, and they only agree in this: that the voyage is certainly dark and dangerous. Is it not better to remain on the firm land, in the sunlight, satisfying the desires of the body?

Such was the Alexandrian position. It seems to me a very strong one; almost, one would say, inexpugnable. Yet these people, who lived as they pleased, who were untroubled by ethical systems or the reproach of conscience, who could satisfy the desires of the body without fear of reproach from within or of censure and punishment from without, were ill at ease. As Mr. W. L. Courtney tells us, when the first century before Christ was drawing to its close, the whole of the Mediterranean shore was anxiously and restlessly seeking for something that it called *soteria* or salvation. And it seems clear that, whatever *soteria* may be, it is not good to eat or to drink. In fine, the red roses and the ivory flesh of the girls had alike grown grey; meat and drink were bitter in the mouth.

The only thing that can be urged against the Alexandrian theory of life is this: it didn't work.

Man, the Mad Mammal

First Critic: "To me civilisation is a matter of sewage."

Second Critic: ". . . Those who to-day tend more and more to feel that every aspiration and every hope of man is a logical absurdity."

These are two recent pronouncements. I believe that there is a link between them, and it may be entertaining to look for it.

To begin with the First Critic, it should be explained that he was criticising. Someone had written a book, a book that touched on music; and the author ventured the opinion that the music of Mozart and Beethoven was the very summit and touchstone of civilisation. Here, he seemed to say, is the purest, the highest, the finest thing that man can do: in a word, civilisation, as contrasted with brutishness. Our critic proclaimed his resolute negative. Not music, he said, nor sculpture, nor architecture make civilisation: for me it is a matter of sewage. And I presume that we may include with music, architecture, and sculpture: painting and literature, though these last are not specified. And a liberal spirit of interpretation will collect under the term sewage everything that makes for the well-being of the human body, every method and every measure that prolongs human life.

I don't think that the position has ever been stated so clearly. Everybody in his senses agrees that physical well-being is highly desirable. Nobody that I have ever heard of has argued that the chief instance of the ancient culture of Athens was the Plague; or that we should praise the Middle Ages not so much for the cathedrals or the Arthurian romances or the *Divine Comedy* as for the Black Death. And it would be over hardy to maintain that the Great Plague of London added much to the merriment of the Restoration period.

Evidently, we all want to live as long as possible, and to be as well as possible. An explorer or an archæologist may say that he is willing to risk catching malaria, even in a bad form, for the sake of making drawings of those sculptures or ascertaining the exact source and course of that river: but he would be much happier if "sewage" in one form or another had abolished the disease.

The case for sewage, then, is proved completely. But two questions arise.

Having got our sewage into the most perfect state possible: having eliminated disease: having found out the complete secret of nutrition: having made wars to cease throughout the world: having reduced accidents and disasters to a minimum: having adjusted the social complex in such a manner that poverty and its result, ill-nourished bodies, have ceased to exist: what are we to do next? John Stuart Mill saw the difficulty and thought, I believe, that man would chiefly occupy himself in reading Wordsworth. But our Critic has swept away the arts. He has declared that they count for nothing. We are perfectly healthy; we have every expectation of living to a hundred, perhaps to a hundred and fifty. But what are we to do with ourselves?

That is the first question. The second is: how is it that taking the human race as a whole, going back to the remotest ages, surveying with Dr. Johnson the world from China to Peru; how is it that men have entirely failed to follow that course which the Critic says is the only rational course? It is not that they have been unaware of the benefits of sound health and long life. These have always been recognised as good things. Of course, men have differed as to the means to attain those ends. We send for the plumber: Black Africa sends for the witch doctor; mediæval man, very likely, sent for the liver of a black dog, torn out under the full moon: on the whole, I suppose that our way is the best. But the end, physical well-being, is the same in each instance.

And yet, man has from the beginning been hugely addicted to the arts; that is, a seeker after beauty. There is no race so primitive or so rude that it does not scratch some sort of a pattern on the bowl from which it eats its dinner; the cavemen painted images on the walls of their cave; there were songs about the earliest camp-fires; and some of our nursery tales were first told by peoples that had perished long before history began. And so it has gone on, ever since, a great pageant of music, painting, sculpture, architecture, poetry, philosophy. How is this? What happened to man at the beginning?

Here, I believe, we discover the link between our two Critics. The second Critic suggests that every aspiration, every hope of man, is an absurdity.

Very good. What should we say, if we saw a swallow trying to gather honey from flowers, and a bee endeavouring to sustain nature on midges; a cat with a violin, in an effort to realise the old rhyme, and a cow, not jumping over the moon, but attempting the art of modelling in mud? I suppose we should say—before we ran—that the creatures were mad, that the beast creation had become maniacal; in other words, that all their hopes, all their aspirations, were absurdities.

And so, combining our information, placing the dictum of the First Critic beside that of the Second, we arrive inevitably at our definition of man: the Mammal that went mad. The monkey, being sane, gibbers, chatters, and screams; his distant cousin, man, being mad, writes poems and romances, and composes music. The clear-headed animal has neither aspirations nor hopes; or, at least, only such as are rational and easily realised. Man, with his wits all addled, is fall of hopes and aspirations, all of them, it seems, logical absurdities. It is evident that if we grant the premisses, the conclusion is inevitable; man is a maniac.

Here, at all events, we have a plausible explanation of what has always seemed to me a tremendous puzzle. We accept the doctrine of science in its authentic form. We are not descended from the apes, as the loose talk ran; but the apes and ourselves come from a common ancestry. Then, at some point in the tremendous past, one set of hairy creatures began to behave in an extraordinary manner. There are people, I believe, who think that the queerness of the divergent stock first appeared in its renunciation of the vegetarian diet that had hitherto been the habit of the whole race and it must be said, in all fairness, that many amiable and enlightened persons of the present time would regard Meat and Madness as almost in the relation of cause and effect. Then, perhaps, the differentiated race learned how to cook. Again, we must admit that some eminent physicians of to-day inform us with authority that to cook our food is to destroy its food value; that we shall never be well, either in body or mind, unless we put out the kitchen fire. And a third step, very possibly, may be symbolised by the Greek mythos of Dionysus, or Bacchus, who civilised men, as the ancients said, by teaching them the strange uses of the vine. We know too well what some of the best people have to say about that step in our career; our mad career, if our two Critics are to be believed. And, after Dionysus had taught our forefathers what to do with the vine, we may well suppose that hopes and aspirations and unimaginable dreams, and all the arts which are born of them, came as a waterflood on this new creature, this transformed mammal. At last, he was Man: and Mad.

It is interesting, I think, to note, as I have noted, the coincidence that may be traced between the old legends and the new science; nay, between these legends and the most modern, the most advanced political thought. You remember how Don Quixote, sitting among the goatherds, took a handful of acorns—it must be confessed they were parched—and delivered his eulogy of the Golden Age.

"Happy the age, happy the time, to which the ancients gave the name of golden—because they that lived in it knew not the two words, *mine* and *thine!* In that blessed age all things were in common; to win the daily food no labour was required of any save to stretch forth his hand and gather it from the sturdy oaks that stood generously inviting him with their sweet, ripe fruit. The clear streams and running brooks yielded their savoury limpid waters in noble abundance. The busy and sagacious bees fixed their republic in the clefts of the rocks and hollows of the trees, offering to every hand without usance the plenteous product of their fragrant toil."

And so forth, and so forth.

Communism, raw acorns, cold water, bee-stings, and wild honey: it must have been almost as nice as modern Russia. And it is practically identical with the nonsense with which Rousseau deluded the world.

Farewell to Materialism

I

The matter of literary survival always strikes me as a curious and difficult question. A year or two ago, that distinguished man of letters, Sir J. C. Squire, addressing some kind of meeting or parliament of bookish men, went so far as to state that in his opinion, hardly any famous man of letters of today would be known by name in a hundred years' time; while renown would belong to a few obscure men, scarcely noted or noticed at the present time. Concerning the second half of this prophetic utterance, I must say that I have very grave doubts. I look for precedents of this long deferred renown, and at the moment I fail to find any, amongst prose writers at all events. All, or nearly all of the great books that we still revere, were heartily and loudly welcomed at their first appearance: *Pantagruel, Don Quixote, The Essays of Montaigne, Tom Jones, Tristram Shandy,* Boswell's *Johnson, Pickwick* were praised and bought and read while they were warm from the press. I am afraid I cannot give much comfort to the neglected of the present; it seems likely that the future will be no more kind to them. Walter Savage Landor said that he would dine late, indeed, but in the choicest company. He has proved mistaken. His dinner party has not come off, though at intervals of thirty years or so we are told by important people that we ought to read Landor and enjoy him very much.

But as to the first part of Sir J. C. Squire's prediction: there I agree. A great many of the writers whose praise fills the review columns of the weighty weeklies, every Saturday and every Sunday of this year 1935, will hardly be known by name to one man in ten thousand in 2035. Mr. Hugh Walpole, indeed, protested warmly at the end of Sir J. C. Squire's speech, but his rebutting example was a little unhappy.

He said that the works of Miss Marie Corelli were still in demand at the circulating libraries; and I can imagine that some of the listening authors were rather shocked than gratified by such a support of their case for immortality. But no doubt Sir J. C. Squire was right. Some of the greatest reputations of our age are destined to dwindle and disappear. To leave the living alone: Arnold Bennett will not survive. Not a single character in any one of his books will be recognisable and quotable as a familiar friend in twenty-five years' time. The quickening juice of life is not in him. I doubt whether people will read Conrad much longer. It is possible, hardly probable, that the Forsyte Saga will be studied a hundred years hence by serious girls going in for examinations. Certainly, no one else will look at it save the mere grubbers in library dust, the men who are only interested in books that are hopelessly and eternally forgotten.

And, then, there is another tiresome question that arises. When we speak of survival, what, exactly, do we mean? Testing the matter by the past, by our knowledge of the old books that we confess are still alive, let us take the most illustrious of them all. How many of us—"us" means men who consider themselves interested in books and more or less acquainted with them—how many of us, without reference or investigation, on the mere spur of the moment, are prepared to comment on one of the most familiar quotations from Shakespeare, "A poor thing but mine own"? How many bookish people are aware that no such phrase occurs in *As You Like It?* To continue the test: name, if you can, the author of the lines:

> See Winter, from the frozen north
> Drives his iron chariot forth!
> His grisly hand in icy chains
> Fair Tweeda's silver flood constrains.

What was *quadrivium,* and how much did it cost on the Great North Road in the first half of the eighteenth century? What did Hafen Slawkenbergins write? What was Teresa Panza's real name—if we are to take her own account of the matter? To put the affair more briefly, I suggest that Mr. Desmond McCarthy was in the right when he suggested that few even among the literate have read the masterpieces that we say have survived; they have merely read in them, which is a different matter. And, to come to the point, the especial point as it happens: to what book were "our fellows" referring when they called Mr. Sparkler, "Quinbus Flestrin junior, or the Young Man Mountain"? The especial point I say, because I want to talk about *Gulliver's Travels,* and I am not sure whether I may take it that this famous book has survived, in the sense that it may be familiar to all the literate. We have all heard of it, I know, and of the Little People, and the Big People, and the Horse People; but is Gulliver an intimate friend, or a mere acquaintance, or nothing but a vague recollection of the nursery library?

Certainly, the book has had a queerer fate than most books; perhaps the queerest fate that any book ever had. In the days of old Holywell Street, that ran parallel with the Strand, I used to wonder at the doom of the profound Rabelais, ranked behind sixteenth-century casements with all manner of cheap rubbish that pretended to be bawdy: *Maria Monk, Aristotle's Works, The Life of Cora Pearl, The Mysteries of the Court of St. James,* and a wilderness of such like trash. But stranger still, I think, is the lot that has befallen Dean Swift's ferocious onslaught on the whole race of men. As I have said, it is, or was till yesterday, an established nursery favourite, and the name of the kingdom of the horrible little men has become a caress, a word of fondness. From that pleasant place of observation, the top of a London bus, I once saw a shop devoted to small children's goods. In the window was a sign: Footwear for Lilliput—as if one were to say Juvenal for the Juveniles. I wondered how the Dean would have taken it; but I hardly think that many people would have seen anything particularly odd or incongruous about the announcement. And that very fact makes me suspect that the true nature of this book, familiarly and commonly as we speak of it, is not generally known or appreciated. Yet one would say that the meaning of the text of *Gulliver's Travels* is neither concealed, difficult, nor obscure. Here is an example, from "A Voyage to Brobdingnag".

> That which gave me the most uneasiness among these maids of honour, when my nurse carried me to visit them, was to see them use me without any manner of ceremony, like a creature who had no sort of consequence; for they would strip themselves to the skin and put on their smocks in my presence, while I was placed on their toilet directly before their naked

> bodies, which, I am sure, to me was very far from being a tempting sight, or from giving me any other emotions than those of horror and disgust. Their skins appeared so coarse and uneven, so variously coloured, when I saw them near, with a mole here and there as broad as a trencher, and hairs hanging from it thicker than packthread, to say nothing further concerning the rest of their persons.

The purport and intent of this and of many other passages in the like vein are surely clear enough. Swift desired to convey a loathing and horror of the very substance of humanity, to make the things that most men consider beautiful and adorable, hateful and disgusting. He does not attack, you will note, this nation or that, this party or that, this religion or that. He is not reprobating the sins, vices, errors, malignities of man; he is not speaking as a moralist. He is not calling attention to the intellectual failings of his subject, to the dimness and feebleness, to the fallacies which beguile us in our search for the truth. Still less is he troubled by the uncertainties of our artistic vision, by the difficulty experienced by his own age in making up its mind as to the respective merits of Handel and Bononcini. He says: "Here is the object and the end of all your desire, of your poetry, of your imagination, of your art; here is woman. And you see that she is in reality a loathsome and disgusting object." And, again:

> They would often strip me naked from top to toe, and lay me at full length in their bosoms, wherewith I was much disgusted, because, to say the truth, a very offensive smell came from their skins.

A pretty book for the nursery shelf, to furnish words for the babies' vocabulary.

This queer fate of *Gulliver's Travels* suggests, however, a singular speculation. There are many writers of the last score of years who have endeavoured to emulate Swift in the science of the disgusting without having, it would seem, Swift's ferocious object, or so far as appears, any particular object save the feeble desire to be in the fashion, and, by the way, to sell their books. It is generally agreed, among our English critics at all events, that the writers of such books are to be treated with the greatest respect, that their frankness, their unflinching veracity, their firm refusal to sentimentalise life, their fidelity to the fact as they see it, are deserving of the most serious consideration and regard. If a writer deck his pages with the words that nasty little boys chalk on obscure walls, we are told that he is moved to do so by the sheer force of artistic duty; that he is more to be revered for the deed than the martyr giving up his soul in the flames. Very well; but how odd it would be if in a hundred years or so these grave and tremendous works appeared in the booksellers' lists under the heading: "Gift Books for the Young"; if tiny tots, just able to read, were found on the nursery floors absorbed in the fantastic unreason of *The New Oedipus,* and gurgling with delight and happy laughter over the very odd adventures of *A Suburban Sappho.* Of course, *we* know that these books have superseded almost everything in English literature; but in a hundred years?

II

The sense of these passages about the ladies of the Court of Brobdingnag is obvious enough on the surface. They are meant to express Swift's horror and disgust at the mere fact of humanity; and there is more to the same purpose in "A Voyage to the Houyhnhnms". What was the cause behind the horror, how much was due to an incipient disease of the brain, how much to disappointed ambition, how much to Swift's firm conviction that, after the death of Queen Anne, England had finally and fatally taken the wrong turning, is hard to say. But beneath the obvious meaning of these passages, which so vilely defame the ladies' charms, there is something hidden, and so deeply hidden that we must suppose it escaped the notice of the man who wrote them. The doctrine that emerges from all this talk of coarse offensive skins, and bloated moles, and hairs like packthread, is simply this: that in the last resort, all science is a lie. That is: supposing the body of the dead Keats had been anatomised, dissected, summarised under the headings of bones and sinews, of veins and arteries, of nails and teeth, of internal organs and glands and processes, of all the complexes which make up the human body; and if the surgeon in charge having put down all the items in his intricate account, had written at the end: "This is Keats": then he would have lied, just as Bitzer lied when he gave his famous definition of a horse in these set terms:

> Quadruped. Graminivorous. Forty teeth, namely twenty-four grinders, four eye teeth and twelve incisive. Sheds coat in spring; in marshy countries sheds hoofs, too. Hoofs hard, but requiring to be shod with iron. Age known by marks in mouth.

Nobody would know what *Hamlet* was by counting and classifying the letters of the alphabet, the nouns, verbs, adjectives and other parts of speech contained in that masterpiece. Nobody would know what a lily was by conning the jargon that the botanists have written about it. Nobody would know what a good dinner was by the recitation of the proteins and carbohydrates that composed it. Nobody would know what Rembrandt's *Mill* was by being presented with a catalogue of the earths and oils which the artist used in painting it. Imagine going to the laboratory for the character of a famous Burgundy of a golden year. The chemist's business is to seek for poisons, not for the secrets of a noble wine.

Or—let it be said again—in the last resort all science is a lie. A lie, that is, when brought to bear witness in the court of the arts, in the court of life, in the secret places of reality. A lie, even, if taken into consultation over a good dish and a bottle of Opimian, though useful, no doubt, in its own confined and inferior region.

And that false doctrine of science is the doctrine which lies beneath Swift's account of the ladies of the country of the giants. With regard to them and their skins and the rest of it, the eyes and nose of Gulliver were powerful scientific instruments of vast magnification. We cannot be Gullivers or become familiar in the land of Brobdingnag; but we can get instruments of far higher powers than his eyes and apply them to the world, if we will. We can put the visage of the Beloved under our microscope and discover it to be an ugly and unseemly thing. With spectacles of the right power we find the painter's masterpiece to be mere senseless and formless confusion; using the same glasses, we see the loveliest landscapes in the world are nothing but blur and mist. In a word, with the instruments and microscopes of the black magic of science, we can demonstrate that all beauty is ugliness, that all form is formless, that the seer's vision is a drunkard's delirium, that the highest sense is nonsense, and that significance is utterly insignificant. Who would be such a fool, it may be asked, as to apply such tests or anything analogous with them?

The answer is that the processes indicated are closely analogous with much of the criticism and a great deal of the creative practice of the present day. It was only a few months ago that I saw an article in a weekly paper of high repute which undertook among other things to restate Keats for us in the light of modern literary science. The first thing done was to apply the Gulliver glasses to the magistral "Ode to a Nightingale"—which, beyond doubt, is sheer miracle and magic. Keats, said our critic, a very well-known man in his craft, had no imagination, but only fancy, a very inferior faculty. And the reason for this notable depreciation and readjustment? Why, Keats wrote: "Thou wast not born for death, immortal bird!"—and we all know, perfectly well, that nightingales are born for death, and that they do, in fact, die. The poet, therefore, has been guilty of making a statement contrary to the laws of science, and therefore again has no imagination but only fancy. I wish the critic had proceeded in this vein of his, and applied his instruments—apparently Sam Weller's "patent double million magnifyin' microscopes of hextra power"—to the work of Shelley, and put him in his place. Shelley wrote an "Ode to a Skylark", and began:

> Hail to thee, blithe Spirit!
> Bird thou never wert,
> That from heaven, or near it
> Pourest thy full heart
> In profuse strains of unpremeditated art.

What an opportunity missed! Here is a man who talks about heaven. We won't press him too hard on that point, we will allow, handsomely, that he does not intend to make the word carry its usual weight of nonsensical theological dogma, or any "Which art in heaven" implications. But we will ask him whether he believes that anywhere in the constitution of things there is a place or a state of perfect happiness and beauty, and if he does believe in any such preposterous nonsense, to be so good as to state his reasons for this belief. Of course, he may say that he simply means by heaven, the sky. If so, it is a pity that he did not say sky, or rather, stratosphere. But even if this explanation be accepted, we must point out that larks are never found in this region, or anywhere near it, and, anyhow, they wouldn't like it if they got there. But there is hardly any need to discuss this or any other matter with a man who states quite definitely that larks are not birds and never were birds, but blithe spirits. And, after that, there is no more to be said. And, if we go on applying our test, our Gulliver Process, what shall we make of the well-known Song in *The Tempest?*

> Full fathom five thy father lies;
> Of his bones are coral made;
> Those are pearls that were his eyes;
> Nothing of him that doth fade,
> But doth suffer a sea-change
> Into something rich and strange.

There is not a word of truth in it; it is a mess of bad science. Where is Shakespeare's imagination now? The man for our modern money is the artist who chose the subject of St. Francis of Assisi preaching to the birds, and made the Saint a squat figure in a friar's frock, and the birds fat geese. The beautiful is shewn to be ridiculous; the artist has the veritable Gulliver touch.

There is one thing to be noted about all these moderns, these Gulliver process fellows, these adepts of a new alchemy, with their *magnum opus* of transmuting all the beauty and delight of the world into filth and ugliness and loathing; and that is that the science which guides them is long obsolete. Sixty or seventy years ago, perhaps, there were dabblers in science, not, certainly, true men of science, who believed that the microscope, let us say, shewed you what the object under observation really was. "Here," they might say, "is a surface which seems to you of an exquisite smoothness, with the tint of a delicate rose: look at it now, and you will see that it is really rough and corrugated, pitted and scarred like a telescopic view of the moon; that the delicate colour you admired is a raddle of great spots, rather resembling a putrid eruption than the blush of the rose." And, if you were simple, you might go away sorry that the thing you had admired was really like that. A later and a deeper science has informed us that there is no "really" in the case, that the reality is no more like the object observed by the microscope than that object when seen by unassisted vision. The thing in itself, the reality, is never to be found; it vanishes into the invisible conjectured land of the electrons; it becomes a manifestation of the eternal energy, a part of an infinite cosmos, like the sun and the stars. Its end is a great glory, a firm order, a shining mystery. After all, even if we make the appeal to science, there is a great deal to be said for the happy ending.

III

Here it may as well be stated, very firmly, that this is no plea for the extreme Victorians and their false axiom, that literature must never touch on anything unpleasant, or on anything that might not be discussed in the vicarage drawing room in the presence of the young people. This nonsense, which would have put most of the masterpieces of the past—certainly the works of Shakespeare—on the index of prohibited books, manifested itself in ways scarcely credible to us, who have gone to the other and the worse extreme, and seem to hold that filth is synonymous with genius. I had occasion some time ago to quote Shirley's poem, beginning:

> The glories of our blood and state

and I was set right by a correspondent, who referred me to some anthology or collection of *Gems of English Poetry,* published in the forties of the last century, in which the line went—

> The glories of our birth and state

I have no doubt that the *Gems* was a book, cloth, gilt, meant to adorn the centre table of the polite drawing rooms of vicarages, mansions, and villas. The editor felt that blood was not a nice word, that its suggestions were decidedly unpleasant; and so it was softened by him into birth. Miss Charlotte M. Yonge was rebuked by an elderly lady for defining the heart as a pump for blood: it might be true, but it was not nice. With this nonsense we have nothing to do, though, by the way, our recognition that it is nonsense need not make us select charts of the intestines, coloured to the life, as suitable ornaments for the walls of dining room or living room.

But, as I was saying, the masters of literature do not shrink from the unpleasant. The topics of the two greatest plays in the world are extremely unpleasant. The Oedipus Tyrannus of Sophocles is the story of a man who murders his father and marries his mother: Shakespeare's *Hamlet* is murder and lust and madness; and it is the Christian, not the pagan poet who is the franker in his speech, the more intimate in his manner of allusion. There are gross things in *Hamlet;* none in Oedipus. The pagans held, and held wisely, that gross speech is matter for comedy; they did not see, as Shakespeare saw, that in art as in life, comedy and tragedy may be mingled. But in neither play is there the faintest resemblance between the unpleasantness or the grossness of these masterpieces and the work of the moderns, who drag in their nastiness by the heels, since it is the real object and the only object of their work. Dickens in *David Copperfield* shews us the man in the debtor's prison, his squalid mistress, and his two daughters with heads of hair all lousy; but it needs not to be said that verminous hair is not the reason of *David Copperfield.* You have your mole, but you do not make it as big as a trencher; you do not suffer your lice to crawl over every page of your book.

It was natural enough, perhaps, that the absurd over-delicacy and false delicacy of some, by no means all of the Victorians, should bring about a reaction, a violent impulse to the opposite extreme. I say, advisedly, "some, by no means all" of the Victorians. We have just seen that Dickens did not hesitate to picture sheer squalor and nastiness if he thought such matter was to his purpose; and those who doubt his ability to be frank on occasion are referred to his description of the birth of Little Dorrit in the Marshalsea Prison. True, there are no lice here; but there are plenty of flies, bloated, as the midwife says, by feeding in the stables, in the premises devoted to the paunch trade and in the burying ground. All thoroughly realistic—to use a term most vilely misapplied. Equally direct in another way were Swinburne and Rossetti: the first series of *Poems and Ballads* is not reticent in its treatment of physical passion, and Rossetti's *Jenny* is a man's meditation on the harlot who is his night's companion. Still, there was a great deal of silly prudery abroad, and the change when it came was naturally violent and excessive. Then, the efforts of Anglican bishops, deans, and dignitaries generally to move with the times and to get abreast with the obsolete science of fifty years before, confused simple minds, and made many hold that the distinctions between right and wrong, good and evil, were childish mediævalisms and terribly unmodern. There was a general desire to be broadminded, not to be passionately certain that triangles had three sides, not to be harshly dogmatic in questions of morals. There was a feeling that the heroic was, at least, suspect, and in all probability rather silly. People smiled a little when General Gordon was mentioned, and I think that there were circles where you would apologise for bringing your friend, the V.C.: "He's quite all right when you know him." Was Florence Nightingale a bit of a sneak, after all? And wasn't there something rather fine (if you could cast off your Victorian limitations) in Charley Peace? You may call him a murderer, but what else (in all probability) is your V.C.? Modern thought declines to make a distinction between the two; saving this point, that whereas the soldier kills to order, Peace expressed himself freely, and so the balance seems on Peace's side. And there are certainly many influential quarters where it is held as an article outside debate that the cause of the Russian Soviets is the cause of freedom, as opposed to tyranny and reaction. And he who can make that profession may be held to be convinced of the existence of two-sided triangles.

To cut a long story short: from one cause and another there was a very general state of mental confusion in most regions of human thought, art, and action. I heard a very well-known art critic declare that he saw nothing amiss in an artist sitting down before a square bit of toast, painting a pink triangle, and calling the picture *Dry Toast.* It is widely maintained, also, that there is something contemptible in imitating the art of the civilised Middle Ages, the ages of Dante, and Rheims Cathedral, and the *Morte d'Arthur;* while the imitation of the art of uncivilised savages is essentially noble and modern. And, when to the various causes I have reckoned up, you add the terrific shock of the war, I do not think that the resultant confusion is to be wondered at.

It is whispered that in those bad old Victorian days, when maiden ladies were quite terrifically virginal and used delicate and complicated periphrases for almost everything seen or done, there were sometimes unspeakable and incomprehensible outbreaks in the dentist's chair. Miss Prymme, the curate's middle-aged sister, recovering from her dose of nitrous oxide, would now and then open her wounded mouth, and to the horror—or amusement—of the dentist and anæsthetist pour out such a flood of shrieking obscenities as neither man had heard delivered so copiously before. Words from old books and old dark walls of railway arches made Landseer's pictures shiver, and may have brought back ancient memories to the figures in "Bolton Abbey in the Olden Time"; and then, in a minute or two, Miss Prymme was murmuring in her gentle faded voice her "thanks to the skill of you two gentlemen, positively no pain at all".

And, really, she was not at all to be blamed. Her outrageous utterance was the result of the gas and the shock of the extraction, producing between them confusion. So the gas of the broadminded bishops and deans, of the advanced and liberal thinkers, generally coupled with the grievous shock of the war, has produced a like confusion, causing our modern novelists to write down in their books the very words with which Miss Prymme turned the doctor and the dentist pale—or purple. Undoubtedly, this said confusion is a grievous one: things have come to a bad pass when many people fail to see any particular difference between self-sacrificing love and a cesspool. Or, rather, I should say that they incline to prefer the cesspool, since it is frank and the truth about life, and stark; while the other matter is certainly sentimental, and is, most likely, a complex, an inhibition, and a libido as well.

And the end of it all? There can be no sure answer to that. It may be that a new barbarism, far worse than the old barbarism that overwhelmed the Roman Empire, is upon us. The Huns and Goths and Vandals were destructive, and that was bad: the new invasion will be constructive, and that will be horrible. Our descendants may live in rooms like this doctor's waiting room, recently described thus:

> Gone is the drab wallpaper, the musty carpet, the Victorian furniture, and last year's magazines laid around a mahogany table. What you see will remind you of a 1935 glass and chromium room in a Cochran revue. It has one wall dead black and the other three bright yellow. The ceiling is black and the carpet near-black. There is a narrow glass table jutting out from one wall, and along it is a long seat of black wood upholstered in bright green. Another L-shaped black and green seat flanks the wall on the other side, and in addition there are three chromium chairs with black canvas seats.
>
> Two recesses, one on each side of what used to be the fireplace, and is now covered in, have glass bookshelves, concealed lighting and huge mirrors at the back.

And we may judge pretty well what the inhabitants of such rooms will be like, what their painting and sculpture and literature will be. But we must hope for better things, and above all for the restoration of the great power of the imagination to imaginative literature. Crass and imbecile materialism is gone forever, and in its place we have the recognition that, in its ultimates, all being is a profound mystery. For my part, I have never felt the need of scientific backing of any kind. The old science, as I have said, was a lie; but it is over and ended. The new science is simply telling us in its own language the secrets which have always been known to the visionaries and the poets and the makers of music and of romances. All these knew, some in their minds but all in their hearts, that we live in a world of symbols; of sensible perishable things which both veil and reveal spiritual and living and eternal realities; and that order and reason (in the high significance which Coleridge gave the word), not disorder and nonsense, are the end and crown of all.

Maurois, the French critic, acutely remarks how Dickens made poetry out of comfort; a homely, a mere bodily thing that apparently has little to do with poetry. Yet, as Maurois sees, out of a dingy London street on a dark evening with a chill and a drizzle in the air, Dickens by cheerful suggestions of muffins well buttered, and cups of hot tea, and the fire stirred into a blaze of welcome for a tired mark's return, makes a something that is an enchantment and a delight; a small thing, if you will, but a wonderful thing; a little glass of vision.

It is strange but it is true that the materialists almost always despise material things, such as muffins for example. But we have done with the materialists. *Conclusum est contra manicheos.*

Can We Trust Tradition?

A little more than forty years ago, I was talking to a small farmer—a very small farmer—who held a few fields and fed a few cows on the top of the Chiltern Hills, near Watlington, in Oxfordshire. Old Mr. Harmon, as he said, was no scholar; that is, he could neither read nor write; and yet he was an interesting man to talk to. There was a keenness about his mind that he may have inherited from his father, a farm-labourer, noted in his day for his strength. "What is the heaviest burden you ever bore?" said a local squire to this elder Harmon. "Well, Muster Fane," the man answered, "the heaviest burden I ever bore was an empty belly."

I happened to mention Chalgrove Field to this man's son, the Harmon of my day.

"Ah," he said, reflectively, "Chalgrove Field: that's where Muster Hampden was killed. *They say it was down in oats at the time.*"

And yet Lord Raglan tells us in *The Hero** that tradition is utterly unreliable, entirely devoid of any historical value, that there is no such thing as folk-memory. I do not think that his proposition is justified by the facts.

My small-holder of the Chilterns is only one instance. Some time ago, a visitor who was being shewn over Tewkesbury Minster realised to his amazement that the verger in charge was giving him what was practically an eye-witness account of the Battle of Tewkesbury, abounding in that sort of minor detail which does not get into the history books; with a picture of the great church after the battle; the dead brought into it, and piled high, as high as the capitals of the pillars. The visitor felt that he was listening to something very different from the tale that the ordinary verger tells, and, making inquiries, he found out

---

**The Hero: A Study in Tradition, Myth, and Drama.* By Lord Raglan (Methuen, 10s. 6d.).

that the man was the last of a family of sacristans and vergers, who had held office in the Minster for 500 years.

Many other instances might be quoted. There was the mound in Scotland where, the folk said, a man in silver armour was buried. The educated laughed and didn't believe a word of it. But one fine day it was noticed that the place had been roughly disturbed. And in the broken and scattered earth the searchers found two or three *laminæ* of silver; all that remained of the armour of the raiding Dane who had lain there for a thousand years or so. And the village poacher or odd-job man—I forget which—had disappeared.

Again; they told in Ireland of a round hill beneath which the People, the fairies, lived, from the top of which flames had been seen to rise at night. The hill or hillock was excavated, and it was found that people—if not the People—had once lived there. The shaft that had carried off the smoke of their fires was discovered. The underground dwelling had been raided, probably by Norsemen, somewhere about A.D. 900. But the folk remembered the flickering of those flames at the top of the shaft; though they had not seen them for many hundreds of years.

There are still older memories. A few months ago I wrote in JOHN O' LONDON'S WEEKLY about the "Buried Church" in a Hampshire village. An old villager remembered a tale his father had told him about a Golden Calf that was somewhere down there. It was a Mithraic Cave; and I wonder when the Rite of Mithras was celebrated there for the last time. Towards the end of the fourth century, perhaps; not later. In my native town of Caerleon-on-Usk the children used to keep the New Year observation of the *Strenæ*—the gilded apple, decked with nuts and raisins, that prayed by its symbolism for a fruitful year. The Second Augustan Legion had gone; the Saxons, the Danes, the Normans, and the Great Western Railway had come; but the Caerleon boys and girls remembered the Roman Rite that they had learnt from the legionaries.

I think, then, that Lord Raglan must allow that there is such a thing as folk-memory. He tells, indeed, of African tribes who have no notion of their past history, who don't remember who ruled over them a hundred years ago, for whom 1870 is the dim and remote past. Yet these very tribes will have their folklore, their tribal laws and observances, their initiation rites. And all these things, in a people which has no written language, are evidence of a very long memory indeed.

The fair inference seems to be that the values of these black people differ widely from our own. Our children are taught in school about the height of Ben Nevis, the principal exports of Calcutta, and the dates of the ministries of Mr. Gladstone and Mr. Disraeli. The little blacks are not taught anything about the number of years since the chief Nbongo led them forth from Nbongaland; they are taught that they must not eat certain kinds of fruit in the presence of their great-aunt, and the reason why—which makes a very odd story.

All these various instances—and many others might be adduced—are urged in qualification of the main thesis of this most entertaining and arresting book. This thesis is: firstly, that no traditional narrative is founded upon fact; and secondly, that all traditional narratives are founded on initiation rites and ritual dramas. Whence it follows that the heroes of early epics and romances never existed at all. Most of them, if not all of them, were originally gods; and the stories that were sung and written about them derive from the rites and ceremonies in which these kingly and heroic and semi-divine personages were the chief figures.

To give examples: the usual view taken of the story of the Argonauts and the story of the Siege of Troy, as told in the *Iliad,* is that they are highly imaginative and decorated accounts of actual events; stories somewhat in the manner of the fashionable biographies of our own age in which the author takes the bare facts in the lives of Henry VIII and Admiral Byng and fills in the outlines, describes scenes which (he says) must have taken place, gives conversations which (he feels sure) must have followed some such course, and from a couple of words scribbled with a pencil deduces a personage, hitherto unheard of, whose existence explains the whole life of his hero.

Lord Raglan will have none of that. The story of the ship *Argo* is no highly ornamented version of an actual expedition: there never was an expedition. The *Iliad* is not the tale of an actual siege of Troy, poetised and mythologised. There never was a siege of Troy, and there never was a Greek overlord called Agamemnon. Agamemnon was Zeus, the principal God of the Greeks, and the story of the *Iliad* derives not from any actual warfare, but from the ancient ritual in which Agamemnon was the principal character. In the same way, we should be wrong in taking the *Morte d'Arthur* as a mediævalised and romanticised account of the struggle between the invaded Britons and the invading Saxons. There never was such a person as Arthur, and—

And here, as it appears to me, we uncover a weak place in Lord Raglan's argument. For that sentence above ought, by analogy, to have ended with: "—and there never was any struggle between the Britons and the Saxons, just as there never was a Siege of Troy or an early Greek expedition to Coichis."

Note the case as it stands. We are hardly in a position to say what did or did not take place in Greece in the twelfth century B.C.—though Dr. Schliemann, exploring in the 'seventies, certainly found the remains of a city that had been taken and burnt somewhere very close to the legendary site of tall Troy town. But the period is remote, and perhaps Dr. Schliemann's findings belonged not to Troy, but to another city of the same day.

But this won't do, if we apply it to our own history. We know quite well that various Teutonic tribes did invade this island of ours in the fourth, fifth, and sixth centuries of our era; and, therefore, as it seems, Lord Raglan's theory is shattered. The Romances of King Arthur and the Round Table are certainly founded on actual, historic facts; they do represent a tradition of events which most assuredly happened. And, therefore again, it is quite possible, nay, it is probable, that the *Iliad* has a core of truth in it, that it is a wild fiction based on fact. Of course, nobody supposes that the *Iliad* or the *Morte d'Arthur* gives a truthful or historically accurate account of the affairs which either professes to chronicle. Nobody has entertained such a belief for many hundreds of years. The Neoplatonists of Alexandria held the work of Homer to conceal profound spiritual doctrine beneath the literal text. A twelfth-century critic ironically congratulates the author of the latest Arthurian Romance on his inventive faculties; and the curious student of the *Matière de Bretagne* is able to point out the very varied sources from which these romance authors drew. As a matter of fact, they invented very little, but, like Mr. Pott's literary critic, they combined their information, and stole consumedly from any matter at their hands. But it is idle to deny that beneath their most extravagant fictions there was this solid foundation of hard fact: the Christian Britons fought the pagan invaders from the North Sea, and were, largely, overcome.

And as to the existence of King Arthur, which Lord Raglan emphatically denies: let us not be too sure of the truth of his negation. For, after pointing out that Arthur has been identified with the raven, the chough, and the bear, he lays down the proposition that "real men are not identified with ravens, or with bears"—that is, presumably, with birds or beasts of any kind.

As my Yorkshire friend used to say to almost every affirmative remark: "A don't know about that."

Wasn't Clemenceau a real man? He was called The Tiger. And Richard III was undoubtedly a real man, though by no means so crooked as the new people said. But how goes the old rhyme?

> The Rat, the Cat, and Lovel the Dog
> Rule all England under the Hog.

And, worst of all. We have all heard of the Swan of Avon. Are we to deny the very existence of Shakespeare because he is identified with a swan?

III. Literary Criticism: First Principles

Aristotle and Art

Last week we made brief mention of Professor Courthope's lecture on Aristotle's Poetics. But the subject of the lecture—the first principles of art—and the Professor's treatment of it invite fuller consideration, and we need make no excuse for examining a little more closely the propositions which the Professor of Poetry at Oxford so admirably expounded and developed. It must be admitted, in the first place, that we live in an age which is not so much intolerant as ignorant of theory in imaginative literature. Aristotle, who has much ado to hold his own in philosophy, has completely faded from the æsthetic sphere of perception and impression. Just as Lord Macaulay, profoundly reflecting that in the ages of philosophy men did not invent steam engines or cotton-mills, concluded that philosophy was useless, so literary critics, having heard of the Unities and having read *Cato,* pronounced Aristotle's æsthetic to be absurd. It must be placed to the credit of the critics in question that they contrived to give the master a double blow. They not only ridiculed his artistic taste, but they also demonstrated their contempt for his logic. "*Cato* is a bad play," they argued; "Addison believed in the doctrine of the Unities; therefore, the precepts of Aristotle made Addison write a bad play."

But it is surely time to clear our mind of this anti-Aristotelian cant. The plays of the pseudo-classical period are certainly dull. The reason, however, is not to be sought in the authors' observance of certain rules, but in the fact that they lived in a period to which the great tragedy was impossible. If Addison had given his days and nights to the study of Shakespeare instead of the Poetics, he would still have written a tiresome tragedy, and no romantic liberties would have set Irene free from her intolerable bondage. The eighteenth century failed to produce grand drama, not because it understood the Stagirite, but because it misunderstood life. Now it is time to restate the great principles which Aristotle enunciated, to apply as far as may be the theories of the Greek philosopher to modern English literature. It is hardly necessary, perhaps, to insist on the first theorem to which Professor Courthope called attention—that the object of art is imitation and not instruction. The illiterate may still maintain that books should be written to do good, to call attention to some injustice, to help the agitation for the abolition of this, the movement for the promotion of that, the campaign for the establishment of the other. But the instructed are fully aware that all such aims are accidental and not essential to literature, which appeals not to our ethical but to our æsthetic sense. As the lecturer very truly remarked, the Georgics of Virgil are not valued for their course of practical agriculture, but for the beauty of the style; and our admiration of Lucretius' poem is quite independent of our belief in his system. Beauty, then, and not truth is the object of all imaginative literature.

We might, perhaps, cavil at the phrase "imitation" if it were not for the second and more far-reaching proposition that art is concerned with the universal, not with the particular, for the artist must not endeavour to imitate nature, but rather to transfigure nature, to consecrate the symbols before him so that they become changed and transmuted into higher things. Literature reflects life, but it should reflect life as the glowing pool mirrors the trees, changing them, illuminating them. A book should be to nature as the dim, rich vision of a city seen in a river is to the actual town—the same, and yet a new creature, a new creation, mystic, wonderful. This, no doubt, is meant by that command to deal with universals, with types, that is, with ideas, with the form and soul and essence of things, and not with the material, outward, accidental appearances. We are to seek for the ἰδέαι, not for the φαινόμενα, by the method of Turner, not by the method of the camera. The artist in literature does not aim at producing a faithful study of a particular man whom he has known and observed, but he rather creates a new man, who stands for all humanity. No one remotely resembling Don Quixote ever stepped the earth, but Don Quixote lives in each of us, and, in a sense, is more real than any of us—is by far more real than the mere "imitations" of the so-called realists. Infinitely clever "realism" may be; Fielding, Thackeray, Jane Austen, George Eliot have, no doubt, achieved much by the method of observation, by a keen inspection of particulars, by the inductive art of the scientific student. But contrast Thackeray with Dickens; compare the "caricature" of Pecksniff with the portrait of Major Pendennis; set Morgan by the side of Sam Weller. In a sense, Thackeray's characters are the more real; we may see Major Pendennis any day if we care to walk on the "sweet shady side of Pall Mall"; we may engage Mr. Morgan in our service if we care to run the risk, and if we can afford to pay that excellent valet his "sellery". But if Pendennis and Morgan are mortals, then Pecksniff and Sam Weller are Immortals. The London of Thackeray stands to-day, perhaps for a long time, but the fields that Dickens loved and created are *glebæ felices æternum libris felicioribus conditæ.* The great Greek drama has survived because the dramatists forsook their age and their friends and the knowledge of the streets and went far back into the misty, legendary past, and saw there in the shadows the awful face and figure of humanity, and shapes greater, more terrible, more beautiful than the citizens of their dear native town. Homer was not content with the cities and the seas that he knew, and so Ulysses sails on the unknown ocean into mysterious harbours, to the caves where giants dwelt, to the Enchanted Island of Circe. Shakespeare did not take his pen to describe Elizabethan manners, but he sought out legends and fables, and old stories of the past, half-forgotten tales of kings and princes who had suffered more than mortal things.

And at no time were these principles and these examples more necessary than they are at the present day. For with us the accidental, the external, the particular pervade both imaginative literature and the criticism of it. A clever young man journeys to the fabled Provence, to the land of the first dawn of poetry and song in modern Europe, to the land that shines in the sunlight, that shines still with the vast white relics of the Roman world, and there, sitting in Villeneuve-lez-Avignon beside the olives and the pomegranates, gazing across the Rhone at the half-oriental magic of "Avignoun", he chatters with an old woman about her son in Tonquin and her cheap trip to Marseilles; and the chatter is headed Villeneuve-lez-Avignon! And the critic praises the "fidelity of the impression". To such petty passes have we come that triviality, snap-shot impressions, Chinese imitations are held as marks of genius, and the artist has succeeded if he have but minutely copied every rent and tear, every foul and greasy patch in the garment of the world. The binding of the volume, the formless quartz boulder, the fashion of a coat are his objects, but the book, and the gold, and the heart are concealed from him.

Let us return to Aristotle, to the first principles, to the great masters; let us forget our science, our microscopes, our weights and scales, our "education", which resembles a nest of Chinese boxes in its laborious and ingenious emptiness. The scientific, inductive, particular method has, with certain rare and eminent exceptions, debased our romance. Let us remember that story-writing is a fine art—perhaps the finest of all arts—not the mere knack of jotting down odd incidents and amusing chatter. Let us educate ourselves in the Aristotelian principles, so that the third axiom—that the object of great art is to please the public—may be true in London as it was in Athens. At present the vast circulation of a book is too often a proof of its utter worthlessness, of its appeal to all the tawdry and vulgar instincts of the modern reader; let us hope that the tide of folly may ebb at last, that the drowned palaces and lovely habitations may once more shine in the sun.

The "Inhumanity" of Art

The lecture with which that sternest of the old school of critics, M. Ferdinand Brunetière, recently disconcerted an audience convened by the Paris Société des Conférences, has since been republished by him as a pamphlet under the title of *L'Art et La Morale.* His views will, no doubt, be received by his readers with more composure than they were by his hearers, whose artless surprise at the lecturer's denunciation of what may be called the Antinomian philosophy of Art was quite refreshing in its way. It is so long since these sensations have lost their original stimulus for ourselves. They have, indeed, been so thoroughly blunted by the psychologists of the daily Press that a discourse on "the relations of art to morality" is one of the last things by which we in England should expect to be startled, and one of the first by which we should apprehend being bored. To M. Brunetiere's hearers, his assertions of the supremacy of morals and his unsparing rebuke of those who maintain that art is its own ethical law-giver, apparently combined the attraction of novelty with the charm of paradox. His contention that "in all forms of art there is a latent germ of immorality which is ever striving to develop" (and which, as we gather, it is the duty of the artist, as a good citizen, to sterilise) appears to be as new to Frenchmen as the first of his three supporting arguments is familiar to ourselves. For, as to M. Brunetière's "firstly"—that the end of art being the pleasure of the senses, it is necessarily directed to what either is, or is continually tending to become, an immoral purpose—was not this thesis expounded years ago with fascinating perversity by the late Mr. Stevenson? And did he not succeed in demonstrating to his own perfect satisfaction that there was no essential difference either in spirit or vocation between the novelist and the *fille de joie?*

These heart-searchings of the philosopher and the philosophising artist are far too familiar to have any freshness of interest at this time of day for Englishmen; so that neither M. Brunetière's "firstly" nor his "secondly" (which is like unto it) need detain us longer. But his "thirdly" is in a different case. His "thirdly" is an argument not nearly so often adduced in this country to prove the essential immorality of art; being, indeed, put forward much more frequently to demonstrate its preciousness as a possession of mankind. The French critic's third reason for pronouncing art immoral is founded on its "isolating" tendency. In proportion to the refinement of his æsthetic sense the artist necessarily becomes segregated from the rest of mankind. Their inability to share his subtle sensations, to comprehend his complex emotions, to discern those elements of beauty in the world of thought and things to which his own perceptions are so keenly alive, produces a constantly increasing effect of estrangement and alienation. In the end the breach between the artist and his fellow-men becomes complete; he gets into the habit of speaking of them as "the crowd", "the herd", and declares, as Flaubert does in his correspondence with George Sand, that they will "always be hateful". And with a gift, an occupation, even an instinct which can induce a comparatively small class of men to speak in so unbrotherly a way of a large body of citizens who are many of them excellent husbands and fathers, pious and benevolent, upright and conscientious, respectable and respected in every relation of life, is on the face of it a thing to be reprobated and reprehended by civilised humanity. It is anti-social, inhuman—in a word, immoral.

These, no doubt, are seriously disquieting thoughts. The democrat in all countries feels the burden of them; but among us at any rate, and we presume in the other English-speaking democracies, they do not beget quite so despairing a conclusion as that to which they seem to have led M. Brunetière. Our own democrats, for instance, decline to accept his minor premiss. While admitting that all things which have an anti-social tendency are immoral, they deny that art is to be included under that category. The artist, they contend, is only temporarily estranged from his fellow-men. In the course of time the advance of "culture" will heal the breach; and the "herd" will cease to be "hateful" to him by becoming a community of art lovers like himself. The expectation may be illusory—in our opinion it is wholly so—but at any rate it saves the logical situation. The democrat of artistic tastes who entertains it is no longer tied down to the conclusion that those tastes have in themselves an anti-social, and therefore immoral, tendency, and thus he escapes the extremely awkward practical consequences which follow from that conclusion, and with which the French critic does not appear to have grappled. From M. Brunetière will find his "thirdly" a desperately disagreeable argument to live with. With his "firstly" and "secondly" it is otherwise. Effect might be given to them without positively fatal results to art. The immoral tendency which is inherent in it either as ministering to sensuous pleasure or as imitating a Nature which is itself too frequently immoral is to a great extent an affair of "subject", and may be corrected by a judicious choice of material. But the deeper, the more vital immorality of spirit—the immorality which belongs to art as art, and which inhumanly estranges the artist from the mass of mankind—is a much more difficult matter to deal with. One does not readily see how art is to be freed from this more essential taint. What would M. Brunetière himself advise "in the premisses"? That the artist should, out of sheer "enthusiasm of humanity", follow the example of the American humourist of whom it was recorded that out of regard for his fellow creatures, "now he never writes, As funny as he can"? Should the artist, in other words, make it his endeavour not to work "as artistic as he can", and so get nearer to the common heart of humanity, after the manner of the famous Parliamentary advocate who used to drink a pot of porter at lunch in order to "bring his intelligence down to the level of the Committee's"? No doubt it is possible for the literary artist to avoid this painful rupture with the rest of his species, and to write in such a way as to win the sympathy of hundreds of thousands of readers, and to insure the periodical sale of many scores of editions. But it is to be observed that in these cases there is no conscious or deliberate debasement of artistic standards. The "art" which these artists offer to their public is simply the best art they know, or, at any rate, can command.

It would appear, therefore, that if the possession of an artistic gift has the "anti-social" effect attributed to it—if art has this essentially "inhuman" tendency—there is nothing for it but submission. Still, it seems necessary to remind M. Brunetière that the possession of *any* gift in which the majority of mankind do not participate tends to the same result. We fancy we have heard of the vanity of personal appearance and physical strength, the arrogance of learning, the pride of science, the mock-humility of self-righteousness, the conceit of connoisseurship in a host of matters which are not even distantly connected with art. The man with a fine discrimination in wine is not unconscious of his superiority. We may be pretty certain that Juvenal's epicure, who could distinguish *primo morsu* between Lucrine and Rutupine oysters, was in the same case. It is possible that the general body of worthy London citizens figure as the "crowd" or the "herd", and as such appear contemptible, if not "hateful", to an accomplished tea-taster in Mincing-lane. The attitude of all these people is more or less anti-social, but we do not on that account exclaim against the essentially inhuman character of the gift or the acquirement which fills its possessor with this sense of superiority to his fellows. The fact is, of course, that the feeling which it is apt to excite is inherent in human nature, and instead of protesting against its particular excitant for the time being—whether art or anything else—it would be much more reasonable, though perhaps not much more profitable, to lament the existence of original sin.

The whole discussion curiously illustrates the prevalence of that malady of self-analysis which is so specially characteristic of the age. It is a malady which, as is the case with maladies of the physical order, is aggravated by dwelling upon it. The artist who, instead of simply following his artistic bent, sits down to consider solemnly whether it is not inhumanly alienating him from his fellow-men is, in reality, ministering subtly to that egotism which he professes to dread. He is going the way to make himself not less, but more, conscious of his superiority to the rest of the world. If he is really haunted by apprehensions of the danger of which he discourses, there are at least two topics of reassurance which he might with advantage accustom himself to consider. In the first place, he might reflect that, if the consciousness of artistic endowment has an anti-social influence, the practice of art, at least in many of its literary forms, has, or should have, a broadening effect on the sympathies; at any rate, the creator of Falstaff and Shylock, of Hamlet and Juliet's Nurse, does not seem conspicuously out of sympathetic contact with his fellow-humans. In the next place, we would remind him that it takes two to make an estrangement, that "the crowd", "the herd", whom he hates, are much too well satisfied with themselves to reciprocate that feeling, and that, so far from smarting under a sense of their own inferiority to the artist, they are, many of them—

in fact, every "practical" man among them—complacently convinced that the inferiority is all on the other side. They themselves feel immensely superior to men who, like some, though assuredly not all, artists, are wanting in "business instinct"; but even here the feeling towards the inferior is not that of inhuman hate, but rather that of good-natured tolerance. If the artist, haunted by a sense of his "isolation", and brooding generally, as M. Brunetière seems to think he should, over his parlous state, has not sufficient sense of humour to feel himself reconciled to the crowd by the very fact that he and they are mutually looking down upon each other—if, after all, he still remains oppressed with the burden of his superiority, we are left without any counsel, save such as may sound a little frivolous, to offer him. We can only advise him to act in the spirit of the injunction laid upon the youthful daughters of the house of Kenwigs, who were instructed to tell their schoolfellows that, though they enjoyed certain domestic educational advantages over other children, they were "not proud, because Ma says it's sinful".

The Paradox of Literature

It seems sad, but I fear there can be no doubt but that Carlyle, whom our fathers regarded as an inspired seer, was, if a prophet, then a prophet of Baal. For many years we have been waiting for that once tremendous reputation to recover the ground it had lost, to emerge, shining again, from the dark cloud of all those squalid, unnecessary revelations, from the effects of a biography written by a friend of "ter-ewth". One thought that those histories of indigestion, heavy bread, and cross Mrs. Carlyle would fade away like the nightmares they were, and that the great figure of the fifties would enter finally on the literary life that is perdurable and immortal. But, alas! people have not only forgotten how Carlyle was dyspeptic and how his wife shewed temper; they have forgotten all else as well, so that of the primeval seer nothing remains except perhaps a dark and threatening shadow—a fetish to which men no longer give sacrifice. It is sad, and yet no lover of literature can say that the fate is wholly undeserved. The man who said that Keats possessed nothing but a "maudlin, weak-eyed sensibility", the critic who admired the whisky-and-sentiment vein of Burns, who went through the Waverley Novels and found all (nearly) barren, because there was nothing "profitable for doctrine, for reproof, for edification", is surely condemned out of his own mouth. But Carlyle was not content with these minor aberrations; he enunciated the major heresy that genius consists of an infinite capacity for taking pains—perhaps one of the untruest things that have ever been said.

For this, it seems to me, is the paradox of literature—of all art, it may be said, but of literature in a more singular degree—that neither genius nor the result of genius has any relation to effort, to the process of taking pains. Some months ago I endeavoured to shew in these pages that the finest charms of the finest books were unconsciously created, and from the theorem thus stated one may deduce the corollary—

that conscious effort, taking pains, in fact, never results in the finest work. I am using the superlative deliberately, not for merely rhetorical purposes. *Marius the Epicurean, The New Arabian Nights,* most of Stevenson's books, indeed, may fairly be classed under the heading of fine literature; but one is confident that neither Pater nor Stevenson will ever be accounted by competent critics as makers of the finest literature. Both these men may stand as examples of the summit to which conscious purpose and effort in literature may attain; their achievement is high and fine, but not of the highest nor the finest. We have heard of Pater's long-enduring patient labours, of the fevers and the chills which he suffered in the writing of his masterpiece, of the elaborate system of notes and memoranda, of the manuscript copied and recopied, interlined and altered year after year. Stevenson told us frankly how from his youth upward he toiled in his vocation; how he sought by all means to learn to write, setting himself in the class of the masters. And yet, with all this infinite taking of pains, neither the one nor the other accomplished anything beyond the second-rate. We know how a certain player, with a smattering of general information and more general literature, took the old creaking dramas, the chronicles, and the story-books in hand, and hacked and slashed and scribbled away for a livelihood, relishing the work heartily, no doubt, but wholly unaware of the dignity of his task. But Shakespeare's taskwork turned out to be the finest literature in the world. Sir Walter Scott, again, wrote his romances partly, it would seem, for the fun of it, partly that he might build a dubious Gothic palace and buy moors and woods. He wrote faster, and still faster, and the less the pains the better the result. The "bow-wow style" was his phrase for his work, which will live while any romance is left in the world. Then there was an Anabaptist tinker—a fanatical, illiterate, and probably most unpleasant person—who tried to write a tract, and succeeded in inventing one of the best *picaros* in literature. It is said that Defoe had the infinitely tedious design of making an allegory about somebody's state of mind—I forget whether it was Defoe himself or a friend of his, who refused to speak to his family for twenty-eight years—but the symbol of *Robinson Crusoe* has happily entirely overshadowed the thing signified.

This, then, is the paradox of literature, that its highest rewards are not bestowed on earnest effort and patient endeavour, but on the elect alone, on those who have "taken the trouble" to be born geniuses. In letters patience and perseverance count, it seems, either for nothing or for very little, or, strangely enough, guide the writer by paths which he had never dreamed of, which he may probably have abhorred, to a goal entirely beyond his conception or desire. Christian in the *Pilgrim's Progress* is a rare *picaro,* as I have said, but how shocked Anabaptist Bunyan would have been if he could have understood the manner of his success. And the principle, which undoubtedly applies to the highest achievements, is not without its application in the lower walks, in the region of the literature of endeavour and studied calculation. For it seems to me that one of the greatest mistakes that a writer can commit is to "read up" a subject with a view to writing about it, to "cram" history for the especial purpose of writing a historical novel, to deliberately make a journey in pursuit of "local colour". This is the dreadful method of writing dull books, the infallible mark which points out the hopeless author. They tell us of persons who spend a fortnight at Paris, and at the end of their visit understand the whole life and humour of the Quartier Latin, and by their works we know them! Burne-Jones, we have heard, drew the inspiration of his pictures from half-forgotten poems, and so must the material of imaginative literature be unconsciously gathered, given to forgetfulness, it may be, for many years, and at last drawn out into the light, having lost and gained somewhat in the darkness. Many of our modern writers, those chiefly of the advertising kind, whom frequent paragraphs proclaim as "studying the cuneiform with a view to writing a romance of early Assyria" or "spending the winter in Barataria in order to investigate the reign of Sancho Panza in the state papers of the period with a view, &c., &c.", are like vintners who bring us their crude new wine, rough from the vat; it is but rarely that we taste the authentic juice, refined and purged by a long sojourn in forgotten darkness.

There can be no question as to the truth of all this; the propositions that the highest art is unconscious, that taking pains does not make for supreme excellence, that even the materials for imagination to work on should be gathered unawares, sublimed secretly, as it were, from the gross substance of life and the world—these are axioms that may be proved by the plainest and most illustrious examples. But the "reason why" might present more difficulty to the inquirer, who acknowledging the fact might very conceivably be puzzled as to the cause. To me it seems that these "irrational" phenomena are to be explained by the very nature and origin of literature, which, in common with all the arts, is so profoundly irrational. Of course, "science", with calm and dignified ineptitude, has "explained" the origin of literature as of everything else; men, it informs us, were tired after their day's work, and felt the need of play; and "plays" were accordingly invented. The explanation is "scientific" certainly, but on the principle of *entia non sunt multiplicanda preeter necessitatem,* it seems a pity that our old friends the early dream and the indefatigable ancestral ghost were not made to account for art as for religion. The truth of the matter is, of course, far otherwise, and though we shall probably never clearly understand the origin of literature, it seems evident that it with all the arts arose from that primordial and universal sense of mystery, from the original ecstasy which separates the man from the brute. Mysterious in its origin it has remained a mystery all through the ages; we can only admire and adore its beauty, and wonder at its work, forced to believe in a miracle which we cannot understand, for which that all-pervading, all-pretending science can furnish no formula. Literature is the key to life, the reflection in a shining and glorious mirror of our imperfect and cloudy actions. And if Carlyle is fast gliding down into the vale of the forgotten it is because, with all his wisdom, he did not perceive the essential things of life, and he was ignorant of life because he was ignorant of literature. Literature is, indeed, a paradox, but it is a paradox that must be most steadfastly believed.

Realism and Symbol

I tried to point out in last week's *Academy* that art is not a trick, not in any way analogous to the performances of the celebrated pony who took port wine with the clown, not in any way related to the shows of dancing dogs or learned elephants. It is not in the nature of horses to drink with clowns, nor have dogs danced *ab initio;* the elephant of the wilds does not ring a bell for his dinner; all these "arts" are things superimposed, they are fantastic upper stories which are no part of the original design of the building. Here is to be sought the fundamental distinction between these tricks and human Art with the capital A. I do not know whether the opposite view—the opinion which holds that art is "artificial", the result of civilisation and gentle manners—has ever been formally proclaimed; but I should imagine that some such opinion might very possibly be found in the works of Herbert Spencer. That deceased "philosopher" would probably maintain that art grew out of some or all of man's physical necessities, and that the primitive man was originally no more an artist than is a hippopotamus. It is not necessary to argue this position, since, as I have demonstrated, it is entirely false. It is from the earliest men, from the dimmest and most remote ages, that the artistic impulse, the whole matter of the arts, has descended to us; and all true art of today is written or painted or carved or sung in the oldest of all tongues, in a language that is ancient, and secret, and universal. Art is the expression of the human soul, of the eternal things in man; and to man it is as profoundly natural as is the song to the bird.

Last week I shewed that art was the true expression of humanity, the grand *differentia* between men and the other animals; but there is another aspect of the matter. From the one proposition follows the other—if art be a mystery-language of the human soul it must have an interpretation. Never a perfect one, since the higher cannot be adequately translated in terms of the lower, and, personally, I always feel the impertinence of the attempt to interpret great music by a flourish of words and phrases. Still, all great art has "a meaning", in other words, it is symbolic. There is all the difference in the world between a landscape by Turner and the best photograph of the same scene. Setting aside the fact that Turner deliberately altered the scenes that he painted, that he treated mountains and lakes, trees, and cathedrals very much as a good stage-manager treats a stage-crowd; setting this quite on one side, one sees that the painting has received that consecration which Wordsworth speaks of: the natural has been assumed into the supernatural; the hills and streams have been exalted in glory, and the fallen world has risen from the dead. In the order of nature there were masses of earth and water and the growth of trees; on the canvas these things have become a sacrament and a symbol.

Hence it follows that all great art is profoundly "realist". It is time that this word with its ancient and honourable philosophical associations should be definitely rescued from the intolerable degradation into which it has fallen. Intolerable, and nonsensical too; for, as a matter of fact, a great part of the literature which has been called realistic is profoundly unreal. *The Mummer's Wife,* for example, which is a painstaking and clever transcript of low theatrical life, is as unreal as any photograph; it has no relation of any sort or kind whatsoever to the eternities and realities. If man were a surface it would be real, but man being a cubical figure it is most unreal. It is, indeed, difficult to say from what complicated attack of folly this perversion of a fine word arose; the notion that a certain skill in the minute delineation of "unpleasant" characters and incidents makes a writer a "realist" certainly seems to belong more to Bedlam and Colney Hatch than to the world that is free of those high walls. Let it be added speedily, in case of misapprehension, that to the artist neither the pleasant nor the unpleasant, the moral nor the immoral, the sordid nor the clean, profit anything in themselves. When there is a true symbol truly displayed there is art. The symbol may be in terms of the darkest pits of human misery and squalor and wickedness, or it may be in terms of the Holy Places. There are seekers for precious stones, not after the flesh nor after the manner of South Africa, who discover jewels in the cesspools and the gutters, for whom there are right Orient pearls "exceeding rich and rare", shining in the foulest middens of humanity. And, on the other hand, there is a far greater multitude who stand in the very sanctuary at the hour of the sacring of the Mass and have the power to retransmute the Blessed Gifts into ginger-beer and mixed biscuits. These are the people who write what are called "good" books—that is, in plain English, books which, by bringing religion into contempt, odium, and ridicule, are more harmful than a wilderness of pornographic libraries. Perhaps I had better explain, by the way, that my phrase about those who find jewels in the gutter is not intended to be an echo of the Banished Duke's most amiable remarks as to finding sermons in stones and good in everything; I do not mean that the moral virtues often exist amidst very deplorable surroundings. I mean that *Wuthering Heights* is a work of supreme genius—a somewhat different matter.

True art, then, is symbolical and realist; and as an example in literature, we may take the *Arabian Nights* as a splendid and typical piece of realism. Not, be it understood, because the account of the manners and customs of the court of Haroun Alraschild is historically correct. I neither know nor care whether this be the case, and in the art of literature, correct information about Haroun's court does not count. It is, indeed, highly probable that many of the incidents in the story of Aladdin never happened, and I understand that modern science is sceptical on the question of the genie. But realism, in its true and philosophical and artistic sense, has nothing whatever to do with correct information; neither a manual of chemistry nor the racing news is entitled to be called realistic literature. No; the *Arabian Nights* is a realistic book because it utters, by means of certain symbols, a profound experience of all humanity.

Perhaps not the dullest dog of us all has been wholly without this experience. One may pass many examinations and yet not miss it, one may yield years to "advanced" thought and yet have one's share in it. I would not utterly deny its occasional presence in the very sanctuaries of Protestant Dissent. Perhaps one exception to this rule may be made; perhaps the one person to whom the tale of Aladdin means nothing is the modern millionaire, who, oddly enough, is the one person who might realise in dull fact a great part of Aladdin's splendours. It is really curious to consider that the egregious Carnegie might have built himself a very splendid palace; "instead of which" he has chosen to devote himself to the erection of free libraries. Perhaps it is better so; there are hands in which gold, and marble, and precious stones, and all the loveliness of the world become changed to something much more offensive than withered leaves. But, setting this interesting and important speculation on one side, I repeat that there comes to most of us, at one time or another, an experience which is only translatable in terms of the *Arabian Nights.* We are walking in the common, grimy street, weighed down with cares or pleasures, or pain or worries, our minds filled with all manner of unimportant, unreal stuff; and suddenly we see the door in the wall, that door that we have never noticed before; and we enter in by it and the Princess awaits us, and we are made free of palaces of gold and crystal, and the slaves with their trays of rubies and emeralds and pearls are our slaves; ours are the magic carpet and the golden water and the enchanted lamp; the fairies are our ministrants, and we see all things in a magic glass of divination. The world, in a word, is transformed; it has put on the glowing and glistening robe of enchantment, every way is a way of wonder, and as one looks on common things and the usual and accustomed passages of life they seem to tremble and waver as if they were a curtain on the point to part asunder and disclose tremendous and most beautiful mysteries. And those who know these times of a strange and mystic exaltation know also how impotent is the logical speech to tell the story of them, how they can scarcely be imagined even in coherent thought; there is nothing for it but to fall back on the *Arabian Nights,* on a world of jewels and lovely ones, and fine gold and brides from fairyland, on a world where magic and enchantment and rapture are latent in every stone, in every blade of grass. And there is a far higher region than this Arabian Paradise. The Catholic alone knows how the denial of the doctrine of Transubstantiation has robbed the world of the fulness of joy, but the initiated Catholic knows also that the final secrets of this matter are to be sought not so much in the formal and logical definition of the Church as in the Romances of the Sangraal. The mystery of the Eucharist is a tremendous and unearthly mystery; no words of the understanding can compass it, but it is (almost) unveiled when the deadly flesh of Galahad began to tremble, being brought near to the Spiritual Things. And this is realism.

Then there is quite another sort of literature that may rightly be called realistic. That is the literature of wandering, named picaresque, the literature that symbolises a sense that we all have at times, the sense that we are bound on a journey of strange adventures, that marvels lie beyond the bend of the road, that we have but to go on and on and wonders will be manifested to us. The wanderings of Ulysses charm by this symbol, and oddly enough the true interest of the *Pilgrim's Progress* is due to a like enchantment. In literature allegory is, on the whole, a vice, as Poe pointed out; this is the weakness of *Jekyll and Hyde.* So far then as the *Pilgrim's Progress* is allegorical it is bad, and yet it is a classic, because in practice we are able to forget the elaborate and minute allegory and to accept Christian as a simple *picaro,* a wanderer by ways strange and unknown. Allied to him are the very different Mr. Pickwick and Don Quixote, and the graceless Roderick Random and Peregrine Pickle have in a lower degree their part in the symbol of the white road climbing the far hill and descending into conjectured country. In *Pickwick,* too, there are the far-descended traces of another symbol, the great Sign of the Vine which is displayed with such splendour of emblazonment in *Gargantua* and *Pantagruel,* the hieroglyph of the ecstasy and joy of life—this also being a portion of the lost Paradise. It is not to be wondered at that ignorant and besotted ecclesiastics have solemnly cursed *Pickwick* as an attack on the great temperance movement. I noted a week ago the curious fact that man alone of all creatures has the power of dispossessing himself of his high privileges. He is the nightingale that, if he will, may bray like an ass.

Literature, then, is (as are all the arts) a book *intus et foris scriptus.* The surface is plain for all to see—comical, or tragical, or tragical-comical. Within are to be found the great secrets of the nature of man, the symbols of our true and essential being; and so all fine literature is profoundly and truly realistic.

Science and Art

The other day I met a fellow-journalist who told me a strange experience that had happened to him. He said: "I am like Tennyson's dog, I often 'hunt in dreams', and spend my night in executing strange variations and fantasies and descants upon the plainsong melody of my daily work. Well, the other night I dreamed that Jones, the news editor, came to me and said: 'Look here, Blank; you know Llandegveth; you get off there as quick as you can; you ought to bring back a first-rate story.' And while I was gathering my notebook and pencils, my hat and coat, and reflecting that most, if not all, of my old friends at Llandegveth were dead; I woke up.

"But the tune that this odd dream had started ran in my head for many days, and still echoes in the inner ear. Llandegveth! I had not seen it for a score of years, I doubt whether I had thought of it, distinctly and specifically, as separate and apart from other remembered places and loved memories, for the last ten years; and thus strangely and whimsically it was summoned back by a crazy dream into the audience-chamber of the consciousness; summoned from that wild outer waste of the soul, from that dim under-world where the dead thoughts still live, awaiting the voice that shall renew their life and quicken them once more.

"No; I had not thought of Llandegveth for years, but now my steps revisit its hidden ways. I am again in the valley of the Soar, that swift shining brook with its everlasting song as it slides and ripples over the big stones, shaded by the grave procession of the alders. I can see the little village in that enclosed valley, the whitewashed cottages in their gardens following the course of the stream, the broad, rich meadows on the western side, the wall of the hillside, and far away the huger height of the rounded mountain. I see where the Soar floats in a shallow flood across the road, and above, the little church on the height. In the churchyard, under the dark yews, and within the church, are the graves and monuments of the villagers and the farmers and the old, vanished gentry of the place. Flourished memorials, beginning 'Here under lyeth', brave coats of arms of Meyrick and Ambrose and Perrott—I can see again the three golden pears for coat and parrot for crest of the last house—whitewashed walls, deal pews, square sixteenth-century east window; they all stand anew in clear, restored light, and through the window the yew-boughs are tossing on a windy Sunday morning in March—in a March of forty years ago. And perhaps I alone of all those who assembled on that March morning and began to sing 'New every morning is the love' am still in the region of the living.

"I pass down the road, the carpenter's shop on my right, lower, the blacksmith's forge on my left—alas! old Watkins and old Cradock are long dead—and go by Waun-y-pwll, where the Ambroses lived; by Lanusoar, the home of the Meyricks—a Meyrick of the thirteenth century gave a piece of land that a candle should burn for ever before the altar of the neighbouring church of Llanddewi—and I get lost in these old memories, and I get lost trying to find my way in fancy by meadow-paths, by winding, narrow lanes. Time flies back; to my nostrils comes the scent of the larchwood on a June evening; it was there that the feathery 'mares'-tails' grew in masses of vivid green. I see again the marvel and the glory of a white winter land, a glimmering, violet sky, the sun a disc of dull red fire on the mountain-top, and a grove of black pines high upon the hill. Again, it is a still evening in October; the bracken is brown on the hillside, and withered leaves are shivering in the hedge; there is a grey-clouded sky, and all seems still in a secret and hidden valley, save for the faint tinkle and ripple of a tiny brooklet."

Such was the "story" that the journalist had brought back from his spiritual visit to Llandegveth, and it reminded me of some literary talk which I have been hearing lately. Wherever I go I make a point of expressing my intense admiration for Mr. Masefield's wonderful poem, *The Everlasting Mercy,* which in my opinion is one of the greatest pieces of pure and exalted literature that has been seen in England for some years. And when I utter this opinion in literary circles I hear something like this:—

"But what have you to say for the psychology of it?"

"Yes; how about the psychology? How much of that poem is village wastrel, and how much pure Masefield?"

"And that woman who bursts out at him just before he is converted; do you mean to tell me that any woman would ever give herself away like that? It's absurd."

"Look here. This man had been a drunkard, and his constitution must have been perfectly rotten. Are we to believe that after a hard fight—and it was a bad fight, mind you—with a heavy drinking-bout to follow, he could have gone up and down that village in the way he is supposed to have done?"

"He puts the scene in the 'sixties; and he mentions margarine!"

"How do you justify that ecstatic peace at the end of the poem? Of course, one recognises the mood—it is that of Traherne; but would it occur so early after conversion?"

And, oddly enough, it seems to me that the most reasonable of all these irritational observations is the caveat as to margarine. Here we have an undoubted anachronism. It is certain, I suppose, that this golden substitute for butter was not known in the 'sixties; and though Shakespeare from end to end is full of the wildest anachronisms which—to quote the first Duke of Wellington—do not matter a "twopenny damn", still there was no margarine known in the days when the Gloucestershire wastrel of the poem witnessed and experienced the Great Transmutation in himself and in the world, and I see no reason why the author should not mend this error in his next edition—provided always that he has nothing better to do.

As for the purely "psychological" objections; I am afraid that I think them all pure, rampant, undistinguished folly. They are as wide of the mark as if I had said to my friend the journalist:—

"Look here, this dream of yours is all nonsense. Your paper only goes in for London 'stories'; is it likely that the news editor would send you to a little place 150 miles from town, where nothing ever has happened or ever will happen? The whole thing is based on an absurd misconception of modern journalism."

Exactly; but to the dreamer the point was that pleasant and goodly recollections were revived for him, that he received anew the vision of his childhood, and heard again with the ear of the spirit the murmur and melody of the rippling brook. To him of what account was it if his dream misrepresented the psychology of Jones, the news editor?

The fact is that when we are considering fine literature—that marvellous spagyric art which renews the vision of our eternal youth in the lost garden—all this chatter about psychology is the sheerest balderdash and impertinence. It is well enough, if the pursuit happens to amuse one, to pause in reading *Vanity Fair* to consider whether Becky would really have thrown the "Dixonary" out of the carriage window on leaving Miss Pinkerton's academy. It might plausibly be suggested that so sharp a young woman, fully aware of her precarious and difficult hold on the world, would have realised the imprudence of making a bitter enemy. And about the end of Josh; would Becky have cut off her source of income? People who like this sort of game can play this sort of game with the secondary literature of the logical understanding, and not much harm is done; it is almost as amusing and instructive as Patience. But when this solemn trifling is applied to the primary literature of the creative imagination, it becomes exasperating to the highest degree; it is a mere repetition of the silly remark that was once made to Turner: "I never saw a sunset like that." It is as if one were to "criticise" Keats by saying, "Well, it seems to me a psychological absurdity to suppose that a half-educated Cockney lad, the son of a livery-stable keeper, and companion of Bob Sawyer and Ben Allen, should write such a poem as the 'Ode on a Grecian Urn'!" It is highly improbable; but the universe—and the arts—are a tissue of improbabilities. To paraphrase Tertullian, *credo quia impossibile;* all true life, all art at its highest is a series of monstrous improbabilities and absurdities. If this were not so, then were our life as the life of the beasts, and our art would have no existence at all. When that furnace of the sages, governed with wisdom, glows white; when the rude dross and the gross matters have been purged away in the burning of that fire, and the pure gold shines recreated and immortal; then the world of life and of art becomes the world of miracles. Then the deaf hear and the blind receive their sight; then the wilderness blossoms like the rose, and in the stony places are found the waterpools. In this hour, then, literature is lifted up from all low conditions, from questions of probable and improbable, and all such unprofitable impertinences. Alas! let us not be found reading "Kubla Khan" and inquiring as to the precise age of the damsel on

Mount Abora, and as to where she could have learned to play the dulcimer, and how much her dulcimer-master charged per lesson, and why she played the instrument on a mountain, and whether her mother knew that she was out. For if we do these things we shall discover at last that the phrase "unheard melodies" is a contradiction in terms, and that the faery seas forlorn are not charted at the Admiralty or so much as mentioned in any geographical work sanctioned for use in elementary schools by the Board of Education; which state of mind is probably alluded to in the Scriptural expression, "The second death."

Indeed all the subject-matter in fine literature with which these poor psychologists are engaged is in reality but the footnote to the poem or the romance, not the poem or the romance itself. It explains how the lyric—the incantation—came to be uttered; it is strictly parallel to Coleridge's note to "Kubla Khan". Had he taken opium on that day long ago in Somerset? Did he awake with a long poem of hundreds of lines present to his mind? Was he interrupted by a gentleman from Porlock on business? I don't know; these statements may be true or they may not be true; and in any case—pleading once more the example of a high heroic shade—it doesn't matter a twopenny damn! There are people who would turn away more in sorrow than in anger from the man who had rescued them from the vision of death in the water, and had restored them to the vision of life on dry land, because his clothes were ready-made and his accent provincial: let me not be found amongst these; let me not be found with the utterers of inconsequence and impertinence.

For their place is in Mr. Squeers' First Class in English Spelling and Philosophy, where they will learn that a horse is a quadruped, and quadruped's Latin for beast; or rather in that far worse hell where Blitzer defined a horse as "Quadruped. Graminivorous. Forty teeth—namely, twenty-four grinders, four eye-teeth, and twelve incisive." A man once told me that the English Army was rationed on strictly scientific principles. "Is that so?" I replied. "Then God help them!"

A Vision

It is an odd thing, but if you want to tell the truth, you must write literature. If you want indeed to tell the highest and the final truth you must go farther; you must not only write literature but poetry. For in the last resort the truth is music—or beauty, as Keats put it—and the difference between prose and poetry is the measured music of poetry.

It is necessary, to be sure, to distinguish between the truth and that which is true. I believe there are—or there used to be—certain arithmetical terrors called "Long tots", addition sums six inches tall or thereabouts. Well, if you added up correctly any two of the lines of figures and gave the result, it would be true.

But it is only when you have added every line and every row of figures and set down your total that you get "the truth" of your sum. This, and this only, is the final result to which those serried lines and columns move; this, and this alone, is the truth of the whole matter. Add, if you like, any one figure to any other figure, any one line to any other line. If you do your addition correctly you will obtain a piece of accurate information. But you won't get the truth.

This doctrine has been otherwise expressed, I think, in the saying that in literature you must contemplate men—and all else—*sub specie aeternitatis,* under the form of eternity. You have, that is, to do a very big, long tot indeed. You have your rows and lines of figures, not orderly disposed as in the horrid examination paper, but scattered and peppered about time and space. Well; you have to make a sum of them, to add them up, as it were, with reference to their final end and significance.

To some of these sums the answer is "Heaven," as in Dante's *Divine Comedy*. To others as, for instance, *Wuthering Heights,* "Hell" is clearly the last line to be written. But in the one case as in the other, all is done with a certain end, a certain final significance in sight. Sometimes you have a writer of immense abilities, of all manner of gifts and graces, declaring that there isn't any sum at all, that the figures don't add up with any intelligible result, that there is no final meaning or significance to men or things. Then you get a book like *Vanity Fair,* which, in a sense, is, indeed a great book. But I don't believe that it is literature, in the real meaning of the term. It does not tell the truth.

Now the truth is beauty—or music—and, as Bacon observed, a certain strangeness of proportion is even essential to beauty. It is through that strangeness that we often attain to the truth which we are seeking in life and in art. If a book, or a building, or a set of verses seems eminently reasonable and sensible and quite what one would have expected in the circumstances; then, I am afraid, that it has very little interest for me. Who ever "expected" Dugald Dalgetty, or Quilp, or Mr. Micawber, till these admirable creations were strangely and wonderfully revealed to the world?

I have just been reading a concrete instance of these abstract reflections. The instance is a slight sketch—it does not cover seven pages—in an extremely agreeable volume of literary essays called *On Falling in Love and Other Matters,* which has just been published by Messrs. Simpkin, Marshall.

Now "At the Shrine of the White Wall" is, on the face of it, an account of an insignificant incident in a walking tour through Normandy. The writer and his friend take refuge from the heat on a patch of turf that lay under the shadow of a long white wall. The writer notices that there are black marks on the whiteness of the wall; seen at a little distance the black marks resolve themselves into a drawing of a bust of Napoleon. The friend, an artist, makes a sketch of the drawing. Then the sound of an iron gate is heard. A beautiful girl, dressed in white, passes through the gate, smiles wistfully, and disappears beyond the wall.

Then the narrator is attacked by violent symptoms of sunstroke. He is taken back to Rouen, and a few days later he sees the white lady who had gone through the gate at the hotel table. The artist passes to her the sketch he had made of the Napoleon bust: "when she saw the picture she smiled wistfully, just as she had done at the white gate, and passed it back to me without a word."

Here, on the face of it, baldly told as I have told it, is a mere jumble of insignificant and unrelated incidents, odd-shaped, or, rather, shapeless pieces of a jig-saw puzzle, without any discernible points of adjustment in any known pattern or design. Yet, by the art of the writer, one is made to feel that he saw a portion of a strange mystery, that everything which he saw was of a quite wonderful significance.

The people at the farm knew nothing about the picture on the white wall: "it must have been done before they settled there," they told my friend. Some years ago two ladies wrote an account, apparently a veridical account, of how they were sightseeing in the gardens of Versailles. Presently, to their astonishment, they saw oddly dressed figures running about in apparent perturbation and distress; they found out afterwards that they had walked, as it were, into a vision. They had been looking at one of the minor scenes of the French Revolution; the very set and arrangement of the gardens, they discovered, were the set and arrangement of 1790, not of 1900.

And in some way or another, I cannot quite make out how, the author of "At the Shrine of the White Wall" has contrived to give his story this sense of vision. I should not have been astonished, though I should have been annoyed, if the last paragraph had explained it all away, as part of the delirium of sunstroke. One knows how the landscape shimmers magically in the heat of burning summer; so this story of the White Wall shimmers in its atmosphere of vision.

The Wonder from Wales

We will begin, if you please, by being extremely homely—by describing a little detail of domestic economy, as practised at Llanddewi Fach rectory about sixty years ago.

At that period then, the rectory, like all its neighbours, baked its own bread. There was a vaulted oven, something like a miniature railway tunnel, in the back kitchen; and on baking day, which was Monday, the odd job man filled it with wood, loppings and prunings and chunks of grubbed-up root from brake and orchard and shrubberies, that were dried and stored for the purpose. After breakfast the maid mixed the flour and water, and had her dough ready in a big red pan. The odd man had in the meanwhile trotted across the fields to the public-house at Croes-y-Ceiliog, a little more than a mile away. Here they brewed on Mondays, and from the brewing the man brought away a small bottle, part froth, part brown liquid, vague-looking stuff called barm. It was mixed in with the dough in the red pan; the pan was placed on a chair right in front of the kitchen fire, and strangely muffled in a blanket. Presently the heavy, stodgy mass of the dough began to behave strangely, as if a spell were working in it and upon it. It stirred and swelled; it heaved and bubbled, till the moment came for it to be ladled out into the tins. The sticks in the vaulted oven had flamed and fallen into ash on the oven floor. The ash was raked out; a lump of the dough was run in on a plank to try the heat—and the final result was excellent hot bread for tea. And if it had not been for the barm from Croes-y-Ceiliog we should not have had bread for tea, but damper, unleavened stuff; nourishing possibly, but heavy and unpleasing.

Very few parables or analogies are perfect; but speaking roughly, I would say that this process of bread-making gives a good notion of the influence of the Celtic spirit of Wales on English literature; the influence of a strange ferment on a mass of good, wholesome stuff, which perhaps might be a little heavy without it. The analogy is imperfect, as I have hinted. On the one side take the barm, the leaven, which stands for the Welsh influence. In itself it was but froth melting in a muddy fluid—force without substance. I would not press that analogy too harshly, though I maintain, as I have always maintained, that in the proper sense of the word Wales has not produced a literature, in the sense that France and England and Spain have produced literatures. I may say that I have no Welsh; and forestalling objections, I declare quite firmly that my ignorance of what should have been my native language has nothing to do with the matter in hand. If I know no Welsh, I know less Spanish; but my delight has been in *Don Quixote* for the last sixty years. No doubt my relish for that mighty book would be keener if I were a Spanish scholar; no doubt I miss a great deal; but what a world of wonder and delight remains. The masterpieces always get translated; and since I have never heard of a Welsh masterpiece in translation, I conclude that there is no such thing in the original. No masterpieces; but amazing and stirring hints; like whispers, half caught, that seem to speak of ineffable secrets. I am sure that the ancient Welsh poem called *The Graves*—*Y Beddau,* if I have not forgotten—is very far from being one of the great poems of the world; but there is one line in it that thrills the heart—*"Vain is it to seek the grave of Arthur."* There is no *King Lear* in Welsh; but there are matters in *The Mabinogion* story of Branwen, the daughter of Llyr, which are of the very mastery of enchantment. There is a life that is all human, both bodily and spiritual, with its agonies and joys, its triumphs and its tragedies of the body and the spirit. That is the life of *King Lear* and of *Romeo and Juliet.* But there is also the life that is almost beyond surmise, and altogether beyond exact speech and definition. It lies on the very verge of imaginable things; its speech is in symbols which are almost music; and its secret tones murmur when, in the tale of Branwen, "there came three birds, and began singing unto them a certain song, and all the songs they had ever heard were sorry compared thereto; and the birds seemed to be a far way off, over the sea, and yet they were clear as if they had been close at hand". A fairy-tale? Perhaps; and perhaps again there are men now living who have listened to the three birds of Rhiannon. Which is as if one remarked casually: "Do you know that Bach's Fugue in C minor is founded on fact?"

So in a sense I apologise for the analogy of the barm; and again I should apologise for the analogy of the dough before the leaven was set in it. England after all is something more, artistically, than a mere heavy stodge. Pure, undiluted Saxon England even, with its Cædmon, has a spirit of its own, and the native goodness of the life-sustaining wheat; but the later England has also the salt vigour of the Norsemen, and the grace which the gallicised Norsemen brought with them from Normandy. The mass ready for the Welsh leaven was a good, sound mass; not devoid of savour.

Yet, after all pardon sought on either side, the analogy of the barm and the dough holds good. From Celtdom at large, and from the Welsh in particular, there did enter into English literature in the making a certain strange leaven. And its work and office were this: that there is an element in our literature wholly peculiar to it, not shared so far as I know by the literature of any other people, whether ancient or modern. It is difficult to define it exactly; as we have seen, its origins in Welsh hover on the verge of intelligible things. It refuses to be brought to the question of the logical understanding; if you ask: "Now what exactly does this mean?" you will get no answer. But before you turn away in disgust, remember that the same question, if asked of pure or absolute music, will meet with the same silence. This strange element has been given all sorts of names; it has been called the sense of wonder, the sense of ecstasy; its product has been defined as "the fairy way" of writing; but I think that it avoids all description and every attempt at definition. It is present mostly in a weak solution, as the chemists would say, in a great deal of our literature; it is to be found, in its pure strength, in such poems as Keats's "Ode to a Nightingale" and in Coleridge's "Kubla Khan". It manifests again in Poe:

"Bottomless vales and boundless floods,
And chasms, and caves, and Titan woods,
With forms that no man can discover
For the tears that drip all over;
Mountains toppling evermore
Into seas without a shore;
Seas that restlessly aspire,
Surging, unto skies of fire;

Lakes that endlessly outspread
Their lone waters—lone and dead—
Their still waters—still and chilly
With the snows of the lolling lily."

And, more perfectly:

"Now all my days are trances,
And all my nightly dreams
Are where thy grey eye glances
And where thy footstep gleams—
In what ethereal dances,
By what eternal streams."

But in its quintessence, as I have said, this strange and unearthly spirit must be sought in "Kubla Khan" and in Keats's Ode. In those lines:

"The same that oft-times hath
Charm'd magic casements, opening on the foam
Of perilous seas, in faery lands forlorn,"

are to be found, as someone has said recently, the very heart and soul of poetry. And the question arises—how did this secret leaven of Wales enter the mass of English literature?

It is not a simple one. The Odes of Horace are a conscious following of Greek models. The French *Gil Blas* imitates pretty closely the picaresque tales of Spain. A great part of the literature of England in the eighteenth century followed, or tried to follow, classic tradition as interpreted by the seventeenth-century French. Kingsley clearly had Rabelais well in mind when he wrote *The Water Babies.* The problem is much more difficult when we deal with the passage of the magic of Wales into English literature. But most of it comes by way of Malory's fifteenth-century book, the *Morte d'Arthur.* This in its turn derives from a number of romances, written in French, roughly between 1170 and 1220. And the heart of these romances is the Legend of the Grail. And whence did that come?

Between forty and fifty years ago the late Professor Saintsbury, most learned of literary critics and historians, was confronted by this question, and was forced to abandon it unsolved. There were magic feeding vessels in plenty on all sides; bowls and cauldrons that never failed to provide meat and drink, and could never be exhausted, were to be found in Welsh tradition, in Irish tradition and even so far away as in the *Kalevala* of Finland. But, as Professor Saintsbury perceived very clearly, none of these bowls, or horns, or cauldrons of plenty was the Holy Grail. That indeed furnished the Arthurian knights with the meat and drink that they desired, but it furnished them with supernal mysteries also, as anybody may discover by consulting no more remote source than Tennyson's Idyll of the Holy Grail. Saintsbury could find no origins, in Welsh literature or elsewhere, for the legend, and had to content himself with the statement that somehow, in the last quarter of the twelfth century, the heather was on fire with it.

And indeed the problem is an obscure and difficult one. Saintsbury and his fellow-seekers did not find what they wanted, because they did not look in the right place. The sources of the Grail legend are not to be found in the remnants of the ancient literature of Wales, but in the lives of the Welsh saints, written in Latin towards the end of the eleventh century, by a Bishop of St. David's, representing certainly very old traditions; also in the Life of St. Columba, written by St. Adamnan in the seventh century. The chalice of the French romances was, in the first place, a portable altar given to St. David: as the eleventh-century Life says: "A certain hallowed altar in which the Lord's Body had reposed, which abounded in innumerable virtues. Never was this altar seen after the death of the Bishop; but it lies hidden, covered with skins. . . . And hence the common people call it the Gift from Heaven." And then of another saint, Caranoc: to him "Christ gave an honourable altar from on high, *the colour of which no man might discern*".

From such sources, from these tales and from many others like them, from all the lingering traditions of the vanished Celtic Church, from whispers that the *Offeren,* a rite that was not the rite of Rome, was still celebrated in secret oratories on the hills and in the forests; from the legend of St. Columba, who was heard to sing "certain spiritual songs which had never been heard before", when he went apart to a place from which a shining glory issued; from the rumour of the altars, the "gifts from heaven" that had once belonged to the holy and wonder-working saints of Wales, now hidden in dark places of concealment; from these fragments of a lost and ruined world of sanctity and wonder, came that sense of enchantment which sets the Grail legend apart, and high above all other legends.

How these stories penetrated into the Anglo-Norman world must be a matter of conjecture. There were castles in South Wales in the middle of the twelfth century where the two races, the Welsh and the Normans, met; at Manorbier, in Pembrokeshire, the lord was Norman and the lady Welsh; there must have been opportunity enough in such a place for Welsh and French ecclesiastics to exchange legends.

And so the wonder from Wales leavened the romances and passed into English literature through Malory, and has haunted our speech to this day.

Romance and Reality: An Introduction

The other day, I was reading an admirable article on "Victorian London". The writer quoted several passages from Trollope, and dwelt with just praise on that novelist's keen eyes and clear record of what those eyes had seen. But then I came to this passage:

> "Those who can remember even the last vestiges of it (Victorian London) will testify that Trollope's London rather than Dickens's goblin city or Thackeray's and Disraeli's sparkling metropolis was the real Victorian London."

And then I said to myself: "This won't do." The word "real" was the stumbling block. What did the writer of the article mean by "real"? As far as I can make out, he meant that the description of an object—in this case, London—which shews it as it appears to a man of good breeding, and of average education and intelligence, with a certain sense of humour, and interests centred in social and political questions—a man entirely devoid of imagination and of all that imagination implies—is a real description; while all other descriptions are unreal, fanciful, or, in a word, false.

Think of the infinite complexity of all things, think of Tennyson's lines:

> Flower in the crannied wall,
> I pluck you out of the crannies,
> I hold you here, root and all, in my hand,
> Little flower—but *if* I could understand
> What you are, root and all, and all in all,
> I should know what God and man is.

It is true of the flower in the wall, and if that little creature be a profound and unsearchable mystery it seems evident that a great city with its myriads of myriads of souls of men cannot be defined really in the terms of a limited social order. Such a definition or description will be accidental, superficial; by no means essential or real. If you say that Mr. Gladstone was a man who wore big pointed collars, and that the Duke of Wellington was a man with a big nose, you will have spoken the truth; but you will not have furnished a real description of the statesman or of the soldier.

It is the office of romance to deal with reality; to unveil, as far as may be, the essential, and real, and eternal truth of things. Mr. Collins's *Romance of the Echoing Wood* is as real (and as romantic) now as in that fabled age of dreams where he must have heard it told.

We hear a lot of loose—and thoroughly unscientific—talk to-day about scientific method as being applicable to everything, and as solving all difficulties and all mysteries. I don't think the real men of science talk this gibberish; their discovery is rather to the effect that the further we progress in knowledge the more profound and illimitable the mystery of the universe becomes. They stand on a peak in Darien, and look out on the boundless ocean of the unknown. But their camp-followers do gabble most unmercifully of the scientific method as applied to art and to everything else. They were gabbling to much the same effect in Dickens's day.

"'Bitzer,' said Thomas Gradgrind. 'Your definition of a horse.'

"'Quadruped. Graminivorous. Forty teeth, namely, twenty-four grinders, four eye-teeth, and twelve incisive. Sheds coat in the spring; in marshy countries, sheds hoofs, too. Hoofs hard, but requiring to be shod with iron. Age known by marks in mouth!'" Thus (and much more) Bitzer.

"'Now, girl number twenty,' said Mr. Gradgrind. 'You know what a horse is.'"

And, as it happened, Mr. Gradgrind was largely right, since Girl Number Twenty had been brought up in a circus, and probably did know a good deal about horses. But in his implication that Cissy Jupe knew what a horse was from Bitzer's definition of the beast Thomas Gradgrind was entirely mistaken. Bitzer was, no doubt, quoting from the school manual; he would have done better to refer Cissy to a very different text-book.

> Hast thou given the horse strength? hast thou clothed his neck with thunder?
>
> Canst thou make him afraid as a grasshopper? the glory of his nostrils is terrible.
>
> He paweth in the valley, and rejoiceth in his strength: he goeth on to meet the armed men.
>
> He mocketh at fear, and is not affrighted; neither turneth he back from the sword.
>
> The quiver rattleth against him, the glittering spear and the shield.
>
> He swalloweth the ground with fierceness and rage: neither believeth he that it is the sound of the trumpet.
>
> He saith among the trumpets, Ha, ha; and he smelleth the battle afar off, the thunder of the captains and the shouting.

There is the real definition of the horse, as distinguished from Bitzer's enumeration of unimportant facts about it. If the body of Keats had been anatomised, and the dissecting surgeon had written an exact report of his procedure, he would not have furnished a real definition of the poet. Reality has nothing to do with teeth, glands, muscles, or bones; you cannot comprehend the genius of Shakespeare by describing the binding of your copy, or by counting the letters and words of the text that it holds.

"He is no writer of romance, no fantastic idealist or dealer in dreams. Mr. Smith (or Jones, or Robinson) fixes his eyes firmly on reality, and sets down what he has seen with the sternest scientific method."

I am sure that is a quotation from some review of a modern novel, the name of which I do not for the moment recollect. I know the kind of book indicated. The method of Bitzer is followed by the author of it. In some parts of it the collaboration of a Sanitary Inspector is indicated, in others a Labour leader would appear to have given expert advice. The writer has looked at life with the vision of a pressman's camera; he has viewed all the surfaces of his scene and of his characters, he has never suspected that life holds anything but surfaces: and the result is called reality.

A good title; but Unreality would be a better—unless Collars is to sum up Gladstone, and Nosey the Great Duke.

If you want reality you must go to romance. Nearly fifty years ago, I remember quoting in a book of mine a strange sentence from a dreamer of the seventeenth century, one Oswald Crollius, otherwise unknown to me. The sentence was: "In every grain of wheat there lies hidden the soul of a star." There is a vague beauty about the saying that enchanted me; but I scarcely thought of translating it into exact terms, of pinning the author of it down to a precise and logical meaning. It has only dawned on me lately that this dreamer, as I have called him, half mystic, half occultist, wanderer in worlds that he had not localised, was understating an exact truth. In his grain of wheat there was not merely hidden the soul or principle of a star; within it there were worlds on worlds, made after the similitude of the starry heavens, the electrons circling round their suns in ceaseless motion and eternal, inevitable order. So far is the secret and hidden truth, the reality, remote from the outward show which is commonly taken for reality. It is the business of romance to penetrate beneath all these outward shows and appearances; to see London (for example) as Syon, in the manner of Blake, or as a goblin city, in the manner of Dickens; to see it, in any event, as a great mystery of black depths and shining heights.

The grain of wheat, the material object, as we have seen, discloses undreamed-of wonders; much more does the whole world and sum of things, the spiritual world of men and all their works, disclose incredible but most veracious marvels to those who gaze on it in the spirit of romance.

IV. Books and Authors

American Letter

Longfellow, perhaps, never quite succeeded in writing a romance, but he certainly understood how romances should be written. Those who know *Kavanagh* will remember that a certain Mr. Hathaway once called on the schoolmaster and proceeded to expound his ideas on American literature.

> "I think, Mr. Churchill," said he, "that we want a national literature commensurate with our mountains and rivers,—commensurate with Niagara and the Alleghanies and the Great Lakes!"
>
> "Oh!"
>
> "We want a national epic that shall correspond to the size of the country; that shall be to all other epics what Banvard's panorama of the Mississippi is to all other paintings—the largest in the world!"
>
> "Ah!"
>
> "We want a national drama in which scope enough shall be given to our gigantic ideas and to the unparalleled activity and progress of our people!"
>
> "Of course."
>
> "In a word, we want a national literature altogether shaggy and unshorn, that shall shake the earth like a herd of buffaloes thundering over the prairies!"

One might quote more of this admirable conversation, but it is evident from these few paragraphs that Longfellow had the root of the matter so far as literature is concerned. He clearly understood that prose and poetry have no relation to external things, that there is no possible analogy between the size of a country and the quality of the books it produces. As he says in the person of Mr. Churchill:—"A man will not necessarily be a great poet because he lives near a great mountain"—any more than one who drives fat oxen must himself be fat.

It is wholesome to recall these sentences of a very charming verse-writer and a very accomplished man of letters because at the present day the absurd heresy which he so wittily opposed is constantly being asserted and reasserted in varying forms. Now it pokes up its ugly head in theology; faith is absurd, because the earth is so small and the universe so large, as if Attica were not infinitely smaller than Australia. Now it appears, under a slightly different disguise, in literature. The nauseous mixtures of the laboratory are decanted before us for our admiration, as if the stuff brewed by "Science and Art" pupils could compare with that shining wine of the ignorant, inspired Homer. And finally, Mr. Hathaway is always calling on us, pushing his wares with the cool impudence of a commercial traveller, insisting that the literature of so huge a country as America must needs be very great. Of course the proposition requires no refutation; it is sufficient if one states it in terms. We may simply answer with Longfellow—

> Switzerland has produced no extraordinary poet; nor, so far as I know, have the Andes or the Himalaya Mountains, or the Mountains of the Moon in Africa.

But we may distinguish a little more minutely. So far as the Americans are a book-producing people they are English, and their literature is and will be English in all essential articles. As a nation, of course, the States are highly composite, but even from this standpoint the direction of affairs is almost wholly English. In literature we need not qualify the truth with an "almost": an American author is simply one who contributes from across the ocean to the splendid archives of English thought. "How about Walt Whitman?" it may be asked. "Was he not purely and exclusively American?" Certainly not, unless Jefferies was purely and exclusively Wiltshire. Whitman was not "American" in his wonderful lament for Lincoln; his *magistral* stanzas recall with no uncertainty the lyrics of Isaiah, the splendours of the Old Testament. And no one would wish to claim as exclusively American his slips and blunders, his occasional outrages on good sense and good taste, his "housetops of creation" phrases. So long as the authors of the United States use the mother-tongue they will be adding books, good or bad, to English literature, and no occasional use of local idioms will cut off their work from the great fellowship. Barnes is as much an English poet as Herrick; the "viery zun" no more dissociates the Dorsetshire writer from English letters than "back of the house", "I want ter know", and "antagonize" can turn a story written in Massachusetts into an American novel.

American writers, then, are English writers, and how superbly some of them have written! If we consider the history of the Colonies and of the States, we may well be astonished at the quantity and quality of the work that has been done. We have no space here to praise the great names; it is enough to mention them. Washington Irving, Longfellow, Poe, and Hawthorne would bring honour to any literature, and we may well push up many British books to make room for Emerson and Thoreau. Two hundred years of struggle with wild lands, with a wild climate, with a wild theology, a desperate battle with the mother-country, the rising of a fearful plutocracy, and fearful politics: these are not the events that make for fine letters, this is not the atmosphere that nourishes imagination. And yet from this ground there grew the "Ode to Helen" and the *Scarlet Letter*. It is almost a miracle that such a barren soil should produce such exquisite flowers. The old generation has died out; the new masters are little masters, yet Englishmen would not have been sorry if Bret Harte and Mr. Howells, Mr. James and Mr. Harold Frederic, Mr. G. W. Cable, Mr. P. L. Ford, and others had been born in Britain; and Mark Twain has written one classic, at all events, in *Huckleberry Finn*—a classic that will outlast the spurious cape and sword romance, the nauseous and pretentious "problem-novels". Of Miss Wilkins it is needless to speak here; we know that at her best she is very near to perfection. And those who love letters will not soon forget the charm of *Colonel Carter, of Cartersville,* or the strange horror of Mr. Bierce's stories. The States have faithfully carried on the magnificent tradition of English literature, and both countries are proud of them and of their work.

At present, perhaps, there is something of a pause in the clear utterance. Here are five recent stories, but only one which seems solidly built, designed from an artistic plan. THE KENTUCKIANS (Harper, 5s.) gives a careful, curious, and admirable picture of two civilisations, or rather of a civilisation and a state which approaches savagery. It tells the old story of the hills and the plains, of the original stock remaining primitive, hardy, and ferocious, occupied overmuch with vendettas and faction fights, living in a rude independence, with the manners of boors and the pride of noblemen. And in contrast with these rough hillmen we have the smooth and modern conventions of their cousins, of the people who have moved down into the "settlemints". Mr. John Fox, the author, has had an artistic idea, and he has thoroughly succeeded in his effort to clothe it with words. JIMTY AND OTHERS, by Margaret Sutton Briscoe (Harper, $1 50c.), is pleasant, readable, quite skilful, indeed, in its manner, but here we find ourselves in comparatively shallow waters. The workmanship is superior to that of the average short story in England, but the matter is poor enough, and there is no trace of any formative idea. Mr. Owen Wister has done far better work than this LIN M'LEAN (Harper, $1 50c.), which is clever and entertaining, and nothing more; and pretty much the same verdict must be passed on THE KING OF THE BRONCOS (George Newnes, 5s.), by Charles F. Lummis, though both these books are amusing and vigorous, and in every way to be commended to those who like to read of cowboys and bears and desperate shots. Last on our list comes THE ROCK OF THE LION, by Molly Elliot Seawell (Harper, $1 50c.), and here, it must be said, we touch on the weak spot of the United States school—a tendency to talk about the Revolution and to dilate on the joys of freedom. Yet the little tale is brightly and sensibly told; one would rather read it than many "great successes" of current British fiction.

The Matter of Romance

The Arthur of the English Poets. By HOWARD MAYNADIER. (Archibald Constable and Co., 6s. net.)

So much has been written recently in THE ACADEMY about the Arthurian Legend, that it would be wearisome to enter into a detailed discussion of the many interesting points raised by Professor Maynadier in the course of his study of the great romances of the Round Table. It may be said, however, that for literary students—as distinct from specialists—who wish to gain a good general view of the rise and flourishing of the Legend the book will be most useful. The writer is evidently ignorant of the valuable assistance rendered by the Welsh Hagiology in estimating the various elements which went to the formation of the wonderful story of the Graal; he makes the mistake of quoting Professor Rhys's nonsense about "Sun Gods" with some appearance of respect; but, with these deductions, the earlier pages of *The Arthur of the English Poets* gives, as we have said, an excellent account of the growth of the great romance cycle that has Arthur as its central figure. There is curious reading, too, in the latter portion of the book, which deals with the fate of the legend in the dark ages of the eighteenth century; and the chapter on Tennyson's treatment of Malory is interesting enough, though it is always melancholy to be reminded how a great poet missed a great opportunity. One sighs as one reads that mighty fragment, the *Morte d'Arthur,* thinking of what an epic the Laureate Poet might have given us; one groans over some of the later Idylls, in which the Mystic King is rapidly being transmuted into a variant of John Halifax, Gentleman, in which Vivien appears as an adventuress from town, disturbing the repose of a country vicarage. The opportunity was lost, the poet was conformed to the world, and it is hardly surprising to find that Lord Tennyson considered the Round Table as a symbol of "Liberal Institutions", which is as much as to say that the central flame of the Universe is in reality a symbol of "The Domestic" Gas Stove, hired, on liberal terms, from the Company. The pages, then, that treat of the Idylls are to be read in the way of warning; and so may increase the usefulness of an excellent book. One may pass over the phrases which demonstrate the selfish, unpractical nature of Galahad's character, his failure to rise to the heights of "Modern Christianity":

> Nor can Galahad (says Prof. Maynadier) . . . be called other than fanatical. As he rides round the world singing, "I yearn to breathe the airs of heaven that often meet me here," he is either not normal and healthy or not honest. . . . Galahad shows himself after all only a knightly brother of the revivalists who manifest their religion nowadays with so much noisy emotion and so little sanity.

This is painful and foolish enough, but it is clear that Professor Maynadier has not heard the command: "Let the dead bury their dead; rise and follow Me." It is idle to attempt to steer a magic bark in faery seas by the assistance of the quadrant, a chronometer adjusted to the meridian of Greenwich, and the mariner's compass.

One point raised by Professor Maynadier deserves some discussion. It is apart from the special matter of the Arthurian legend, and concerns the whole question, so often debated, of the Celtic Spirit or Celtic Genius. Speaking of the tale of "Kilhwch and Olwen", the author remarks:

> It is not a tale to impress human imagination for centuries, like the legends of Lancelot, Perceval, and Tristram and Iseult, for it is after all best characterised by that adjective which Matthew Arnold applies to Celtic Art in general, "ineffectual." Celtic Art, he says, so long as it remained purely Celtic, has never profoundly impressed the world like Greek or Roman Art, or the best German, French, English, Spanish, and Italian Art. Now, it was because French Art was able to join reason and significance to the fantastic poetry of such Celtic tales as *Kilhwch* and *Olwen,* to give the old charming but "ineffectual" stories substantial meaning, that they have become effectual and permanent contributions to the literature of the world.

And here lies a matter of perennial interest to all lovers of literature. It is, perhaps, idle to insist on the term Celtic; for, as Mr. Yeats has confessed, the spirit that we often call Celtic is, in reality, the spirit that is common to many if not all primitive peoples. It would be difficult to express its qualities in a phrase; it is the spirit of enchantment, of ecstasy, of wonder, of adoration; it is the spirit which protests for ever against all modern materialistic theories; it is the eternal witness, as some of us think, to the existence of that Avalon from which we have been driven, for which we long during the days of our banishment, *exules filii Hevæ*. The existence of the Brook by the way may be deduced from the thirst of the wayfarer; and so Paradise may be inferred by our longing for it. It is this longing, and the expression of this longing, which distinguish, in the last resort, Art from Artifice; without it a book, or a picture, or a statue is nothing but a mere or less ingenious contrivance, with the excellence, perhaps, of a beehive or an ant hill, but no true work of art.

And here is the tragedy to which Matthew Arnold made allusion in the adjective "ineffectual". Take the *Morte d'Arthur* of Malory even; there the material which came from Celtdom—or, let us say, from a primitive race—had been worked over by many hands, both French and English, for more than two hundred years. And yet: compare Malory's book with the average "clever" modern novel; not with the dregs and drivel of the publishers' stock, which is, surely, the most offensively pretentious stuff that ever found expression in writing or print or articulate speech, but with the well-made, well-dressed, decently written story of these "educated" days. Well, of course, the modern book is nought, and worse than nought when compared with Malory; it is as the ingenuities of an amiable bee, or of an observant butterfly beside the *Morte;* and yet, how vastly the latter is excelled, in mere artifice, by the former. The modern writer "jines his flats", he has a story to tell, and he tells it in more or less logical order; the old romancer, not content with the wanderings of his heroes, must wander too; breaking off, turning from the track, indulging in episodes without end, returning to the high road of his story, only to stroll away from it again in the course of a few chapters. In a word: the spirit is undoubtedly present in the romance, but the body which the writer has provided is often deplorably ill-jointed and shapen in strange sort, and sometimes in no sort at all. And, nevertheless, we know that the old romance is a part of the lost paradise; while the new novel is just very entertaining reading. One may call this a tragedy of literature, that the perfect spirit—the one element which makes literature, which transmutes the lead of human things into the pure gold of art—has so often been manifested in very dim and imperfect vessels; while well-chased flagons hold but poor, thin liquor, small wines of a second growth, agreeable enough with one's dinner, but not apt to serve in the celebration of the Greater Dionysian Mysteries. Of course, there may be people who think the faults of the old tales are beauties, just as there may be persons who think that the bad drawing of early stained-glass and illuminated manuscripts is an added charm; but these are not tenable opinions. A glowing and glorious saint in his dyed robes is the less, not the more beautiful by the obvious dislocation of his neck; and so the wonderful old tale loses, not gains, by its awkward and rambling construction.

Here, then, is a great task for the writer who has the requisite vision, who is willing to be brave in his recounting of it. Let him think of this as his life's work, to tell the great dream truthfully, and yet to tell it coherently. The vision, of course, is above all things necessary; the chosen one must above all see the real things, he must be able to gaze on Paradise; and even if the especial gift have been vouchsafed him, he will have much ado to keep his eyes clear, to dispel, to dispel continually, the mists that rise from the rotten fens and dunghills of modern civilisation. He must purge his mind of cant; especially and principally of that noxious form of cant that caused Professor Maynadier to pen these dolorous pages concerning the selfish, fanatical, and unhealthy nature of Sir Galahad, which made poor Tennyson see in the marvellous imagery of the Round Table simply a pretty way of putting one's respect for the House of Commons, the County Council, and the School Board. The man who is to clothe the shining spirit with the perfect body must forget all this rubbish, he must forget that it exists, or the vision will be taken from him, as it was taken from the eyes of Tennyson; and Avalon, the isle beyond the glassy floods, will, perhaps, turn into a picture of modern society, or (worse still!) of "modern Christianity". Nay; he who is to write our great romance must himself be a knight-errant; he, too, must turn his back on the city, on the places where people sit by the cosy fires of social and convenient morality, and do business, and do each other, and deduce obvious moral lessons from everything, and pass Acts of Parliament, and make Religion a sort of shabby Moyen de Parvenir; he must fare forth on the wild ways, by the dark wood, by the bare mountain heights, through fires and storms, over the billows of the great deep. In other words, he must be firmly and utterly convinced that man is here, not that he may be good-natured and kindly (so far as kindness and good-nature are consistent with business principles), but that he may be worthy of the Vision of the Most Blessed Cup of the Sangraal.

Now, this is no easy task. Our corruption is so profound that we have well-nigh lost the measure of all things; we have quite lost the measure of the highest things. Professor Maynadier's view of Galahad as a selfish and fanatical revivalist is probably quite a representative opinion in these sorry and besotted days; or rather, let us say, it is the representative opinion of the natural, bestial man of all ages. Since man was man the Primæval Pig has dwelt in him, grunting out the Pig Gospel: that the end of all things is Wash, that the Pig whose trough is full is a good, pious, religious, and perfect Pig, and that, since one must work for Wash, the Pig who is always "doing business" is highly to be revered. These dogmas, as we have said, are a portion of the early curse, of the doom that was laid on man when he lapsed from Paradise, when, according to William Law, the fluid and glorious universe became a grim and solid and brutal mass and fell upon "Adam", so that he was crushed beneath its weight. In every age the Bestial Evangel has been preached; Labour, which in the great Mythos of the Garden is denounced as a curse and a punishment, is proclaimed as a blessing, a pious exercise, a reward, in itself a heaven; and though the Christ denounced this vile heresy in no uncertain terms, though He stigmatised the saving of money and business forethought as wicked and senseless follies, though He placed before men the example of the lilies, though St. Paul declares that all actions of practical benevolence even are but dust and ashes if the secret fire, the divine ardours of Love are not present; still, in the Bright Ages there were doubtless many people who thought that the men called monks, who did nothing but pray and worship God, were useless idlers, that building cathedrals was a dreadful waste of money, and that the price of the incense at the Sacrifice would have been much better expended on "the poor"—that is, on themselves, on the hard-headed, practical men who usually keep the bag. If this were so—and it doubtless was so—in the

Golden Ages of true faith and true reason and true art, what is now the depth to which we have fallen? Well, it may be said that we have almost reached the limit of utter confusion, of profound denial of all that is true, of firm asseveration of all that is false. The other day a bishop of the Catholic Church had the great opportunity of addressing certain of his flock, of confirming them, one might conjecture, in some dogma of the Faith, of unveiling to them some secret treasure of the Great Mysteries, of instructing them in some of the transcendent morals of the Christian religion. One would have conjectured all awry; for Dr. Diggle talked about the Lusitania's "record", and hoped that the proud and swelling, though legitimate, feelings aroused by this great achievement would move the people of Liverpool to a more liberal support of the Seamen's Orphanage! And it would not be true to say that this virulent nonsense is peculiar to Anglicanism or Protestantism; it is not many months since Father Bernard Vaughan allowed himself to speculate as to the probable conduct of St. Paul if he had edited a daily paper, and as to the likelihood of his appointing St. Timothy as assistant-editor.

Well, it is of all this *cochonnerie* that the man who would write great romance must clear his mind; he must silence, and silence effectually, the gruntings and squealings of the foul creature who dwells within him; he must pay no heed to the voice of the body of death to which he is chained in the valley of this pilgrimage. Utterly must he dismiss from his soul the thought that "success" means anything, that a man who has made a great deal of money or earned a great deal of praise, is anything but a *prima facie* suspect; for the dogma of success is one of the chiefest articles in the great Creed of the Stye. It is to those who are able to cleanse themselves of these defilements that the Vision may be vouchsafed, in them the old dream of the Celts may be renewed, and with clearer eyes for the struggle that has been endured they may see the wonder of the world and the wonder of man—the "things that really are" of Plato.

"Darkness and the shadow of death" is a very familiar phrase to many people; and one wonders to how many of these people the slightest gleam of the true meaning of these words has been given. As a matter of fact, one conjectures that ninety-nine out of a hundred, asked to explain the phrase, would reply that a thief, a pickpocket, an adulterer, a murderer might be described as being in this condition. The reply would, very likely, be true—in a sense; in the sense in which scarlet fever might be defined as an appearance of spots, or a great statue as a block of limestone, or a great picture as a collection of coloured earths, combined with oil, and applied to wood or canvas. But, essentially, such a reply would be imbecile; it is highly probable that the people who have never broken a single commandment are in a deeper darkness, in a more profound shadow of mortality than the criminals whom they scorn, or hate, or pity. The shadow of death and darkness, in reality, describes well enough the utter error and confusion of all men, "good" and "bad" alike, their ignorance as to what they are, and why they are, and what their end should be. The baser sort reply that they are here to make money, the better sort that they are here to do good, or even to be good; who answers that he is here to enjoy happiness, that he may enjoy a more perfect happiness in the life of the world to come? The people whom "the good" and "the respectable" call wastrels, Bohemians, vagabonds, have a sort of dim vision of this truth; they realise that happiness is man's true end; their mistake is in a confusion as to the means. Still, with all their error, they are infinitely nearer to the truth than the Scribes and the Pharisees, than the "practical men", the apostles of "plain common-sense", the vermin who infest church and chapel and the very altar itself. And it was no doubt because of this clearer vision that the Christ loved those whom the world called disreputable, while He hated all the representatives of respectability.

The hero of the Great Romance must, therefore, set his face continually to Syon; his ardours must consume him ever; through the wild and waste lands he must still wander, seeking Corbenic and the Blessed Vision of the Sangraal. "Liberal institutions", "modern Christianity", "practical philanthropy"—all the Nine Hundred and Ninety-Nine Articles of the Great Pig Philosophy have for ever vanished from his eyes. His are the delights that are almost unendurable, the wonders that are almost incredible—that are, indeed, quite incredible to the world; his the eternal joys that the deadly flesh cannot comprehend; his the secret that renews the earth, restoring Paradise, rolling the heavy stone of the material universe from the grave whence he arises.

Of such matters will the High History treat—that High Romance which is yet to be written.

A New War Poet

Lord Dunsany's Discovery

There is a picturesque story about this book and its author. Francis Ledwidge was born in the Irish peasantry. He was a labourer on the land. He learned shorthand, hoping to be a journalist. He was a shop-assistant in Dublin. He was a miner. He was a hypnotist, and so banned in County Meath as a wizard. He had always written verses and destroyed them till Lord Dunsany became his patron in the best sense of the term, and so these songs have been printed. And now patron and poet are fighting together in the ranks of the Royal Inniskilling Fusiliers, on the Gallipoli Peninsula.

This, I say, is a most interesting story, but as Lord Dunsany wisely cautions us, its interest has nothing whatever to do with Mr. Ledwidge's poetry, as poetry. Art is neither aristocratic nor democratic, or rather, its high and low have no relation to the high and low of the political and social order. The psychologist may find it deeply interesting when the peasant becomes a poet; perhaps a more subtle psychologist may wonder how anybody save a peasant can become a poet; the inept "Baconian" will eject his futilities as to the impossibility of the "Stratford yokel" ever having written Shakespeare's plays.

But in the high court of literature all these pleas and writs cease to run; the only question is as to the value of the accomplished work. And I think that these *Songs of the Fields* are of high value.

Before comment, I take an example that strikes me; not as the author's best work, but as a text for what I am about to say:—

EVENING IN FEBRUARY.

The windy evening drops a grey
Old eyelid down across the sun,

The last crow leaves the ploughman's way,
And happy lambs make no more fun.

Wild parsley buds beside my feet,
A doubtful thrush makes hurried tune,
The steeple in the village street
Doth seem to pierce the twilight moon.

I hear and see those changing charms,
For all my thoughts are fixed upon
The hurry and the loud alarms
Before the fall of Babylon.

Now one sees, I think, in these lines an observation and expression both faithful and felicitous; note the entire fitness and happiness of that "grey old eyelid" to figure the dim February twilight. The landscape is all veiled and filmed over with grey, the rising moon is of the faintest silver, hardly illuminated, everything is still and dim, sinking into darkness and a deeper silence.

It is all very well done; but it is the last stanza that transmutes the lines from verse into poetry; when one sees the peaceful Irish village suddenly lit up by the red glare of those frantic torches that rushed and hurried and flamed to and fro in the awful hanging groves and terraces of Babylon.

It is with difficulty that I express my meaning—for poetry by its definition is the last and essential truth, which can be defined no farther; but I would say that the poem of "Evening in February" seems to me to picture of eternity itself.

Then there is a minor consideration. It is this; that though the author has been a peasant and is a poet; he is not what is called a peasant poet. Burns was a peasant poet; and when Carlyle remarks on the sad disadvantages of Burns's education he told the truth in a manner that he little suspected. The true disadvantage of Burns's education was that he had any. It was his misfortune that he smattered a little cheap learning, and so called the sun Phœbus instead of plain sun. His true education was in the tradition of the Scots poets that were before him, in the legend and fairy tales of the country that the old woman taught him when he was a child, in the Scottish breath of the winds than blew upon him. It was well that he knew a few books, it had been better if he had known none.

Quite otherwise is the case of Mr. Ledwidge. The poem that I have quoted is a "literary" poem; that is, it is the work of a man who has been influenced profoundly by his reading. Its phrasing shews that; that "grey old eyelid" could only have been written by a lover of books. And so the illuminating appearance of Babylon: that is a touch that speaks of the lettered man.

Now and again, it must be said, he does strike a certain Celtic note, but it is the simplicity, not the glamour, of the Celtic spirit that he attains. Thus:

> Had I but wealth of land and bleating flocks
> And barnfuls of the yellow harvest yield,
> And a large house with climbing hollyhocks
> And servant maidens singing in the field,
> You'd love me.

is Celtic in its primitive simplicity, not only of manner, but of fact.

SONGS OF THE FIELDS. By Francis Ledwidge. With an Introduction by Lord Dunsany. (Herbert Jenkins.)

Books of To-day

THE RED HORIZON. By Patrick MacGill. (Herbert Jenkins.)

Vivid, humorous, and picturesque sketches of the nightmare of the trenches and the dug-outs—which Mr. MacGill and his brave companions do their best to laugh into a happy, jolly dream.

Read "The Dug-Out Banquet." A bullet whistled through the door in the middle of the feast and struck a tin of condensed milk, which hung by a string from the rafter. The milk oozed and fell on the table.

A menu is given; it ends with "God Save the King: Gott Strafe the Cooks."

GERMAN CONSPIRACIES IN AMERICA. By William K. Skraggs. (Unwin.)

This detailed and elaborate account of German "activities" in America is by an American, who feels that his country has not exactly exalted its fame in the manner in which it has met a campaign of insolence, outrage, and murder.

> If we entertain pirates and conspirators, if we connive at arson, murder, rape, and piracy, if we submit to indignities and insults under the plea that we are too proud to fight, we shall find that those who fought for their homes and country will be too proud to sit at the council-table with us.

WAR LETTERS OF AN AMERICAN WOMAN. By Marie van Vorst. Illustrated. (Lane.)

A book of lively impressions, emotions, fears, and hopes.

> We over here [in England] hope that the pulse of America is not too tightly compressed by the thumbs of the Wall-street clique.
>
> I remember that you told me some time ago that no one dreams how America is influenced by that colossally rich Hebraic band.

WHAT OF TO-DAY? By Father Bernard Vaughan, S. J. (Cassell.)

Essays on "burning questions" of the day, with special relation to the problems of the war.

Father Vaughan makes a good point when he shows that it is idle to ascribe the abominations committed by the Germans in Belgium to sudden fury and blood lust breaking out among the soldiers.

He says truly: "The German soldier is far too strongly disciplined to dare to commit such outrages as have been proved against him without the express sanction of superior officers who dominate him."

THE STAR-TREADER AND OTHER POEMS. By Clark Ashton Smith. (Robertson, San Francisco.)

Seventeen often longs to write, above all to write poetry; and seventeen usually makes a sad mess of it, and spends long years of anxiety afterwards, lest some enemy discover that thin volume of sorry verse.

It is understood that Mr. Ashton Smith is seventeen; but he at least will never blush for "The Star-Treader." He is not far from the true vision of the world.

FAIRY LANTERNS.

'Tis said these blossom-lanterns light
The elves upon their midnight way;
That fairy toil and elfin play
Receive their beams of magic white.

I marvel not if it be true;
I know this flower has lighted me
Nearer to Beauty's mystery,
And part the veils of secrets new.

The author shows in many poems of his verse a great admiration for "the grand manner"; he builds his poems up as if they were cathedrals.

Often he is justified by his results; but one would urge him to admire above all simplicity and lucidity. Rheims cathedral is—or was, alas!—a miracle of rich adornments; but how lucid, how clear and self-illuminating is the vast scheme of the west-front.

AMONG THE RUINS. By Gomez Carrillo. Translated by Florence Simmonds. (Heinemann.)

Senor Carrillo was one of the first journalists to see the work that the Germans had done in that first furious fight of theirs through France.

There was a landlord of an inn at St. Menehould (famous for its method of cooking "trotters") who was more cunning than the army of looters.

He put vinegar labels on his best wine-bottles; so they escaped. And:

> "Do you see those pictures?" he cried, showing us a series of eighteenth-century French engravings, charming in their spritely malice, their ironic grace, and French elegance.
>
> "When the Boches came . . . I thought of a device. I ran to the market and bought twenty chromos representing coarse scenes of monks and fat wenches in Flemish public-houses. When the Boches came they hastened to put them into their bags, and despised the pale engravings."

PHOTOGRAPHS OF THE YEAR 1915. Edited by F. J. Mortimer. (Hazell, Watson, and Viney.)

The review of the world's photography during the past year. Some of the examples are of extreme beauty.

In "The Adventurers," by Mr. W. H., Porterfield, of Buffalo, N.Y., and in "Storm-twisted," by Mr. H. C. Mann, of Virginia, for example, there is an atmosphere and an "intention" which one finds very rarely in photography, even of the best.

SELF-GOVERNMENT IN RUSSIA. By Paul Vinogradoff. (Constable.)

A very valuable analysis of Russian society, and of the "materials" available for schemes of self-government.

Professor Vinogradoff finds that the present situation in Russian politics "is in no way an accidental one. It has been produced and prepared by the whole course of Russian culture and politics."

AUSTRALASIA TRIUMPHANT. By A. St. John Adcock. Illustrated. (Simpkin, Marshall.)

This is the only complete story of the achievements of Australia and New Zealand in the great war; not only in Gallipoli, but in southern seas, and in Egypt.

There is a brisk and thrilling account of the action between the Sydney and the Emden.

> As soon as she was clear of the island the Emden opened fire on the Sydney, and at first made excellent practice, but the Sydney answered by pouring in such an accurate and deadly fire that the enemy's three funnels were shot away, some of his guns silenced, and all the speaking-tubes smashed, so that the captain had difficulties in transmitting his orders, and his firing began to fall of considerably. . . .
>
> The cheerfulness and reckless ardour of them [the Sydney's crew] all were amazing; nobody thought of danger; nobody thought of anything except that they were at grips with the enemy at long last, and did not mean to let him go.

May the whole English Navy come before long at grips with the enemy "at long last," with a like issue!

Jack London the Man

Jack London. By Charmian London. 2 vols. 41 illustrations. Mills and Boon. 36s. net. Published to-day.

Jack London was pitchforked into life. His father was of the class of the pioneers, the men who are said to have come from the log cabin, if they get on in life. But John, father of Jack, never arrived. He died a poor man, something in the police, after having tried to do many things. He was foreman of a gang of navvies, farmed, was a building contractor, a market gardener, a speculator under poor enough guidance, and fades ineffective out of life.

It cannot he said that his son Jack—he insisted from the first that his name was "Jack", not "John"—had any particular upbringing, though his half-sister, Eliza, always did the best she could for him, though his old negro "mammy" loved him dearly and helped him with her savings. He found himself, somehow, on the streets, selling newspapers. His father—this was in the policeman stage of his career—took his son with him in his official parade of the "tenderloin night life of the town"; and one gathers that tenderloin life is far from decorous.

> "Here again, he could not but be struck by the fool-making effects of too much alcohol; and when these effects exceeded foolishness, and drinkers were jangled off in 'hurry up wagons' to jail, he was confused by the fact that drinking was a licensed pastime for the young as well as the matured, not frowned upon by the men who sat in the high places. On the contrary, in saloons he beheld such exalted personages also imbibing the potent draughts, little recking that often their joviality was but a cloak for ills that urged them towards the inhibitions of alcohol."

There! It must come sooner or later, and it is as well that I confess at once that there are whole pages in these two volumes that are to me quite unintelligible. I do not know what that last sentence means. And later in the book when Mrs. London wishes to tell us how her husband came to write:

> "He shortened his tools, focussed more intently, and began hewing unique art forms, of unmistakable purity of design, out from the blocks of empirical and idealistic material so long storing in his mind against this inevitable day."

I do not know what that sentence means. And, again, I do not know in the least what this means:

> "I have seen him quite white with distress that he had to spoil a party by depriving guests of the spectacle of himself routed from his materialistic terra firma and driven upon the impalpable ground of the metaphysicians with their, to him, colossal evasions of mundane interpretations."

I do not know what it is about. I say with Martin Luther, quoted, oddly enough, in the paragraph above that last sentence: "Here I stand. I can do no otherwise so help me God!" And I must say that through the clouds and fireworks of this extraordinary diction the character of Jack London is difficult to discern.

But with this granted, and with the further caution that Mrs. London's literary manner is so grand that it is hard to know sometimes what her hero is doing, not merely in the spirit but in the body, we may go on with the Life.

Jack sold his papers in the "tough districts" of San Francisco; he swept out stores, helped icemen, stuck up skittles, went to school a little but not very much, fished in the bay, learned to love sailing and to be skilful in that craft, and drank, at intervals, exorbitant quantities of the "whisky" of the longshoremen of the bay, a liquor which is no doubt well defined chemically and scientifically by its pet name of "rot gut".

At fifteen or sixteen Jack London turned his attention to Oyster Piracy, the illegitimate delving in the oyster beds of the San Francisco waters, taking with him as partner a young lady of his own age, known as "the Queen of the Oyster Pirates", who had deserted in Jack's favour an older pirate lover known as "French Frank". Jack had been savagely worked, before the oyster piracy episode, in a "cannery"; it was a relief and a joy to be out on the fresh waters of the bay. Then, according to his biographer, he became a philosopher, or, as she puts it:

> "I think it must have been right here, aligning his equipment for immediate benefit of all concerned in his province, that the budding philosopher forever renounced idle dreaming. Henceforward he appeared to range his conclusions with more or less logical application to practical solutions."

Again! What does it all mean?

On sea and on shore, Jack lived wildly. In his own words,

> "If I should serve sentences on end for pranks I did in sheer pursuit of the tang of living, from time to time during the scattered months I was busy 'finding myself' on the Bay, or tramping, or ashore with the 'Boo Gang' and the 'Sporting Life Gang' that terrorised Oakland, I'd languish behind prison bars for a hundred years!"

And in this period of his life there is a curious strain which reminds us of Lord Northcliffe's recently published article on Prohibition in America. Lord Northcliffe writes to the effect that America, having banned alcohol, seems to have got it on the brain; and so with Jack London. He and his biographer are always protesting abhorrence of the accursed thing. He hates the taste of it; he much prefers candy and buttermilk. He hates the effects of it. He is horrified by the results of it—and he drinks furiously. Again, in his own words:

> "I have not only been drunk, beastly, hopelessly drunk, unnumbered times, but once I was drunk for three weeks on end. I mean, literally, that I did not draw one single, sober breath for 21 days and nights."

Having tired of oyster piracy, he became a "fish patrol", the keeper instead of the poacher of the waters. Then he went on a sealing ship, and had a spirited discussion with one of the older seamen.

> "Suddenly boiling over, the incensed giant let go the coffee-pot he was carrying and gave the boy a back-handed blow across the mouth. Like a flash Jack landed on the other's eye, dodged the return swing of the sledge-hammer fists, and the combat was on. . . . With that cat-like swiftness he later described in his "Sea Wolf", Jack had outflanked the foe and sprung upon his shoulders, where he clasped powerful short legs in a strangle-hold about the roaring bull-throat, while his fingers sought eyes and windpipe of the confounded, raging brute under him. The only recourse left the Swede was main strength, which he used, perhaps by

> mere instinct, in butting his captor against the deck beams. This inflicted bloody and painful damage to the young tiger's scalp and crouched shoulders. But those excruciating pointed digits in larynx and eye-sockets settled the issue, and the tormented viking was forced to give in."

A very pretty irregular kind of warfare, as Dugald Dalgetty said of the Highland bowmen.

Well, the sealing boat touched at the Bonin Islands off Japan, where Jack, loathing alcohol more and more fiercely, indulged in a "jag" on "rot gut" and sake. At Yokohama "all we saw of Japan was its drinking places, where sailors congregated". On board of another American ship Jack drank a pint of malt whisky at a draught. But this was merely because he did not know what the bottle of water on the table was for.

Sealing was succeeded by work at a jute mill, at coal shovelling, by a little experience of the "hobo" life, with its perilous stolen journeys underneath the cars, and on top of the cars, and between the cars. Then to High School and the University, to Klondike, and finally into literature.

In this last pursuit he achieved an enormous success: it will be for time to say whether, in the American idiom, he "delivered the goods".

Le Morte Darthur

The Noble and Joyeus Boke, Entytled Le Morte Darthur. "The Shakespeare Head Press Malory." (Basil Blackwell, Oxford. Set of Two Volumes, Nine Guineas.)

The wise are wary in dealing in superlatives. It may be due to the Fall, as Mr. G. K. Chesterton (I think) would say; but it is dangerous to predicate perfection of any mortal work. But, bearing this in mind, I must say that I think the "Shakespeare Head Press Malory" is very nearly perfect. The sumptuous paper, that is thick enough to be rich, and not too thick for comfortable handling, the pure and clear font, the balance of the page, with its nicely observed proportion of text and margin, the fine rubrication, the "colore di fiamma" of the binding: all seem to me of the best and choicest. It has all the reverence and devotion of a Missal, and such a show is well fitting for this rare old book, which represents for Englishmen one of the noblest legends of the world. The romances of King Arthur and the Round Table, of Lancelot and Guinevere, of Percival and Galahad, and of the Holy Grail were first written in the French of the twelfth and thirteenth centuries. For the France of to-day, these romances are literary and antiquarian curiosities; the preserve, or almost, of experts, and matter for discussion and argument of the intensest interest—to experts. But so far as I am aware, the matter of the romances has hardly entered at all into the literary life-blood of France. The tales have not been made of the general consciousness. The modern French writer does not feel them even vaguely in the background of his dreams. To him, the Percival and the Merlin, the Quests and the Grand Saint Graal are no more present than the poems of Cædmon to an English novelist.

It is our good fortune that, through the blest work of Sir Thomas Malory, King Arthur and the Holy Grail, Sir Lancelot and Queen

Guinevere have been children's books and grown-up books, too, for the last four hundred years. It is true that Roger Ascham cursed Malory, but God before cursed him. Malory and all the legends he collected and collated are part of the living substance of English literature. With better fortune Tennyson might have renewed their life in a modern epic—though it seems hard to believe in the possibility of a modern epic. He began well with the fragment "Morte d'Arthur", but then, towards the middle of his life, some faintly scented delicate breath from vicarage drawing-rooms swooped upon him, and he mingled the decorous image of the Prince Consort with the vision of King Arthur, and all was lost. Indeed, he said himself that he meant the Order of the Knights of the Round Table to symbolise Liberal institutions. After which, there is, clearly, nothing to be said.

The chief consequence, then, of this new-old story of King Arthur and his Knights and the Grail is the fact that it is one of the greatest stories in the world, and that it is part of our literary consciousness. But that granted, I am free to aver that I quite appreciate its other aspect, as a golden quarry of research and argument and learned dreams. To catalogue the various theories that have been formed, merely glancing at each one in passing, is in itself a rich entertainment. Old Rossetti, the Italian exile, father of Dante Gabriel, held that all the romances of chivalry were elaborate allegorical treatises against the Pope. According to this school, when you read in your romance book of a Distressed Damosel, you are to understand that she symbolises the hidden church of the true believers, which turns out on examination to be the Albigensian sect—and though the Albigenses were savagely persecuted they were not really nice or wise people. Then, Wolfram von Eschenbach, author of the *Parzival,* speaks of the Knights of the Grail Castle as "Templesiens". This was enough and more than enough for another set of researchers, who forthwith made the romances a manifesto of the Order of the Temple, and incorporated all the tiresome twaddle that has been written about the Templars with their theory of the legend of the Grail. A more modern author, Miss Weston, expended vast and conscientious labour in proving, as she thought, that the Grail legends and tales were built upon the ritual of a Gnostic sect, which had persisted in Wales up to the eleventh century. She found also traces of sexual symbolism and of a Fertility mythos. Still later, a gentleman whose name I do not recollect, has derived the whole cycle from the Greek mythology. And a favourite sport has been, and still is, to regard all the Christian and sacramental elements in the romances as impertinent excrescences on a pagan Irish story about a miraculous feeding bowl.

And, in a way, all these vanities and vexations are but tributes to the splendour and the majesty of the text whereon they comment. It is the mark of a great book to have a wilderness of ardent and ingenious nonsense written about it.

The judicious booklover now has his Malory complete. All that remains for him to do is to choose some suitable moated grange as a habitation for this wonderful book in its sumptuous edition.

In a brief notice of the first volume, I indicated some aspects of the problem of the Arthurian legend and its origin. It must be said that, after all the exertions of the learned and ingenious, the problem remains unsolved, and, in all probability, unsolvable. The raw material was, undoubtedly, of the Celtic stock. It is clear, also, that the Anglo-Norman poets and romance writers did not receive it as a compact and coherent legend, which only required to be translated into French. Rather, they received an incoherent mass of legends; some British or Welsh, some Irish, and some, no doubt, of mixed origin. There was an element, and a strong one, of pagan folklore; there was another element of ecclesiastical legend and legendary history. Chrétien de Troyes left his tale unfinished, and though he mentions the Grail, we do not know in what sense he used the word, or what powers he assigned to the vessel. On the other hand, Borron, writing soon after Chrétien, tells what is, practically, a missionary story of the evangelisation of Britain. Every country wished to trace back its Christianity to an apostolic, or at least, a scriptural origin. Borron fixed on St. Joseph of Arimathea as the Apostle of the Britons; and it is interesting to compare his legend with the parallel Provençal story of the Saintes Maries de la mer. Borron, no doubt, had heard of what we may call the folklore Grail, the magic feeding vessel of the pagans. But with him, the Grail is wholly sanctified. It provides a feast, it is true, but the feast consists only of a fish, and those familiar with the Ichthus symbolism will know what is implied.

These two poems, one by Chrétien, the other by Borron, are the earliest examples of the Anglo-Norman cycle of the Grail. It is likely enough, though it cannot be certain, that Chrétien set out to retell the old story of Percival, his Exile, Return, and Vengeance—a majestic variant of the tale of the Ugly Duckling—without thought of any special Christian significance in his story or in the Grail vessel which he barely mentions. Borron, on the other hand, has not heard of Percival, and writes his missionary narrative rather in the mariner of a monk engaged to enrich the Legendarium of his monastery.

Between these two extremes the Romances move, mingling the two motives, Christian and Pagan; but resolving them at last into the great mystery of the book of Galahad; a romance of the very heart of the Faith.

Poet and–Cockney

Keats, the Despised Immortal

In the eighties of the eighteenth century there was a prosperous livery stable in Moorfields, which we now call Finsbury. The address was 28, The Pavement, and the business was carried on under the sign of the Swan and Hare. John Jennings was the name of the proprietor.

To John Jennings came a boy of unknown origin called Thomas Keats. He not only lacked a pedigree of the simplest kind—nothing is known either of his father or of his mother—but the place of his birth is uncertain. It was somewhere in the west; it was either Devonshire or Cornwall.

Thomas Keats entered Mr. Jennings's service as a stable-boy. He did well; and at twenty he had risen to be head ostler. And soon afterwards he married his employer's daughter, Frances Jennings. To this couple was born in he year 1795 John Keats, a seven-months' child.

In due course young John went to a private school at Edmonton, where he received a decent, lower-middle-class education; an education distinctly below the level of the small grammar schools of the age. The curriculum included the ordinary English subjects, with, I suppose, a good deal of learning selected "pieces" of prose and poetry by heart, and elocutionary delivery of the same by the prize pupils. There was, it is supposed, a little, a very little, French and a little Latin, which went, if I remember rightly, as far as Virgil.

There were books for the boys who cared to read them. John Keats read everything he could lay hands on; he was especially fond of Lamprière's Classical Dictionary, with its stories of Jupiter, Venus, Apollo, the Nymphs, Pan and the Satyrs, and all the mythology of Greece and Rome.

John Keats, in fact, did the best he could with the tools that were given him. But at fifteen he was taken from school and apprenticed to a surgeon and apothecary. He did not much care for the work, but he applied himself to it, and studied seriously. Then he quarrelled with the doctor, and the indentures were cancelled by mutual consent. Keats began to write poetry; he got to know Leigh Hunt, and made other literaery and artistic friends.

He published three volumes: *Poems,* 1817; *Endymion,* 1818; and *Lamia, Isabella, The Eve of St. Agnes, and Other Poems,* 1820. These volumes were received with offensive personalities, vulgar abuse, and the extreme of literary contempt from all the exalted, learned, dignified, and academic quarters of the day. None of the critics who wrote the "reviews that counted"—to use our modern phrase—had a good word for the vulgar little Cockney apothecary.

Then Keats became consumptive. He also fell in love with an entirely commonplace, silly young woman who was very properly named Brawne. There was what is sometimes called "an understanding", a sort of an engagement between them, but Miss Brawne would dance a good deal and flirt a little with young officers, and so wrung John Keats's heart. There is one thing: if they had married, she would have broken that heart.

But the consumption grew worse and worse. It was thought that the climate of Italy might give Keats a chance. So his friend Severn, the painter, one of the best friends a man ever had, took the poor poet to Italy in the sailing brig *Maria Crowther.*

This was in November, 1820. Keats plucked up in body and spirit for a while. Like a good poet and a man of good sense, he threw the bad dinner that the Roman cookshop sent in in tin dishes out of the window, tin by tin. But the relapse came, and on February 23, 1821, John Keats, the despised, the immortal, died as to his body in the arms of his friend.

Nobody cared: nobody that wrote reviews that "counted". Shelley wrote his lament, *Adonais,* in Keats's memory. *But it was almost thirty years before the people who "counted" knew that John Keats was one of the very greatest of the English poets.*

And now, a hundred years later, the whole world praises him. The house in the Hampstead byeway—still peaceful, still remote from the roaring and the rumour of these late, unquiet years—this house with the old garden where Keats listened to the nightingale—is not to be turned over to the speculative builder or to be supplanted by a monstrous, raw, red barrack of terrifying and penal aspect, known as "flats". The house is to be preserved for ever, in pious memory of "Mr. John" who was advised to go back to his gallipots. And here comes a noble book, issued by the Keats House Committee: *The John Keats Memorial Volume* (John Lane), all in honour of the little valiant man—he "bashed" a Hampstead butcher in his day—who knew not a word of Greek: and yet knew more Greek than all the Classical Tutors, the Classical Fellows, and the Classical Professors who have been since the foundation of Dondom.

All the great names acclaim him now.

Introduction to *A Handy Dickens*

"Dickens? Dickens is next to Shakespeare."

Thus spoke the late Sir J. M. Barrie, in colloquy with that amiable American, Professor "Billy" Phelps of Yale University. And, upon my word, I don't see how you could sum up Charles Dickens in a better phrase.

It is, of course, an accidental rather than an essential definition. It does not tell us what Dickens was. It does tell us his place in the great roll of letters. And the only alternative to Barrie's sentence seems to be the writing of a tome on the whole work of Dickens. And this is not the place for such a huge exercise. But there are one or two points that may be considered.

The common charge against our author is, I suppose, that he exaggerated and caricatured his characters. Hence, it was urged, they are not lifelike. Nobody had ever met or would ever meet anybody like his Micawber, or Mrs. Gamp, or Quilp, or Cheeryble Brothers, or Mr. Pecksniff, or any of that marvellous company. Again: they are not characters but caricatures. Well; this is a very minor point, a small jotting by the way: but have you ever noted that a really good caricature is vitally and essentially much more like the true man than his portrait in the Academy? The caricature often presents the essence, the vital significance of the man; the portrait often conceals it, and sometimes falsifies it.

But this, as I remarked, is by the way. I believe the real error in the talk about caricature and exaggeration lies in a misunderstanding of Aristotle's dictum, that art is imitation. It is an old misunderstanding. Plato may be said to have misunderstood the definition of Aristotle before Aristotle uttered it. Plato said that the man who painted a bit and bridle in his picture was a vastly inferior person to the gentleman who gave the order to the smith and the saddler to make him a bit and bridle; inferior also to the two artisans who carried out the order. Knight, and smith, and saddler understood about bits and bridles; the painter understood nothing at all about them; he merely made a likeness of them in his pigments. But the more vivid example of this ancient misunderstanding is in the tale of the painter who was so great an artist that when he painted grapes, the birds came and pecked them. I do not know that there is any record of a visitor to the National Gallery trying to climb one of Turner's hills, or of a sculptor's friend whispering soft nothings in the marble ear of Venus in the studio. But when we talk of literature, something of the old false attitude survives. I think I have read, and read more than once in book reviews the sentences: "This is not art. This is life", and the critic supposes that so saying he praises the book. The countryman at Madame Tussaud's, according to the legend, was apt to ask the waxen policeman the way to the Chamber of Horrors; the figure was so lifelike. So, early on a rather dim London morning, riding on the top of a bus, and peering ahead, I noticed an assistant looking at a group of figures in the window of some big shop. As we passed, I found that the supposed assistant was but another dummy. Art deals in illusion, but not delusion, and we are not to conclude that the maker of the assistant-dummy was a great artist. Aristotle, who gave his definition of art as imitation, was thinking of the Greek drama; and he knew full well that he would never meet Œdipus, or the Furies, or anyone like them in the Athenian streets. He knew also that, off the stage, no one chatted in iambics.

As with Œdipus, so with Micawber and the rest of them. We have never met them, and we never shall meet them; though we often pay an unconscious tribute to their artistic reality by saying of one: "He's just like Micawber"; of another: "He reminds me strongly of Dick Swiveller"; of a third: "Mrs. Gamp come to life." As if these fictions of Dickens's creation were living beings; and we, the living creatures, were copies and imitations of his dreams. We touch Plato again, and this time to happier issues. "A regular Pecksniff", we say of some florid professor of virtues which he does not possess; and so saying, we make Mr. Pecksniff the Archtypal Hypocrite, to which our friend imperfectly conforms; the Platonic Idea of the hypocrite.

I once met a man from Sheffield, and being always willing to consult experts and authorities, I asked him if he would tell me what steel was. He considered a little, and then said: "Steel is iron after its impurities have been removed." So, perhaps, with these alleged caricatures who walk and live in the world of Dickens: they are the very steel of humanity, purged of its impurities, its insignificances; evident, bright, and shining; while we, who think ourselves real, are only actual; the dull and obscure iron, without form or light. Nature (said a Quarterly Reviewer) had a certain Idea in her mind. She tried to realise this idea in Socrates, she tried again, and we had Dr. Johnson. Then Dickens, as he so modestly and simply expresses it, "thought of Mr. Pickwick". Nature was satisfied; her idea was fulfilled, in the spirit if not in the flesh.

As I was saying just now, we speak of these Dickens characters as if they were the real glowing and living people, while the actual men and women that we know or know of are more or less shadowy and misty reflections of them. Yet it remains true that, as the sourer critics say, the Dickens people are like nothing on earth. This is true; I acknowledge and I reaffirm its veracity. But, if we come to think of it, I believe that we shall find that this unearthly quality is shared by many of the greatest figures of romance. Aristotle, we have noted, who held that art was imitative, never expected to meet an Œdipus or a Chorus of Furies; but do we expect to meet Ulysses, or Sir Galahad, or Don Quixote, or Sir John Falstaff? We may meet Quixotic men, we may know one or two fellow-mortals who may be called Falstaffian: but these, we readily acknowledge, are but shadowy imperfect copies of the great originals, who remain and ever will remain like nothing on earth. Charles Dickens may rest well content; if in this particular he errs, he errs with Sophocles and Homer, with the twelfth-century authors of Arthurian Romance, with Cervantes and Shakespeare.

And that last name reminds us that some of the greatest men of letters have suffered in a way from which their lesser brethren are free. To cite another name on our list of Immortals: it was discovered a very long time ago that even Homer sometimes falls below his high standard: *aliquando bonus dormitat Homerus.* This, That, and T'Other, on the other hand, elegant authors of *vers de société,* never fall short of perfect point and elegance, in matter as in form. And so with Shakespeare: he was a man, we know, of the highest genius—but he was also a theatre playwright. He had to rewrite the old play founded on the older legend of the ninth-century Prince of Denmark, to bring the ancient story up to date, to turn Amleth into Hamlet, a rough Viking warrior into a cultured gentleman of the Renaissance—and yet, whatever happened, to keep in the Ghost. I suppose the Management was convinced that the Pit would never suffer the Play of Hamlet without the Ghost. Well; there was Shakespeare's task, and he achieved it, and produced the greatest of all tragedies. And yet, there are evidences, I think, which shew that the task was an uneasy one; that there were great difficulties in running the ancient legend into the mould of a modern play. Take, for example, this matter of the Ghost. The more enlightened Renaissance didn't believe in ghosts. It didn't believe in fairies—see Sir John Falstaff in *The Merry Wives of Windsor.* It was inclined to doubt whether life were worth living; in a word, it was profoundly agnostic. And so Renaissance Hamlet has to speak of the undiscovered country, from whose bourn no traveller returns, though Viking Hamlet has seen his father's ghost, has listened to the spirit's story, and means to act on it.

It was clearly a difficult and a delicate labour that Shakespeare undertook; this mingling of the Norseman, of wild and dark and ancient days, with the polished courtier of the sophisticated Renaissance world.

And Dickens, too, had at times a thorny and a troubled path to tread, though his difficulties were of a very different sort from those of Shakespeare. Alike in this sense, it is true, that both writers stood between two worlds. But with Shakespeare, the trouble was purely external; he had, somehow, to make his wild man of Dark Denmark into a modern Elizabethan gentleman, and yet give the latter the adventures of the former. With Dickens, the contest was internal. The central fire within him was pure and primitive romance; but "things" and the world being as they were in the 'thirties and 'forties of the last century, and Dickens's circumstances and upbringing in Camden Town, Somers Town, Lant Street, Borough, and the Marshalsea being what *they* were: why, there was nothing for it but to write novels. And the novel had its conventions; and one of them was that the chief interest must centre about a hero and a heroine. It is true that in the later 'forties *Vanity Fair* was announced by the author as a novel without a hero—Thackeray, you see, felt that he was perpetrating something strange and new—but Dickens neither would nor could have followed any track laid out by Thackeray.

There it was, then. There was no vehicle, no medium for the exhibition of the pure romance that was the mainspring of his creative life save the modern novel, and so he wrote it. Sometimes he wrote it magnificently. Is there anything in English fiction that can compare with the early chapters of *David Copperfield?* Sometimes, the results are piteous; take the terrible case of the loves of Esther Summerson and Dr. Woodcourt; consider the dull, lifeless propriety of Clennam, as the hero of *Little Dorrit,* the book with a plot which nobody can remember, which, anyhow, doesn't matter. Of course, even in such bad cases as these, there are splendid things. In *Bleak House,* infested as it is by mock-modest Esther, there is a wonderful Fog, which has rightly aroused the admiration of M. Maurois, there is the malignant grotesquerie of old Smallweed and his family, there is the gargoyle Krook with his burning death, there is the madness and the pathos of Miss Flite, there is the dinner at the Slap-Bang. As to *Little Dorrit,* the "lead", to use the actors' phrase, must be divided between Flora and Mr. F.'s Aunt; and their price is beyond rubies. And let not the Marshalsea Prison be forgotten. The actual Marshalsea was, no doubt of it, a foul hole of misery and semi-starvation, punctuated by poisonous stenches beyond the nightmares of any Sanitary Inspector. Mr. Bryant, in his *English Saga,* has told us that in those Dickens days, there were fifty cesspools under Windsor Castle, and that Queen Victoria's apartment at Buckingham Palace was ventilated through the main sewer. The thick stink of the Marshalsea must have ascended to the stratosphere.

And yet, in Dickens, the Marshalsea Prison is a great adventure. We love to read of it; an enchantment is laid upon it. So, in the old romances, we read of the valley of the Deadly Pool, where the rocks above grin like demons, and the black twisted trees are the outward shape and manifestation of spiritual wickedness, and that which is below the dark water begins to heave up and rise as the Knight goes down into the valley. So we read, or—perhaps, it might be more just to say—our fathers in the old time read all this with a mingling of terror and delight. This, perhaps, is not a bad instance of what I have called the central fire of pure and primitive romance which was the heart of Dickens. He falsifies nothing, he doesn't make-believe. Here is the Marshalsea Prison, as painted by Mrs. Bangham, the prison messenger and general odd-job woman. The scene is the birth of Little Dorrit, in which Mrs. Bangham officiates in the character of midwife.

"'The flies trouble you, don't they, my dear?' said Mrs. Bangham. 'But p'raps they'll take your mind off it, and do you good. What between the buryin' ground, the grocer's, the waggon-stables and the paunch trade, the Marshalsea flies gets very large. P'raps they're sent as a consolation, if we only know'd it. How are you now, my dear? No better? No, my dear, it ain't to be expected; you'll be worse before you're better, and you know it, don't you? Yes. That's right! And to think of a sweet little cherub being born inside the lock! Now ain't it pretty, ain't *that* something to carry you through it pleasant? Why, we ain't had such a thing happen here, my dear, not for I couldn't name the time when. And you a-crying too?' said Mrs. Bangham, to rally the patient more and more. 'You! making yourself so famous! With the flies a-falling into the gallipots by fifties! And everything a-going on so well! And here if there ain't,' said Mrs. Bangham as the door opened, 'if there ain't your dear gentleman along with Dr. Haggage! And now indeed we *are* complete, I *think!*'"

Dr. Haggage is described as a medical scarecrow; very dirty, very drunk. It is all as greasy and grimy, as squalid and deplorable as may be: and yet as I say: the Marshalsea in Dickens becomes the Adventure of the Marshalsea.

And so with *The Old Curiosity Shop,* a book full of wonderful scenes and wonderful characters who live in the light of that pure romance of which we have spoken: Dick Swiveller, Sampson Brass and Sally Brass, Mrs. Jarley and the other wandering showmen, the Marchioness, and above all, that creature who is intensely humorous but hardly human: Quilp. He, it is clear, was once an inhabitant of some great and magical cathedral of the thirteenth century; it is possible, indeed, that he had confabulated with the Lincoln Imp, and with him had driven flocks of gargoyles through the dreams of sick men. Somehow, he had escaped from his stony prison, and appeared in a fog, rising out of the mud of the Thames, where Dickens found him. And yet, to read of all these wonders and terrors and delights, Little Nell and the Grandfather must be endured; for if you leave them, you will fail to meet Mrs. Jarley, and Codlin and Short, the Punch and Judy men, and Jerry with his dogs, and the talk of retired Giants and Dwarfs, living in a house in Spa Fields. And Little Nell and the Grandfather are worse than Clennam.

He is so flat and dull that he fades readily from the view of the reader; but the pathos of these two, the doited old man and the tedious child, is insistent, irritating, maudlin, inescapable. Yet, read the chapter I have chosen concerning the passing of Quilp, read of the haunted streets of London withdrawn into the darkness of the fog, of the black river that flows hidden beneath it, hear the cries of the lost bargemen on the invisible waters; and see a city translated into the very mystery of terror.

So, in one way or another, Dickens had to compromise in most of his books, and with varying success, in his mingling of the two elements. In one of them, he found a solution of his problem which I think is very nearly satisfactory. In *Nicholas Nickleby* he does not attempt to give his hero and heroine individuality or character. As in the old romances, the hero is brave, virtuous, and victorious, while the heroine, also virtuous, is fair beyond comparison, persecuted by evil enchanters and caitiffs, but delivered from all evils by the hero: so Nicholas and Madeleine play their old parts in a modern scene. The lady is beauty in distress, the young man is her appointed lover, rescuer, and husband, and that is all we know about them, or want to know. Andrew Lang tells of a friend who observed that Ralph Nickleby was "too steep for him". He was judging the book as a novel, and he no doubt meant to imply that Nicholas's uncle was too villainous to be probable or even tolerable. And, no doubt, from the standpoint of the modern novel, Andrew Lang's friend was quite right; and yet, if Ralph had been made into an ordinary, though somewhat malignant, money-lender, who had taken a very decided dislike to his nephew; it is quite clear that he would have been a blot on the book. For all the purposes of the scheme of *Nicholas Nickleby,* Ralph is a Wicked Enchanter, and as any student of the Romances of Chivalry will tell us, Wicked Enchanters never relax from their unholy and malignant activities. All their hours are office hours. And so, as I say, *Nicholas Nickleby*—which every good man must love with few reserves—represents a successful solution of the problem which confronted Dickens all his life. Another success is *Great Expectations.* In this there is not the breathless excitement of *Nicholas Nickleby,* the continual sense of adventure that the earlier book affords; but the tale of Pip has its own sure magic, though its enchantments are uttered in quieter tones. But *Pickwick* is the one book where there was no problem to be solved, no difficult adjustments to be made, no need to weave into the story you wanted to tell fragments of the story which your readers and the rules and conventions of the chosen form demanded. Mr. Pickwick was a retired man of business, who had wound up his affairs in the year 1827: but he is of the race of Ulysses. As the book begins, Mr. Pickwick finds out his real business, which is to go on and on, continually encountering strange scenes and strange adventures; at every turn of the road he finds some new thing.

Ulysses? No doubt, ultimately; but naturally Dickens drew from a source nearer to his own day; in the letter that is, not the spirit. The immediate stimulus which lay behind *Pickwick* and also *Nicholas Nickleby* was, no doubt, Smollett's *Roderick Random,* which had enchanted his early boyhood. Then, as he confesses in one of the *Uncommercial Traveller* papers, in those young days he had believed Roderick "to be no ruffian, but an ingenuous and engaging hero". Roderick Random, no doubt, appeared in his true character in later readings: still, it was he who made Mr. Pickwick acquainted with Mr. Dowler, the boastful coward—it was an ensign, I think, who hid in the straw of the waggon, when there was a false report of a highwayman on the Great North Road. Roderick, again, contrived the affair of the middle-aged lady and the mistaken bedroom at the Great White Horse at Ipswich: a comic but most decorous version of some of his own disreputable adventures. Roderick ordered Mr. Pickwick to Bath and procured his imprisonment in the Fleet: and there, one may say, his office and influence ended. There was a hardness and a cruelty in Smollett which neither he nor any man could pass on to the compassionate Dickens: the traces of these evil things which appear in some of the tales in *Sketches by Boz* are mere boyish imitation. There is but one flicker of the old unkindness in *Pickwick:* the passing sneers at Mr. Wardle's Poor Relations.

I would not dare to say that *Pickwick* is the best Dickens; there are finer things in *David Copperfield.* But it is the most faultless Dickens: the one book which he wrote without compromise, without the necessity of complying with the accepted conventions of the novel. As he said, he thought of Mr. Pickwick, and that thought excluded the entrance of those dull and disastrous Esther Summersons, Woodcourts, Clennams, Little Nells, and Grandfathers who work such sad mischief in their several places. And the thought of Mr. Pickwick and his adventures did more: it excluded the necessity of a plot; one might say that it was definitely contracted between Dickens and his publishers that there should be no plot. In all the books that were to follow, a plot was a necessity of the case, save only in *David Copperfield*, the best of them all. In that book, there is no contrived plot, though there is a story. And though Dickens could sometimes contrive an ingenious and elaborate plot—see *Bleak House*—it was not his real business, and, at its best, was always the work of Dickens the artificer, never of Dickens the artist. And then, there are cases in which the plot is very bad indeed: *Oliver Twist* and *Martin Chuzzlewit* are instances of these unhappy fables. The only thing to be done with them is to forget them: to think hard of Fagin, Bill Sikes, and the Artful Dodger in the one book; of Pecksniff, Mrs. Gamp, and Mrs. Todgers in the other.

"He is next to Shakespeare," said Sir J. M. Barrie. It is true; and at one point, in the celestial tent where the Immortals notch, the score is in favour of Dickens. On the whole, Shakespeare saw the world sadly: on the whole, Dickens saw it gladly. In the first of the selections which follow, we have the picture of "a dark, dull, murky winter's night" with a heavy, lazy mist in the air, and a slimy moisture on the pavement. It is a mean little street, of mean little houses; a wretched picture enough. But the muffin boy comes down the street, ringing his cheerful clamorous bell; and Mrs. Walker, and Mrs. Peplow, and Mrs. Macklin throw open their doors; and there is a talk of the "kittle just a-biling, and the cups and saucers ready laid". One divines fires blazing in the little grates—with hobs, I think—of the little parlours, and a genial glow, and cheerfulness over such small blessings as "a nice hot comfortable cup o' tea". Indeed, the end of the evening, when the nine o'clock "beer" comes round with a lantern in front of his tray, and hands Mrs. Walker "Yesterday's 'Tiser", is rendered all the more cheerful by the potboy's remark: that he's blessed if he can hardly hold the pot, much less feel the paper, for it's one of the bitterest nights he ever felt, 'cept the night when the man was frozen to death in the Brick-field.

At this, be sure, Mr. Walker, who had walked home from his work at the Docks through the dirty, chilling streets, poked the little fire into a renewed blaze; and Mr. and Mrs. Walker drank their supper beer with a keener relish.

This passage, which I dare say many English lovers of Dickens have never noted, is selected by M. André Maurois as of high significance in the consideration of our author's work. Indeed, it gives the key to much that is most precious in the writings of Dickens. I can well imagine that there are not a few who find the symbolism of a dark and bitter night contrasted with a nice hot comfortable cup o' tea poor and contemptible enough. So far as these unhappy persons are concerned, I am afraid that we must adopt the phrase and attitude of Miss Fanny Squeers: pity their ignorance—of spiritual things—and despise them.

Dickens saw the world gladly, and, therefore, he saw it wisely. He knew that the great everlasting book has a happy ending.

Mieulx vault de ris que de larmes escripre, parceque le ris c'est le propre de l'homme.

And with Dickens, as with the waves of Homer's sea, there is laughter beyond all measure.

V. Fantasy, Horror, and the Occult

Review of *The War of the Worlds* by H. G. Wells

Schiller," said Coleridge, "has the material sublime; to produce an effect, he sets you a whole town on fire, and throws infants with their mothers into the flames. . . . But Shakespeare drops a handkerchief, and the same or greater effects follow."

It is evident that Mr. Wells has thrown in his lot with Schiller, and one is sorry, since *The Time Machine* gave promise of far higher things. That wonderful "Time Machine" was, it is true, a mechanical and material contrivance, not unlike a bicycle in shape, but the conception of it was purely metaphysical, and the main idea of the story would have interested Berkeley and Kant. Hence, one hoped that Mr. Wells had thoroughly grasped the essential and necessary truth that it is the things of the mind, of the soul, that are alone really wonderful; that the achievements of the hand and the inventions of the laboratory, however well described, are fundamentally unimportant in imaginative literature. *The Time Machine* had a splendid and original idea underlying its mechanism, and we hoped that the author would ride very far, that he would one day cry:—

With a heart of furious fancies,
　　Whereof I am commander:
　　　　With a burning spear,
　　　　And a horse of air,
To the wilderness I wander:
With a Knight of ghosts and shadows,
　　I summoned am to Tourney:
　　　　Ten leagues beyond
　　　　The wide world's end:
Methinks it is no journey.

There can be no doubt that if Mr. Wells had chosen he could have discovered a new world for romance; he had only to look less and less into his test-tubes and crucibles, to forget by degree all the wisdom of Gower-street, to think lightly of electricity, and to scoff at the Röntgen rays, and in place of peering through the microscope to peer into the soul of man. Tennyson wrote with true instinct—

> Tho' world on world in myriad myriads roll
> Round us, each with different powers,
> And other forms of life than ours
> What know we greater than the soul?

But Mr. Wells has convinced himself that the stars are greater than the soul, and, by consequence, we have *The War of the Worlds,* which relates the story of England invaded by Martians, burnt, scorched, poisoned, and destroyed by the Handling-machine, the Fighting-machine, the Heat-ray, the rockets which discharged the Black Vapour. The Martians were made after this sort:—

> They were huge round bodies—or rather, heads—about four feet in diameter, each body having in front of it a face. This face had no nostrils—indeed, the Martians do not seem to have had any sense of smell—but it had a pair of very large, dark-coloured eyes, and just beneath this a kind of fleshy beak. In the back of this head or body . . . was the single tight tympanic surface, since known to be anatomically an ear, though it must have been almost useless in our denser air. In a group round the mouth were sixteen slender, almost whip-like tentacles, arranged in two bunches of eight each. These bunches have since been named, rather aptly, by that distinguished anatomist, Professor Howes, the *hands.*

And here is a perhaps more vivid, if less technical, description:—

> A big, grayish, round bulk, the size perhaps of a bear, was rising slowly and painfully out of the cylinder. As it bulged up and caught the light it glistened with wet leather. Two large, dark-coloured eyes were regarding me steadfastly. It was rounded, and had, one might say, a face. There was a mouth under the eyes, the lipless brim of which quivered and panted, and dropped saliva. . . . There was something fungoid in the oily, brown skin.

There are many pages of elaborate and careful writing, telling us how these octopus-like creatures made for themselves gigantic metal bodies, and dire machines such as the inhabitants of Erewhon shuddered at in Mr. Butler's famous satire. We read of vain attempts on the part of the English Army to withstand these armoured monsters, of whole parks of artillery consumed in a moment by the terrible heat ray, of London left desolate as Babylon. And, finally, the Martians are destroyed, skilfully and scientifically, and in death, as in life, they were punctilious in their observation of the laws of evolution.

But the laws of romance? We may say to Mr. Wells:—

> Let argon, helion, science crammers die,
> But leave us still our sense of mystery.

An impatient schoolmaster once remarked to a little boy who had failed in his arithmetic, "If you divide yards by feet you will get neither pigs, sheep, nor oxen." And in the same way Mr. Wells should understand that though he may add chemistry to physiology, and astronomy to bacteriology, he will never get romance. He may vie, indeed, with Jules Verne; but he has imagination, if he would use it, he has an excellent sense of style, he comprehends the art of dialogue, and with such qualities he should aim higher. *From the Earth to the Moon* was well enough—from Jules Verne—but we did not expect the author of *The Time Machine* to furnish us with a companion volume to the French masterpiece.

We have shewn that Mr. Wells does not understand the true nature of the wonderful, for he writes as if Mr. Edison were his ideal hero; but there is another emotion concerning which he holds totally mistaken ideas. He confuses the terrible with the disgusting; he follows the example set by Mr. Rudyard Kipling in his story of the horrible ape, rather than that real achievement in the terrible, "At the End of the Passage". He strives to make us realise the effect of the Martian heat-ray on the human body, he gives us the picture of a respectable citizen being sucked of his blood by the monster, and at the end we have "a dog with a piece of putrescent red meat in his jaws". There was the same fault in *The Island of Dr. Moreau,* in the murderous achievements of *The Invisible Man;* and the two sins of Mr. Wells, his "material sublime" and his "material horrible", both spring from the same source—his failure to recognise the axiom that the only wonder and the only terror are not in the material universe, but in the soul, the creator of the world as we know it.

Let it be said at the last that, though the idea of *The War of the Worlds* is unimpressive, the execution is admirable. Mr. Wells writes vigorous, unaffected English, he knows how a picture should be "bitten in" with a terse, decisive phrase, and he carries the reader on triumphantly through the stench and gore and the green smoke of the Martian furnace. The judicious will regret not so much that the book was written, as that the author of *The Time Machine* should have written it.

Science and the Ghost Story

Sir William Crookes' declarations at the meeting of the British Association on the subject of psychical research had a significance even greater than that which they have been generally recognised to have borne. They may be said perhaps to have marked time in the progress of the relations between science and "occultism". They did not really go much beyond a suggestion of some possible material explanation of all that is included under the term "telepathy", and an insistence upon a purely scientific and experimental study of similar strange phenomena. The necessity of such study most intelligent persons are now beginning to recognise, and this result is due to nothing so much as to the investigations of the Society for Psychical Research, of which Sir William is President. But his attitude illustrates a general change of feeling as to the whole range of subjects on which people have hitherto been either too sceptical or too credulous. Hardly anyone but a schoolgirl, or—so advanced are girls' high schools and their teachers—perhaps we should say a schoolboy in the fourth form, would now ask the question, "Do you believe in ghosts?" That belonged to the days when supernatural occurrences—or what appeared to be so—were only believed if they squared with one's own private ideas as to how a "supernatural" world should be conducted. "I believe in ghosts," people would say, "when they appear to save some one's life or to do some good." Evidence as to what a ghost did was of no weight at all compared with a hazy individual conception as to what it ought to do. This *a priori* method is becoming more and more discredited. The reply which the schoolboy would, or should, receive might be something like this:—"Belief in such a subject can only be based on a series of observations, extremely difficult to verify, which, so far as they have at present proceeded, hardly satisfy the canons of induction." And we should like to see the schoolboy's face when he heard the answer. What Sir William Crookes said of the study of the direct action of mind upon mind is true of the whole range of these mysterious phenomena:—

> This delicate task needs a rigorous employment of the method of exclusion—a constant setting aside of irrelevant phenomena that could be explained by known causes, including those far too familiar causes, conscious and unconscious fraud. The inquiry unites the difficulties inherent in all experimentation connected with mind, with tangled human temperaments, and with observations dependent less on automatic record than on personal testimony.

Hence it is that both on the scientific and popular sides only slow progress can be made. The President's Address at the British Association shews that science is making a serious advance into regions which the older psychologists knew nothing of, and it will also help to regulate men's notions as to what we still describe as "the supernatural". The tentative and transitional stage at which the subject stands has affected both scientific and other literature during the past year. There has been a good deal of psychological work bearing on it in America—some of which has been expounded in the Contemporary Science Series (Walter Scott)—notable Mr. Scripture's *New Psychology,* which we reviewed last November, and which dealt with the study described by the author as "Psycho-physics", or the application of experimental methods to the processes of the mind. In the same series came Mr. Parish's *Hallucinations and Illusions: A Study of the Fallacies of Perception* (Walter Scott), which we noticed in January. Another useful book bearing on the direct action of mind on mind is *The Elements of Hypnotism,* by Mr. R. H. Vincent (Kegan Paul), which has run to a second edition. A fresh chapter has been added on the *Physiology of Hypnotism,* in which is given the author's view of the relations of the various forms of nervous activity, a view which differs from the teaching of the accepted schools of physiological psychology. He classes the various kinds of nervous action under three heads. If the response to a stimulus be one which is "physical"—*i.e.,* giving no evidence of modification due to the external environment, he includes it in the elementary class of nervous action—the "inaptic". If the response be of such a nature as to shew that there has been a modification due to the environment of the moment, but without consciousness, it is "aptic". Responses which are associated with a conscious process form the third class. It will be noted that the differential elements vary from those usually put forward as the criteria of classification. The term "reflex" has been omitted, on the ground that reflex actions belong to all three classes. The author insists that a fundamental distinction exists between the inaptic and aptic classes of action, and cites some remarkable experiments which seem to support the theory that the essential qualities of a psychical process do not require the co-existence of consciousness. He admits that the classification is not a perfect one, but argues that it matters little as to the exact point at which we may deny or admit the interposition of an unconscious intelligence, so long as we recognise that amongst the functions of the nervous system one of the most important parts is played by this unconscious intelligence. Some valuable indications are given as to the method by which scientific investigation of the hypnotic phenomena may enable us to gain a more thorough appreciation of the processes employed in the execution of suggestions which are psychical in their nature, and a more definite state of knowledge as to the memory.

In Mr. Podmore's *Studies in Psychical Research* (Kegan Paul) one of the author's main objects was the exposure of spiritualism. Nothing has more wholly contravened the maxims of Sir W. Crookes quoted above than modern spiritualism. The representative spiritualistic book of the present year—and here we pass from scientific to wholly unscientific literature—was Mr. Stead's *Letters from Julia, a Light from the Borderland* (Grant Richards, 2s.). Here we have nothing of the old respectable "high priori" belief that spirits can only appear to do dignified and beneficial actions. But its place has not been occupied, as it is, we think, being occupied in the minds of most sensible people, by the inductive experimental habit. One must begin at the end. "Julia" has indicated to Mr. Stead a method by which soul may converse with soul, by which the dead and the living may hold parley together. It is a simple thing, this "Open Door to the Open Secret"; one has only to sit in a dark room and think of a friend, and presently he will appear, but this statement, "so precise, so positive, and yet so marvellous, seemed too astounding to be published even on the authority of 'Julia'". So Mr. Stead was puzzled, and his bewilderment has crystallised into an appendix. He dared not publish, he says, this astounding secret of "Julia's" on his own responsibility, but:

> In such matters I usually take counsel with Mrs. Besant, but Mrs. Besant is in the United States. I therefore sent proofs of the communication just as it was received to Mr. Leadbeater, to whom Mrs. Besant told me I could refer any question upon which I wanted advice in her absence.

It is one of the strange puzzles of "occult" imposture that the men of affairs, the shrewd "men of the world", are often the readiest victims. The philosopher, the metaphysician, laugh at "Mahatmas", at the clumsy conjuring, at all the second-rate Egyptian-hall exhibition. Those who have really studied the secret things of the human soul and the human will, who have listened to the clear voices of Plato and Berkeley discoursing of mysteries, are never to be found in the back-parlour sessions, where the spirit of Shakespeare speaks as a fool, where Milton has learnt the American accent, where all the holy and venerable and awful things of the Temple are trampled in the gutter of a London street. And the man of letters is almost as secure; even though he may believe nothing and care nothing for spiritual truth, yet this mere æsthetic sense preserves him from the charm of the "trance-medium"; he is enabled to say, *non credo, quia putidum.* The student of physical science is not always so safe; the gulf between the materialism of biology and the materialism of the medium is not unbridged, and often there are few steps between the laboratory and the séance.

But the "man of affairs" supplies the best soil for the growth of all the foolish and squalid beliefs which American and English dreamers have held and propagated. Our age, which has vulgarised everything, has not spared the unseen world, and superstition, which was once both terrible and picturesque, is now thoroughly "democratised". The seer and the prophet have been transformed into the medium and the *clairvoyante,* the Sabbath has become the séance, the demon has turned "spook". With awful prayers, with hushed supplications, with aspirations for purity of heart, they gazed of old time into the crystal, hoping to look into the eternal mirror of all things, into the immarcescible light. Now, in our days, some wretched woman, half-drunken, half-hysterical, glares at the grounds in the tea-cup, and gabbles her lesson to the half-educated inquirer.

It is lamentable to think that Mr. Stead should make himself responsible for these *Letters from Julia.* One cannot be surprised, for, as we have remarked, he belongs to the class which is often captured by the rudest "spiritual" traps. The shrewd civil servant, the enterprising journalist, the dabbler on the Stock Exchange, those who flatter themselves on their actuality, on their businesslike habits, seem utterly defenceless when there is any question of the intellectual and spiritual sphere; their appreciations of the wonderful are on a level with the opinions of an agricultural labourer as to the merits of an old Bordeaux. For there is no palliation possible in this case of "Julia" and her letters. One may search the book through for one dignified sentence, for one thought that transcends, not the known world, but the commonplace thoughts of commonplace people, and the quest will be utterly in vain. Look at this opening of the fifth chapter; it is "Julia" who speaks, and Mr. Stead answers her:—

> MY DEAREST FRIEND,—What am I now going to write is for *Borderland.*
>
> *I have not the ghost of an idea what it is to be about.*
>
> Oh, what an opportunity you have this year of making a memorable and permanent memento of the Queen's Jubilee!
>
> *Humph! Does the Jubilee interest you?*
>
> Yes, we are interested in this as in all that stirs the heart and moves the soul of man. We see what you are thinking, and we see what you are doing. And we see also what you ought to do if you would but use the opportunity aright.

And (we quote "Julia" again):—

> The Angel Guardian who came to me had wings, as I have said. It is not usual, but if we please we can assume them. . . . We think, and we are there. Why, then, wings? They are scenic illusions, &c.

And Julia wishes Mr. Stead to establish a "Bureau" or a "Bridge Bureau" of communication between this world and the next. And Julia preaches a flabby Unitarianism, a species of deliquescent Dissent, redolent of the atmosphere of Pleasant Sunday Afternoons; she alludes gracefully to conjugal relations, in the best manner of the quack doctor's book of America; and she wishes to see the Rosary modernised, brought up to date. And we laugh at the credulity of the Middle Ages!

In the thirteenth century Dante saw the Angelic Rose in Paradise; in the nineteenth century Mr. Stead receives the *Letters from Julia* by automatic writing.

It is a relief to pass to the old-fashioned ghost story which honestly scoffs at science and makes a candid appeal to romance. One remarkable fact strikes us at once and is perhaps due to the change in men's ideas on the subject of apparitions—viz., that the ghost story is much less *en évidence* than it was. One of the few good supernatural tales of recent months was Mrs. Oliphant's *Lady's Walk* (Methuen). As a rule, the novelist fights shy of it; the *raconteur* recognises that its vogue is past, and it finds but scanty refuge even in the "Christmas number". But here again, Mr. Stead rushes in where the *raconteur* fears to tread. That delightful book of our childhood, *Communications with the Unseen World,* has not, perhaps fortunately, had many imitators. But *Real Ghost Stories,* reprinted from the *Review* of *Reviews* (Grant Richards), will supply adequate matter for those who want to have their blood curdled or, like Mr. Wardle's Fat Boy, to curdle that of others. From the scientific point of view the book is very instructive. The spirit in which Mr. Stead entered upon his task may be gathered from the following remarkable passage in the introduction:—

> Of all the vulgar superstitions of the half-educated none dies harder than the absurd delusion that there is no such thing as ghosts. All the experts, whether spiritual, poetical, or scientific, and all the others, non-experts, who have bestowed any serious attention upon the subject know that they do exist.

That being so, of course there is nothing more to be said, though one confesses to a desire to hear the views of a "poetical" expert on ghosts. If Mr. Stead would have us take him seriously he should acquire a little wholesome science, and learn, among other things, the way in which sensory stimuli act suggestively on the process of false perception. A little course of logic, also, would not be amiss, as with the aid of logic we might eliminate such arguments as this, that inasmuch as there are at least as many persons who testify that they have seen apparitions as there are men of science who have examined microbes, therefore both are matters of testimony and not of personal experience. Mr. Stead claims to have treated ghosts scientifically, although he generally assumes what has to be proved, but apart from the manner in which the subject is presented the book has a certain scientific value. It is a collection of ghost stories, fairly representative, which shews the nature of the evidence upon which such stories too often rest, and the ignorance on the part of the narrators as to what constitutes evidence. It is interesting, also, to note the *naïveté* with which in many cases the narrator, all unconsciously, discloses the physiological genesis of the apparitions which he sees.

But we need hardly take such a book too seriously. Its interest lies in the curious exception which it presents to what we believe to be the trend of public opinion about ghost and supernatural phenomena generally. To readers of a literary journal perhaps a more interesting subject than either the new experimental psychology or the decline of the sensational ghost story is the literature of occultism proper, and to this we hope to recur.

Folklore and Legends of the North

The ideas of Aristotle became the fixed ideas of the Middle Ages. This was well enough in logic, but in physics it was a bar to all progress, and the poverty, or rather the nullity, of the mediæval chemistry and biology is the only excuse for the ignorant epithet "dark" applied to ages which contained some of the acutest thinkers that the world has ever seen. In sciences which are tentative and depend upon research and inquiry there must be no axioms, and no infallible pronouncements; if men of science had certainly believed that a deal board was impervious to light, we should never have seen the shadow-pictures of the unknown rays. This horror of the axiom is well established in the minds of those who deal with the sensible properties of matter, but when we cross the boundary and try to trace the secrets of the soul, we find ourselves at once in the intellectual atmosphere of the Aristotelian tyranny of the Middle Ages. The curious may study early consciousness, beliefs, and legends as deeply as they please—on the condition that they bear in mind the axiom that the unusual never happens, that the supernatural (or supernormal) does not exist, and never has existed.

Unfortunately, Mr. Léon Pineau, the author of the learned and entertaining *Les Vieux Chants Populaires Scandinaves* (Emile Bouillon, Paris, 10f.). has given in his fullest adhesion to this scientific dogma. The first *fasciculus* of the work, which is before us, has for its subject the Magical Songs of the "Époque Sauvage"; and the book, besides being a study in comparative literature, is also a history of Northern folklore, and more particularly of the stories of transformation. M. Pineau lays down the laws of the primordial consciousness in an elaborate preface. Here is his demonstration. In the beginning primitive man had one and only one object—the struggle for life. Those who fought against him in this struggle were other men—and animals. *Therefore,* he came to the conclusion that there was no distinction between animal and human consciousness, and he naturally called himself by the name of some animal. Hence arose the "tribe of the Wolfs", and hence, in process of time, totemism, the belief that this tribe was descended from a wolf. Indeed, the author has heard a farmer's wife in Touraine talking to her goat as if it could understand her; *therefore,* this belief of animal descent still exists. Later, man discovered that he had a "double", a soul, and so, of course, had animals, since animals and men are the same, and since for primitive man all things are animated, not only animals, but stars and rocks and winds have "doubles" also. Next, primitive man dreamed a dream; his double had gone abroad. No doubt animals and trees and the sun had similar experiences; *therefore,* there were wandering doubles everywhere, and by consequence a man might find himself turned into an animal. This, briefly, is the theory on which the author explains every song, every legend, and every belief that he encounters in his Scandinavian researches. Later, in the book, it is true, we find traces of "Sun myth", and "corruption of language"; but these are, in the phrase of the geologists, mere "traces", and the whole work is virtually founded on the above analysis of the primitive consciousness. It will be seen that M. Pineau inclines rather to the doctrine of Mr. Andrew Lang than to that of Mr. Herbert Spencer, since he apparently holds animism to be part of the original human thought, but we find no indication of Mr. Lang's fruitful suggestion that myths are the result of misunderstood ritual.

Now, although there are links in M. Pineau's chain of argument that seem weak, yet there is no doubt a good deal to be said for his position. It is possible that sometimes our early ancestor, having formed designs against a hare, found himself thwarted by a bear; it is possible that he argued from this that the bear was a creature of like passions with himself, capable of similar designs and of superior strategy.

But M. Pineau has only one explanation for the strange beliefs of early man—a series of hazardous deductions from uncertain premisses. Mr. Herbert Spencer tells us that primitive man came on earth sane, and without delusions of an animistic kind, but that afterwards he dreamed and entangled himself in a mesh of vain superstitions. Mr. Andrew Lang says that from the first man was an animist, and he thinks that a wild belief was strengthened by the occurrence of "hallucinations" of the dead and the living. One need hardly trouble to mention the good old teaching of the eighteenth century and the rationalists—that everything was invented by the art of crafty priests trading on the simplicity of a clear-headed and virtuous people; and, perhaps, the "sun myth" and the "corruption of language" theories are more extinct than the superstitions which they professed to elucidate.

But are any or all of these explanations adequate? Does anyone of them cover the whole field of legend and belief?

Let us take an example from the work of M. Pineau. He lays stress on the peculiar importance of the "runes" in Northern folklore: by runes and runic art all the marvels are achieved, by them the lover wins his mistress, by runic charms the ship is brought safe into the haven or overwhelmed by the storm, by runes the good sword kills, by runes the maiden becomes a deer amidst the woods. And the runes, it seems agreed, were the mystery of the dwarfs; again and again we meet the daughter of the dwarf-king by a Christian mother, who teaches her lover the magic art of those potent letters and words. M. Pineau, very properly, interprets these dwarfs to mean the aboriginal Turanian race which inhabited Europe before the coming of the Aryans, and passes on, without dwelling on the subject. But can we not get more out of the dwarfs? Every one is aware of the great part played by the fairies in old legend, and in spite of the "literary" fairy, the tricksy elf of Shakespeare, and the minor divinity, sometimes benevolent and sometimes maleficent, of Perrault, there yet survives in Ireland the older conception of the "good people", the "fair folk", who must be given a pleasant name precisely because they are evil. Of recent years abundant proof has been given that a short, non-Aryan race once dwelt beneath ground, in hillocks, throughout Europe, their raths have been explored, and the weird old tales of green hills all lighted up at night have received confirmation. Much in the old legends may be explained by a reference to this primitive race. The stories of changelings, and captive women, become clear on the supposition that the "fairies" occasionally raided the houses of the invaders. And M. Pineau, after saying that everything in Scandinavian folklore is effected by runes, admits that the runes came from the dwarves. We might deduce the whole mythology from a confused recollection of the relations existing between the tall Aryans and the short Turanians, but how fallacious such an explanation would be! No doubt the fairies count for something. The ballad of Sir Tœnne of Alsoe, for example, may very well be a poetical and decorated account of an event which really happened when the "good folk" inhabited the lonely rounded hillocks, and haunted the remotest recesses of the forest. One day, the song tells, Sir Tœnne went hunting in the woods, and there encountered the "daughter of the dwarf", surrounded by her maidens. She took her harp, and began to "play the runes".

> And the harp sang afar
> And the wild world of the wood was still
> And the bird upon the bough left his lay,
> And the little hawk high in the hedge
> Fluttered his feathers.
> The field grew fair with flowers,
> And bright the boughs with leaves,
> So strong sang the runes.
> Sir Tœnne spurred his steed,
> Yet he could not fare free.

The knight was obliged to follow the "dwarf" girl to the mountain (the fairy rath), where the "wife of the dwarf" tells him that she was born a Christian, and carried away by the dwarfs. To adopt the manner of the bard, the whole song may very well be sooth; such incidents may have often occurred in the early history of the Aryan invasion, and there are many of the old ballads and traditions which may be explained on similar grounds. But though all "magic" is worked by runes, and though the runes came from the fairies or "dwarfs", yet we must beware of making the "little people" responsible for all the marvels of story. M. Pineau forces the whole wonderland to rest on his somewhat doubtful argument as to the primitive consciousness; we must not let ourselves be entangled into following his example, and, above all, we must beware of M. Pineau's almost suppressed but all-pervading minor premiss—the supernormal never happens.

A large portion of the book deals with metamorphosis, with songs telling of how the princess was changed into a doe, how the wicked stepmother made her stepdaughter assume the form of a pair of scissors. That all such stories arose from the fact that primitive men, fighting with beasts, concluded that a beast and a man were the same thing, that after a few dreams they found out that not only all men but all beasts have doubles, and that not only beasts but all existence, from the sun to a sword, has its double, and therefore, since these "doubles" wandered away from their bodies, any one thing could be easily changed into any other thing appears to be an unthinkable proposition. We have said that the whole chain of argument seems so weak that, even if we allow M. Pineau's very doubtful deductions to stand good, there are many other factors which may have gone to the making of this curious superstition.

In the first place, "lycanthropy" is a fact of human nature. Men and women have actually been possessed by the belief that they are wolves or other animals, and they have, no doubt, acted on their delusion. In the old legends we are told that such a person was a woman by day and a wolf by night, and no doubt the "fit" which transformed the human being into a creature of blind ferocity, running on all fours, gnashing its teeth and tearing to pieces all whom it encountered, occurred when the darkness came on, at the hour in which all that is morbid in mind and body is strongest. The were-wolf, then, is not a superstition but a fact, and a fact which goes very far in clearing up the early belief in metamorphosis.

Secondly, the whole group of stories which deal with mermen, mermaids, Melusines, and "ladies from the sea" may be explained in a manner which renders our author's theory quite superfluous. Mr. J. Russell-Jeaffreson, the author of *The Faroe Islands* (Sampson Low, 7s. 6d.), relates the legend of a man who went sealing, and hid himself by the shore.

> In the morning the seals came up on to the rocks. But what was his surprise on their landing to see them slip out of their skins and assume the form of very beautiful damsels.

We know how the story must proceed. The fisherman, of course, catches one of the seal-maidens before she can put on her skin, and takes her home and marries her, and they become the parents of a large family. The skin is kept carefully locked up by the husband, but one day he leaves the key at home, and the seal-wife returns to her old shape and her beloved element. The legend has been told again and again, but Mr. Jeaffreson's tale has a touch of actuality that is new, inasmuch as he was assured that the descendants of the mermaid were alive and had webbing between their fingers. Now this legend, and all legends that resemble it, may be clearly traced to the sea-going Lapps, who, covered with seal-skins, drove their canoes through the stormiest waters and sometimes visited, not only the Faroe Islands, but the coasts of Scotland. The seal-skin, which covered the man or woman, was attached to the boat and kept out of the water, and without this protection the Lapp was helpless.

Thirdly, there can be no doubt that the collective memory of the human race is a very long one. At the present day, in quiet Somerset and Derbyshire villages, there are women who follow the same arts, and, on some matters, think the same thoughts as the sorceresses of antique Babylon. The readers of Mr. Elworthy's admirable book on the "Evil Eye" will remember the instances of modern witchcraft, and the account of the horrible objects which have been found within the last ten years, hidden in the chimney-corners of witches' cottages. The methods of sorcery have not changed, the clay images are made as they have always been made, and here is a memory that goes back at least 6,000 years. If, then, the people of our modern England, surrounded by every hostile influence, have remembered the black art of Babylon, what shall we say of the memory of early man? For no doubt the singers of these Northern songs worked on old materials—one song may be the product of a hundred revisions. The earliest men of whom we know anything were artists, and scratched pictures of the creatures they hunted on horn, and where there is the art of line, there will be the art of literature; consequently, the earliest form of any given song may probably have been chanted by Palæolithic poets. And who shall put a limit to the dim and remote antiquity of which these old makers knew by a still older tradition? Is it not possible, and, indeed, probable, that these earliest inventors had an inherited memory of a time when men had scarcely emerged from the company and state of the beasts, when individuals, here and there, fell out of the great march of evolution and lapsed into the low condition from which they had scarcely risen? Here, then, is another cause which in all likelihood influenced the belief in the possibility of a man becoming an animal. So far as we are aware, no legend tells that a beast became human; though if M. Pineau's theory were satisfactory we should expect to find many instances of reversed metamorphosis. A princess may turn into a swan, but a swan never becomes a princess.

Fourthly, there may be the influence of the human consciousness. We know what strange, almost incredible, tricks the mind of man can play on itself; how children (those eternal "primitives") can "make believe"; how an actor can for the moment change his personality, how a dreamer may lose all idea of self-consciousness, and become another person, and, more rarely, an inanimate object; how a lunatic accomplishes for himself the wildest transmutations in idea. The imagination of primitive man, luxuriant to extravagance, and almost wholly unrestrained, must have been capable of feats of which we can form but a poor and inadequate conception.

And, lastly, there is hypnotic suggestion, called witchcraft by our ancestors, and the primitive hypnotist is, no doubt, responsible for many of the metamorphoses which startled the early community. And after we have allowed for all the sources, there still remains the great question of Montaigne—What do we know? Every day thinkers are becoming more and more convinced of the absurdity of saying that anything is impossible, every day it becomes clearer that the universe and man are mysteries. The Marquis of Lorne in *Adventures in Legend* (Constable, 6s.) tells of a recent case of undoubted "second-sight", the scene of which was at Loch Awe, close to a hotel, crowded every summer by tourists. A young man was drowned a year or two ago in the loch, and his body could not be recovered. At last an old woman in Perthshire, who had never seen the loch, was consulted, and by her vision and description of the loch and the islands the mother of the drowned lad succeeded in an extraordinary manner in obtaining the body. In a recent number of the *National Review,* Dr. Herbert Coryn gives the case of the lady who saw a heavy window-sash fall on three of her child's fingers, cutting them off. After dressing the wounds the surgeon turned to the mother, whom he found moaning and complaining of pain in the hand. "Three fingers corresponding to those injured in the child were discovered to be swollen and inflamed. Purulent sloughing set in." So a mental impression can affect the tissues of the flesh; and what is this but magic? And if this be possible in our late civilisation, what might not have been possible in the far-off ages which moulded the human consciousness? Let M. Pineau consider again all this matter of legend and magic. He will find, we believe, many marvels which his philosophy cannot explain, which cannot for a moment be understood in the light of his crude hypothesis. And as the "worms" and "dragons" of the ancient songs, and the "roc" of the Arabian tales are doubtless memories of the iguanadons and plesiosauri and pterodactyls, so the wildest myth may prove to be founded on a, perhaps, wilder reality.

The Literature of Occultism

There is a sense, of course, in which all fine literature, both in prose and in verse, belongs to the region of things mysterious and occult. Formerly it might have been maintained that music was the purest of all the arts, that the shuddering and reverberant summons of the organ, the far, faint echo of a distant choir singing spoke clearly to the soul without the material impediment of a story, without that "body" which must clothe the spirit of pictures and sculptured forms, being as they are representatives of the visible things around us. But since Wagner came and conquered, music has become more and more an intellectual exercise, and to the modern musical critic every bar must be capable of interpretation, of an intelligible translation, if it is to be absolved in the judgment.

Since then music has frankly become a "mixed" art, a "criticism of life" in the medium of sound, we who try to understand literature may well insist that our fine prose and our fine poetry have a part in them, and that part the most precious, which is wholly super-intellectual, non-intelligible, occult. The lines of Keats, the "magic casements, opening on the foam Of perilous seas, in faery lands forlorn", will occur to every one as an instance of this mysterious element in poetry, Poe's ode to Helen is another example, and there are passages in the old prose writers, sentences in Browne and Jeremy Taylor, and sometimes a sudden triumphant word in Ken, which thrill the heart with an inexplicable, ineffable charm. This, perhaps, is the true literature of occultism. These are the runes which call up the unknown spirits from the mind.

But there is a literature which is occult in a more special sense, which either undertakes to explain and comment on the secrets of man's life, or is explicitly founded on mysterious beliefs of one kind or another. Books of this sort have, it is well known, existed from the earliest times; perhaps, indeed, when the last explorer leaves Babylon, bringing with him positively the most antique inscription in the world, he will find an incantation written on the brick or on the rock. It will be said, no doubt, that there would be nothing strange in such a discovery, that early man living in a world which he understood either dimly or not at all, would naturally devise occult causes for occult effects, would imagine that he too by esoteric means could pass behind the veil, and attain to the knowledge of the secret workings of the universe. But we know that such beliefs were by no means peculiar to the Egyptian and the Accadian of prehistoric times, we are able to trace all through the ages the one conviction of an occult world lying a little beyond the world of sense, and probably at the present day, in our sober London streets, there are as many students of and believers in magic, white and black, as there were in the awful hanging gardens of Babylon. But though belief is as fervent as ever, the expression of it has lamentably deteriorated, as may be seen in Mr. W. T. Stead's *Letters from Julia,* written by the hand of Mr. W. T. Stead, which we reviewed some time ago. The modern disciples of Isis speak in a tongue that differs from that of the ancient initiates. They who wish to learn the message of the new hierophant may read the review, or even the book in question, but here, where we discourse of literature and of literature only, we cannot enter into the squalid chapter of back-parlour magic, into the follies of modern theosophy and modern spiritualism. And here we must not even speak of "imposture", for we know nothing of most of these persons, save that they cannot write books.

But this literature of occultism was not always vulgar. Futile, perhaps, it was always, or perhaps, like the ritual of Freemasonry, it did once point the way to veritable enigmas; if it could never tell the secret, it may have whispered that there was a secret, that we are the sons of God and it doth not yet appear what we shall be. But no one could look into the alchemical writings of the Middle Ages and deny them the name of literature. Alchemy, in spite of all confident pronouncements on the subject, remains still a mystery, the very nature and object of the quest are unknown. The baser alchemists—there were quacks and impostors and dupes then as now—no doubt sought or pretended to seek some method of making gold artificially, but the sages, those who practised the true spagyric art, were engaged in some infinitely more mysterious adventure. The Life of Nicholas Flamel is decisive on this point, and Thomas Vaughan, the brother of the Silurist, was certainly not hinting at any chemical or material transmutation when he wrote his *Lumen de Lumine* and the *Magia Adamica.* The theory has been advanced that the true alchemists were, in fact, the successors of the hierophants of Eleusis, that their transmutation was a transmutation of man, not of metal, that their "first matter" was "that hermaphrodite, the son of Adam, who, though in the form of a man, ever bears about him in his body the body of Eve, his wife", that their fine gold, glistening and glorious as the sun, symbolised the soul, freed from the bonds of matter, in communion with the source of all things, initiated in the perfect mysteries. However that may be, there can be no question as to the beauty of the best alchemical treatises, of that strange symbolism which spoke of the Bird of Hermes, of the Red Dragon, of the Son Blessed of the Fire. The curious in such matters may consult Ashmole's *Fasciculus Chemicus,* and the extraordinary *Opusculum* of Denys Zachaire, at once an autobiography and an alchemical treatise.

In the space of an article it is, of course, impossible to sketch out even a brief scheme of old occult literature. We must pass over the Greeks, in spite of the songs of the Initiated that Aristophanes has given us, in spite of that Thessalian magic which Apuleius moulded to such exquisite literary ends. We must decline the question of the origin of alchemy, which a distinguished French chemist has characteristically referred to some misunderstood trade recipes, relating to methods of gilding and bronzing the baser metals. Then there is the great question of the Sabbath. History tells us that in the Dark Ages people were mad about witchcraft, and that they tortured old women till they confessed to anything rather than suffer another turn of the rack. It was a familiar superstition, that of the poor old woman with her black cat, but it may be noted that Payne Knight's monograph on the *Worship of Priapus* throws a very different light on it, and that Hawthorne understood something of the real Sabbath. The terror and the flame of it glow behind all the chapters of *The Scarlet Letter,* and those who can read between the lines see the same red glare in "Young Goodman Brown". We must leave, too, the problem of Rosicrucianism, concerning which Mr. A. E. Waite has said the last words in his *Real History of the Rosicru-*

cians, a kind of historical counterblast to the fantastic and entertaining, but wholly unreliable work by the late Hargrave Jennings. The "Black Mass", which M. Huysmans exploited to such purpose in *Là Bas,* is a degenerate, *décadent* descendant of the mediæval Sabbath, and is really only a revival of the blasphemous fooleries that went on in France about the time of the Revolution, when great persons assembled to adore a toad, which had received "all the Sacraments of the Church". Indeed, there seems to be a constant Satanic tradition in France; in the Middle Ages one finds Gilles de Raiz, and about ten years ago a clever writer described an appearance of Satan in Paris with extraordinary effectiveness, and this, be it remarked, was long before Léo Taxil had invented Diana Vaughan, and the diabolic rites of an inner Masonry. Those who know anything of occultism will be aware that we have scarcely touched the fringes of the subject; we have said nothing of the Kabbala, nothing of the Evil Eye, perhaps the most widespread, ancient, and persistent of all beliefs, nothing of the malefic images, such as "Sister Helen" made in Rossetti's ballad, which are being made in our Somersetshire at the present time by village women who love and hate. And all these beliefs and many others have left deep marks on our literature, and perhaps on our hearts also.

So far our subject has been chiefly the "expository" literature of the secret sciences, we have noted some few of the forms which occultism has assumed, and have mentioned one or two of the leading books and leading cases. The imaginative literature inspired by or dealing with the mysteries is a far smaller field for criticism. Passing by the *Golden Ass* and all the mass of legends and songs that the Middle Ages have given us, doing reverence to King Arthur as we read that "here in this world he changed his life", leaving the strange Hermetic Poems of Sir George Ripley, and that mystical romance the *Chymical Marriage of Christian Rosycross,* we may glance at the fiction of the present century and see how it has been influenced by the occult idea. Sir Walter Scott dabbled slightly in the subject, as he dabbled in most antique and curious things, but occultism to him was merely a "property" with which he decked some of his pages, as he chose to deck his hall at Abbotsford with helmets, and broadswords. *Mervyn Clitheroe,* by Harrison Ainsworth, and the *Lancashire Witches,* by the same writer, are books to make boys quake of dark nights when they pass the black end of the lane, but Bulwer Lytton's *Strange Story* strikes a genuine and original note of terror, and few will forget the appearance of the *Scin Læca,* the Luminous Shadow of Icelandic belief. And perhaps the "Haunters and the Haunted" comes still nearer to perfection, with its theory of the malignant dead, of the instruments by which they work. Hawthorne and Poe, so utterly unlike in most things, were at one in their love of haunting, but while Hawthorne suggested the presence of the infernal army camped all about us and around us, Poe found his terror and awe in the mortal human body, in his theory of a living death. He wrote the story of the corporal frame that rots in death, and thinks while it decays. Those who have read Mrs. Oliphant's *Wizard's Son* have seen a splendid theme spoilt by weak and diffuse execution, but her *Beleaguered City* may stand with Mr. Kipling's very different "Mark of the Beast", that is amongst the little masterpieces of occult fiction. In the one case spiritual awe, in the other panic terror, and the hint of awful possibilities are developed with the extremest skill, and after such successes as these it would be painful to contemplate the sorry imitation, the lath and plaster mysteries of *Mr. Isaacs,* a book which recalls Madame Blavatsky and her sliding panels. At the outset of our article we barred all discussion of "Theosophy", so it will only be necessary to say that Mr. A. P. Sinnett once wrote two novels, which may be Theosophic but are certainly not literature. *Jekyll and Hyde* remains to some of us Stevenson's most perfect work, and it may be that a too obvious undercurrent of allegory is its only flaw. But those who revel in the creations of a bizarre and powerful imagination may perhaps find something to satisfy them in Mr. M. P. Shiel's *Prince Zaleski,* and *Shapes in the Fire,* stories which tell of a wilder wonderland than Poe dreamed of in his most fantastic moments. And *Pierrot,* by Mr. De Vere Stacpoole, stands alone, perfect in its pure and singular invention. We must say at the end as at the beginning that perhaps the true occultism is to be found in the books of those that never consciously designed to write of hidden things, that the "melodies unheard" are the mightiest incantations, that the "magic casements" open on the very vision of the world unseen.

Mr. Algernon Blackwood: Some Brilliant Short Stories

THE LOST VALLEY AND OTHER STORIES. By ALGERNON BLACKWOOD. (Nash. 6s.)

I suppose that everybody recognises a certain influence in landscape. We say, when we get out of London for a few weeks: "Don't these rocks look terrible?" "What a cheerful country!" "Aren't those dark woods depressing?" We say such things and many things like to them, and then the excursion steamer, or the char-a-banc, or the train whirls us away, and we have lunch, and we forget the rocks and the valley and the woods and come home and tell our friends how we have been to an hotel which "does you splendidly at six francs a day—wine included," or perhaps, "haven't had a decent bit of meat since we left England." So we forget and go our ways, and make the sight of strange hills and unknown waters as dull and as insignificant as the daily work which we resume after the holiday is over.

It is Mr. Algernon Blackwood's business—or a chief part of his business—to keep us in memory of those awful heights and Titan woods and utter depths that we have gazed upon and forgotten. And then he does something more; he makes us wonder as to the source of our wonder. We have gone as far abroad as the Canadian forest, let us say; we have felt the awful silence and solitude of those primeval woods sink into the very depths of our being. Or we have been appalled by the icy heights of the Swiss mountains, our souls have been subdued by the stillness of remote valleys which no foot of man has ever touched. We read these files, and we ask ourselves as to the origin of these emotions: why have we trembled at the icy walls, why have we been afraid in the awful depths of the forest?

Mr. Blackwood answers these questions in the language of symbol;

and as the language of science, once appropriate, has become obsolete to-day, there is justification for such a story as "The Wendigo" in the collection of tales before us.

The story is of a hunting party adrift in the trackless forests of Northern Canada. There are a Scotch doctor, his nephew, the divinity student, an American guide, a French Canadian guide, and an Indian cook and handy-man. The author takes us with these people, all ordinary enough, beyond the verge of civilisation, into the very depths of the wilderness, into a solitude that it is difficult for a European to conceive, and then he embodies, in the shape of an Indian legend, the very horror of desolation.

Our immediate ancestors, in their folly, believed, or pretended to believe, that man was solely and simply a logical animal, into whose being you could only pass by the gate of logical demonstration. Mr. Blackwood, more wisely instructed, shows us humanity as a strange and terrible complex of sensations and imaginations and emotions. Take a man away from the lecture-room and set him in the heart of the wild wood, he seems to say, and you will find that he is much more than a syllogising animal. A certain faint odour floating between the trees will become to him a symbol of terror; the sound of the wind will shake his soul to its depths; the shadow of the twilight will appal him. The blackness of the forest midnight will be as a spell. In his soul there will rise emotions that he never dreamed of; terrors and joys that seem to belong to another being.

In a sense, most of Mr. Blackwood's characters have "seen the Wendigo." They are not super-sensual; they have not risen into the world of pure intelligence—if there be such a place at all. Rather, they have been forced to realise, in one way or another, that the whole of the sensuous and material universe is but the veil, the symbol, and the sacrament of things secret and eternal. Not only thoughts are significant, but also sights, and odours, and sounds.

Such are the grounds, then, on which we may justify the art of Mr. Algernon Blackwood—with the art of Edgar Allan Poe. Each deals in vague terrors, and in the shadows that sometimes hang over the stoutest souls, and each, one may say, treats of things which are as truly "real" as death and taxes.

Poe the Enchanter

A Study in Æsthetics

The name of Edgar Allan Poe was once mentioned in Emerson's presence. The age of Concord lifted his eyebrows, and said, "Oh, the jingle-man!" and changed the subject. One understands the point of view; Emerson had read "The Bells" and perhaps "The Raven". Then there are many readers to whom Poe appeals as a capital concocter of "shockers"; others who rather like his detective stories; others who pronounce his work morbid and unnatural; and some who think he was a bad man given to excess in drink. I believe, indeed, that Poe's intemperate habits have excluded him from an edifice in America called the Temple of Fame—a circumstance which must move the Shades to inextinguishable mirth. And it may be as well to say at once that all these criticisms are mentioned that they may be dismissed as impertinences and irrelevancies. Poe is one of the most important figures in the whole history of the fine art of letters, and those who have not been initiated into this mystery must be requested to regard themselves as profane, unfit to approach the shrine and oracle of the great American.

I am glad to find that Mr. Arthur Ransome, author of *Edgar Allan Poe: A Critical Study* (Secker. 7s. 6d. net), is fully possessed of the true faith as to Poe. He analyses the collected works of his author with that subtlety and sense of æsthetic beauty which they demand; he is absolutely convinced of the supreme dignity of the masterpieces on which he comments. And his study is "critical"; it is not a mass of undiscriminating laudation, of that "praise, praise, praise" which is the negation of the critical spirit. And I cannot help announcing my gratification in the discovery that Mr. Ransome feels about Poe as I have always felt. I have always been convinced of the fact that Poe's work is supremely great, that the charm of it is unique in letters; but I should have been perplexed if I had been asked to justify this belief "in black and white", to give plain reasons for the faith that is in me. So Mr. Ransome:

> I had become dissatisfied with my own respect for Poe, because I could not point to tales or poems that accounted for its peculiar character of expectancy. I admired him, but, upon analysis, found that my admiration was always for something round the corner or over the hill.

Well, as Mr. Ransome says, very truly, "an admiration or contempt that we do not try to understand is more humiliating to the mind than none at all", and so he has written this study to justify to himself his sense of Poe's very high value. What is the secret? According to the author, Poe's supreme merit is not to be sought in the excellencies of his poems, or tales, or critical writings, but in the fact that he "tried to teach, even in broken speech, the secret of beautiful things, and the way not to their making only, but to their understanding". Poe's palmary greatness then, according to Mr. Ransome, is as a discoverer of æsthetic principles in literature, and I am not quite sure that I agree. Let it be understood that I quite admit the excellence of Poe's æsthetic work; considering the circumstances of the man's life and his surroundings, considering the nature of the barbarians amongst whose tents he dwelt, to whose deaf, and stubborn, and evil ears he preached his sublime doctrine, considering this reward—poisoned arrows of calumny, and the sharp stones of starvation—considering all this, his achievement in proclaiming the first principles of art was little short of miraculous. He told that stiff-necked generation that the object of poetry is to create beauty, and, consequently, to excite joy in that beauty. To us this is a commonplace; but to Poe's audience it was nonsense, and blasphemous, immoral nonsense, and just the sort of delirious wickedness that you might expect from a man who occasionally took more drink than was good for him. We can laugh at these people whose descendants are apparently in charge of the American Temple of Fame; but I agree with Mr. Ransome in thinking that the prophet who prophesied such things to such an audience is, indeed, an amazing figure.

Still, we must not forget Carlyle's very valuable caution—forgotten by Carlyle himself now and then—that the difficulty or ease with which a thing is accomplished has nothing really to do with the worth or worthlessness of that thing. A bad poem may have been written with great difficulty, and an immortal lyric may have flowed from the pen in an hour or two. Besides, I do not believe that Poe's vision of essential principles in art is the supreme reason for our admiration of his work. I am inclined to think that Mr. Ransome is nearest to the mark in that sentence, "My admiration was always for something round the corner or over the hill." "Over the hill"; exactly. Other writers shew us the hill of our mortality—the side visible to us all; they picture to us the long white road thronged with the pilgrims of this earthly life; but in Poe there is the ever-recurring hint, expressed by mystic symbols unintelligible to the profane, that over the hill there are forms and figures of which we have never dreamed; that round the corner of that road there is an unimaginable country. Take for example the famous "Fall of the House of Usher". Considered from the point of view of the logical understanding, I could not justify my conviction that this is one of the finest stories that have ever been written. Logically, you have here a tale of an old house, of a melancholy brother, of a sister who is apparently dead, who rises from the death-chamber to affright the living, of the brother's madness, and of the house itself falling asunder and crashing down to destruction. Honestly, I cannot say that this plot, *quâ* plot, strikes me as a work of supreme genius. Indeed, I think I could name many better inventions by writers of quite inferior excellence. But read the story and meditate on it; contemplate the extraordinary atmosphere with which Poe has invested the tale; consider the mysterious thrill with which you are affected. You will find, I think, that you experience sensations and emotions similar to those produced by listening to wonderful music; you have been charmed by a certain combination of sense and sound and suggestion, into another world; you have ascended the hill, and looked on a wizard land; you have seen the dread vision that lies beyond the corner of the road. Then there is another tale, called, I think, "A Story of the Ragged Mountains". It is, on the face of it, a tale of reincarnation; and, again, though the thing is deftly done, I cannot find the highest merit in the logical invention of it. But there are a few words descriptive of those forlorn and outland hills, of the mists and heats that brood over them, that sound on the ear like a spell, that echo within the spirit an unknown, unearthly message, from a world that is beyond the veil.

I have spoken of music and of charms and spells; and here, I believe, we must seek for the palmary excellence of Edgar Allan Poe. Allowing him, with Mr. Ransome, all his merits as a discoverer in æsthetics, giving him due praise for invention that is sometimes supremely good, for craftsmanship that is often superb in its accomplishment, I hold that his great secret lies in the fact that he was an enchanter, that he approximated to the primitive incantation which is the essence and fount and origin of all true literature; that his work was of the family of "Kubla Khan". Pater, whom Mr. Ransome calls an unconscious follower of Poe, laid down the far-reaching law that music represents the point to which literature should aspire; it is another way of saying that literature should be an incantation. It should rise, that is, into a world which is above all logical definition, which cannot be explained in terms of the understanding or in terms of common sense, for the good reason that it transcends all these things; it speaks a language that is not of earth; in the last resort it is the communication to mortals of immortal and ineffable beauty. And all through the work of Poe, with varying degrees of intensity and clearness, we can hear the solemn and awful cadences of this inexpressive song. As men in the market-place, buying and selling, cheating or being cheated, speaking of common things in common tones, hear now and again the far-off triumph of the organ, and clear voices chanting the eternal mysteries, so in the tales and poems of Edgar Allan Poe there is a secret sense beneath the open sense, the sound of a voice that is not of man.

The Black Art

The Book of Ceremonial Magic. By Arthur Edward Waite. (Rider. 15s. net.)

"The cesspools of spiritual life and the pit of the second death"—these are the words with which Mr. Waite describes the extraordinary mass of material which he has in this volume edited and elucidated; if a region compounded of Tartarus and Bedlam may be considered as capable of elucidation. Of course there are many people who will chide Mr. Waite for having wasted his time in commenting on these frantic follies. I think that any such persons will be wrong, and for the following reason.

There is deeply implanted in every sane human heart the love of mystery, the desire of wonder. Indeed, it is not too much to say that the man without this desire is no longer a man; for this aspiration for the mysterious, the secret, and the marvellous is but one expression of that quality which makes man to be what he is, which differentiates him from the cleverest of monkeys and the wisest of pigs; and causes a human community, however vicious and senseless, to be something infinitely above the best regulated ant-hill or beehive. It is the sense of wonder which lies behind all religion and every art; it is this consciousness of a hidden, awful, and transcendent reality latent in the whole process of the material universe, from the grain of sand up to the great circle of the starry heavens, that makes us human, and not bestial. Hence it is of the utmost and most vital importance that this sense, that this desire, should be regarded as a pure well of supersubstantial water springing up to eternal life. These fountains, at least, are not to be defiled; no one, if we can help it, shall adulterate the springs of everlasting bliss. Yet, in the nature of the case, when man desires pure drink, there always have been, and always will be, the false taverners and the vintner of Sodom and Gomorrah with their poisonous, "substituted" drenches, their vats holding nothing but venom, who are always ready in the way, who stand in the streets and in the market-places holding out their chalices of perdition and madness. There is Theosophy, there is "New Thought", there is "Christian Science"; there is Spiritualism, "Liberal Christianity", Gnosticism; the list is interminable; to the catalogue of follies, past and present, there is no end. What is the result? The exhibition of these poisons may turn out in one or another of two ways. One man tastes, and, having a strong palate of common sense, perceives that the draught offered him is rubbish and poisonous rubbish. He turns away, loathing; but in too many cases he confuses the adulterated draught with the pure and true springs; perceving that occultism is nauseous nonsense, he includes the veritable marvels in his sentence of disgust, and says in his heart that there is no God, that the world of vision has no real experience. This is bad enough; but the fate of him who swallows what is proffered and rejoices in it, and believes that he has found the truth is even more lamentable; he becomes an occultist; he joins the ranks of that dreary host who march to the land of everlasting nonsense.

Hence the importance of detecting the imposture, of prosecuting the vendors of wicked absurdities with all the rigour of the critical law, of displaying the tomfoolery that lies behind all occultism so clearly and manifestly that the most credulous may see and beware and avoid. This, as I conceive it, is the office of "Ceremonial Magic", and Mr. Waite has well discharged a duty which he has undertaken before. Who has not felt the glamour of the word "Rosicrucian"? who has not cherished a vague but inspiring belief that there was once on a time a secret Rosicrucian Society, and that it did wonderful things? Well, Mr. Waite wrote many years ago a book called *The Real History of the Rosicrucians;* and the famous order evaporates, turns out to be nothing more or less than the *jeu d'esprit* of a German scholar who concocted an entertaining mixture of Lutheranism and Paracelsianism. There never was a Christian Rosencreutz, there never were any Rosicrucians in the proper sense of the word, any more than there was an Abbey of Thelema save in the imagination of Rabelais.

A similar work has been done by Mr. Waite in the book before me. I have often cherished a kind of uncritical belief in the wonder of magic rituals. They may be, and very likely are, utterly futile, I have said to myself, but no doubt they possess a certain weird and awful splendour;

the evocations will, no doubt, fail to bring up an inhabitant of the spiritual world but they will shake the heart with their dark solemnity. So I suffered myself to fancy; finding in the revelations of Madame Blavatsky, in the comment of Mrs. Besant, in the fooleries and trickeries and futilities of spiritualists nothing but tedium; I still harboured a childlike faith in the dignity of ancient magic. And this is ancient magic!—

> PROCEL appears in the form of an angel, and is a great and strong duke. He speaks mystically of hidden things, teaches geometry and the liberal sciences, and at the command of the operator will make a great commotion like that of running waters; he also warms waters and tempers baths. He was of the Order of the Powers before his fall.

He seems to combine the virtues of Mr. Wackford Squeers, of Dotheboys Hall, with those of a bath-geyser. There are better things in ceremonial magic than this specification of a fiend; some of the invocations have a certain ring about them, though the scraps of Hebrew are mostly ridiculously corrupted. But there are also worse things—matters which are disgusting as well as silly; and the languarge which the editor uses to describe his material is not too severe. And if the methods used for compelling the fiend to appear are ridiculous—I have just noticed that in one conjuration the spirit is evoked on the authority of "Genio and Liachide, Ministers of the Tartarean seat, chief princes of the seat of Apologia"!—the uses to which you put your demon when you have got him are squalid and earthly to the last degree. The devil is brought up from the abhorred and flaming lake that the magician may know Euclid without the trouble of learning it, get money without the toil of earning it, and be taught a royal, if infernal, road to the affections of the cook and housemaid. In a word, black magic is stuff, and very sad stuff at that; it is as silly and futile as modern occultism, than which no more dismal sentence may be pronounced.

There are, however, one or two interesting considerations which arise from this book. Firstly, there is the literary and historical point: are the documents illustrated by Mr. Waite "the real thing"? Some of them go back as far as the late Middle Ages; more are concoctions of the eighteenth century, a fruitful period in false doctrines and sick inventions: how far are any of them invented in good faith by people who really believed that by killing poultry and talking a lot of nonsense you could compel the spirits of eternity to become manifest? Personally, I am inclined to think that almost all of the conjurations and evocations and formulæ were "made to sell"; I do not think that the authors of the nonsense believed in it. So far as one can see, the formulæ are the dregs and lees of the Jewish Cabala in its most unworthy aspect; they are the work of a kind of pseudo-scholarship; but one fails to detect in them any real root of genuine popular tradition. There are still those in England who have preserved in lonely cottages, in dwellings by dark woods, and in wild places the ancient tradition of witchcraft. It is still possible, if you know the right quarter, to procure the making and wasting of the waxen man. But those initiated in these secrets know nothing, we may be sure, of the demon Procel, or of the infernal region called Apologia. And there is another aspect of the subject which I hope to treat in some subsequent number of *The Academy*.

Has Spiritualism Come to Stay?

I hope not, and I will tell you why. Four years ago I wrote: "Separate a man from good drink, he will swallow methylated spirit with joy." I was speaking on the curious collective delusion which is best known under the heading of "The Angels of Mons". I was asking how a nation plunged in materialism of the grossest kind had accepted on the vaguest rumours, on evidence that was no evidence, a wild story of the supernatural as certain truth. And my answer to the problem, which I still regard as satisfactory, was this: that it was exactly because our whole atmosphere was materialistic that we were ready to believe anything—save the truth. And then I gave the instance; if a man cannot get good drink he will go to bad drink, and even to the nauseous horror of methylated spirit.

And so far as I remember I gave this answer on general principles as it were. That is, I did not know as a matter of fact that there was such a vice as methylated spirit drinking. And now I find my extravagant instance was no extravagance at all, but the exact literal truth. People have been separated by restrictions and regulations from good drink; and they are drinking methylated spirit. The Liverpool magistrates have been talking of petitioning the Home Office to take some measures to stop a horrible and destructive vice; every other day I see some reference to it in the paper, now a woman goes raging mad, now a boy is all but dead from his dose of methylated.

And practically the same tale has been told, is still being told, in the courts; though here it is not a case of poor folk and their tin of methylated, but of well-to-do people and their "dope"—cocaine, heroin, trional, veronal, morphia, or opium. It may have been necessary in war-time to tell London to go home quietly at ten o'clock, to make the little supper party with champagne at the smart restaurant an impossibility; it may have been necessary to do this, as it was certainly necessary to plunge London into the terrific and perilous gloom of the darkened streets; but the result was none the less certain. The big bottle with the gold foil on it being taken away, the little gold box with the cocaine in it came immediately in its place. And then there is the strange and terrible example of Russia. Russia "went dry" by Imperial ukase. I do not know that Russia has discovered any material poison in place of Vodka, but it has certainly found a spiritual substitute in the form of Bolshevism.

Well, it is clear enough that that proposition of mine as to the results of separating man from good drink is absolutely true in the literal sense; he does take to methylated and cocaine and other horrid and unwholesome drugs. But it is true also in the metaphorical sense in which I first applied it. It was true of the monstrous mass of legend that got itself called "The Angels of Mons" four years ago; and it is true now, I think, of the system of belief and practice which is known as Spiritualism. Just as I cannot open a paper without reading how someone has died or almost died of drinking methylated spirits, of sniffing cocaine, so in another column of the same paper I shall most probably find a paragraph, an article, an interview, or a review dealing with communications, of various orders, which are supposed to have been received from ghosts of the dead.

Of various orders! Sir Oliver Lodge receives a communication from an alleged spirit containing a reference to one of Horace's odes, which, by the way, does not very well fit the facts of the case, since that "blow", the death of Raymond, was not averted. Or more recently, an excellent dissenting preacher has news, per medium, of his son Rupert, killed, as Raymond Lodge was killed, in the war. Or again, Sir Arthur Conan Doyle is present at a sitting with a medium and several other persons. The medium is tied up with ropes, the room is darkened, and things begin to fly about in a manner which strikes Sir Arthur Conan Doyle as inexplicable; save on the assumption that disembodied spirits are rattling tambourines and throwing the medium's coat into the air. Now, I think this is all "methylated".

You can debauch your physical palate. And all sorts of causes have continued to make us at the present day a race of materialists, to deprive us of the faculty of discerning and appreciating the true mysteries of the universe. Darwin confessed towards the end of his life that his imaginative faculty had almost perished, he could no longer relish literature, but only cheap and rubbishy sensational fiction, and Darwin may stand as an example of his age. We are plunged in physical science, and we have tried to put that in the place of religion. Our religious teachers avoid as far as they can the mystic side of the faith and dwell almost exclusively on the ethical or philosophical side of it; and we have tried to put that in the place of religion. And so far has the real meaning of mysticism—which I take to be the heart of religion—been lost that only the other day I was asked what I meant by calling myself a mystic and disbelieving in the miracle of the philanthropic tambourines in the darkened room.

And so I say that those people, the necromancers, as Robert Hugh Benson called them, not being able to obtain or appreciate the veritable wine of the spirit, have betaken themselves to the methylated beverage of spiritualism.

I have been to only one séance in my life, and that began as a joke. A party of five actors found the Sunday evening going rather slowly. One of them suggested a séance. I stood out; the other four sat down at a small table and made a ring of touching hands upon it. The gas was left full on. One of the sitters somewhat profanely—as I consider—recited the Lord's Prayer. They were all of them grinning. But presently I noticed on the face of one of the two women sitters a look of extraordinary eagerness, which presently heightened into a singular aspect which I find some difficulty in describing. There was a certain ecstasy about it; but I would not say that it was ecstasy of a heavenly order. This strange look faded away and was succeeded by an aspect of gloom and depression. The other three went on grinning and uttering—two of them at all events—burlesque evocations to the "dear spirits", till they got bored and returned to the whiskey and soda and cigarettes. There were no "phenomena", no raps, no quaking of the table, no disturbance of anything. But the sitter whose face had looked so strangely told me afterwards that she had at first experienced an acute sense of delight, which was succeeded by deep horror. Then she had felt as though an icy wind had blown upon her, and at the same time as though a dear friend, dead some three years, was present. And she told me also that she had very steadfastly resolved never again to take part in such business.

I tell this story to point my belief that Spiritualism is not all knavery, fraud, and conjuring. Occasionally, I have no doubt, as at this exceedingly informal and irreverent séance in the actors' rooms at Bath, something happens. I do not know what that something is. I do not begin even to conjecture what it may be. But the sitters, I am willing to believe, do, very occasionally, lay unskilled, blundering, ignorant hands on some concealed door in the house of life and produce queer results—just as a child meddling with the works of a clock will also produce queer results, perhaps making the clock go backwards, perhaps causing it to strike 201 at noon; but, clearly, not doing the clock any good, or improving its time-keeping qualities.

There begins and ends my "belief" in Spiritualism. As for its formal revelations and communications: they cannot be true. For even the dullest of us here in the flesh have our rare moments of exaltations and of spirituality. We will not believe that the casting off of the muddy vesture of the body condemns the spirit to an eternity of platitude, to a dulness and insipidity which would arouse comment in the most limited company of the dullest country town.

These spirits are "methylated".

An Ancient Mystery

In this authoritative and final volume on the matter of Alchemy,* Mr. Waite, who has known all the cities and castles and temples of the magicians, has to deal with a most curious and entrancing hypothesis. This hypothesis owes its existence mainly to an obscure writer, Mary Anne South, afterwards Mrs. Atwood, who in the year 1850 published a volume entitled *A Suggestive Inquiry into the Hermetic Mystery.* No sooner had the book been issued than the author felt that she had told too much and spoken too openly. The book was withdrawn from circulation; it was said, I think, that there were only twenty-five copies in existence. It enjoyed a sort of cryptic fame well worthy of its subject, and I remember looking into a copy that came my way with a very eager curiosity. I retired beaten; the book was as luminous as a London fog—that is, where all detail and logical exposition were concerned.

But the main thesis was certainly, as I have said, an entrancing one. In brief it is that alchemy is a sublime allegory. The object of the alchemist is not to make gold; it is to make himself divine or all but divine. The lead that he is to work on is himself, undeveloped, imperfect humanity, full of impurities; the gold, glistering and glorious as the sun, which is at last to be discovered in the crucible, is the perfect man, as gold which is tried in the furnace, purged of all dimness and heaviness and base alloy of earth, and already having his conversation in the heavens. And thus, according to this theory, the technique and terminology of alchemy are purely symbolical. The Gross Work, the Engendering of the Crow, the Birth of Luna, the Red Powder, the Furnace of the Sages governed with wisdom—all these it is true relate to a sure and certain though secret process, but to a process concerned not with lead and mercury, sulphur, salt, and gold, but with the life and spirit

---

**The Secret Tradition in Alchemy: Its Development and Records.* By Arthur Edward Waite. 15s. (Kegan Paul.)

and soul of man. And I may say at once, speaking from my own casual and limited knowledge of alchemical literature, that many passages in the works of the masters are patient of this sense. Again and again the alchemist will break forth, amidst his talk of furnaces and sulphur and antimony, into such songs of praise and thanksgiving to Almighty God, Who sheweth His glorious and marvellous works to them that seek patiently; that it is difficult to believe that the writer is speaking of successful chemical experiments.

But Mr. Waite suffers from two misfortunes—scholarship and honesty. It is his office to shatter our illusions. A short while ago he issued *The Brotherhood of the Rosy Cross,* a work of the most minute and elaborate learning. But no one who has read it can believe in the Rosicrucians any more; in the Rosicrucians, that is, in whom Lord Lytton believed, a secret body of mighty and mystic power, whose very name carried a thrill with it. The brotherhood that survives Mr. Waite's investigation is hardly more mystic or more thrilling than the Society of Antiquaries. And so with Mrs. Atwood's theory; it cannot survive the assaults of the scholar in alchemy. The alchemists of history were men who tried to make gold, the gold that we once knew in sovereigns and half-sovereigns, the precious metal; and perhaps some of them succeeded. And as to those songs of praise and thanksgiving to which I have alluded, how are these to be explained? I give the answer in the author's admirable words:

> "We may find that their furnaces were erected occasionally 'on a peak in Darien', and that through the smoke of their coals and their chemicals they beheld illimitable vistas, where the groaning totality of Nature advanced by degrees to perfection. 'A depth beyond the depth and a height beyond the height' opened beneath and above them, and glimpses of glorious possibilities in all the kingdoms overlighted their barbarous language and transfigured their strange symbols. . . . In those days a world of wonder opened wherever any quest began, because it was ever pursued in a great unknown, the unmeasured cosmos of Nature, where never a plummet could sound the vast abysses and never a shaft of light penetrate the starry height. The occasional greatness of alchemical literature is accounted for in this manner . . . the work which they watched in alembics was for them like God's work in Creation, when there was 'darkness upon the face of the deep'. . . . For them also, or

> many who ranked among them, it was like the work of redemption and the work of God in the soul."

That is the end of the matter, and the solution of one of the greatest difficulties of alchemical literature.

Mr. Waite, then, destroys the fantastic, though alluring hypothesis of the "Suggestive Inquiry into the Hermetic Mystery", but to do so he is forced, very fortunately for the reader, to traverse and survey the whole history of alchemy from its very obscure and dubious origins onward. Obscure and dubious, for the first traces of it are to be found in a Greek papyrus attributed to the third century of our era. This is a technical handbook of metallurgy, with formulæ for the composition of alloys, recipes for gilding, silvering, bronzing and so forth; the note-book of an artisan, as Berthelot, the famous French chemist, calls it. And briefly Berthelot's conclusion is that these trade recipes, falling into later and more barbarous hands, were misunderstood. The early craftsman would have said: "This is the way to make lead look like gold"; the man of a later time misread the text into "This is the way to turn lead into gold." Mr. Waite thinks that there was more than this in the generation of alchemy; that from the beginning there was a sense of the transmutation of metals being a high and magic art. I should not dare to dispute with him; but I would insinuate that there are periods and states of man when there is a tendency to involve the simplest processes in a veil of magic and secrecy. In my own county forty years ago, and to this day, for all I know, there was a sacred magic in the killing of a pig. The beast was always slaughtered under the waxing moon; else its flesh would wane and shrivel as the moon waned. How many *paters* and *aves* did Don Quixote recite during the concoction of the Balsam of Fierabras? I remember reading that certain Arabs tried to keep their discovery of Quadratic Equations a close secret; I heartily wish that they had succeeded. So I would urge that the occurrence of magical formulæ in these early alchemical tracts is hardly evidence that the work was regarded from the first as a wonder of the Most High.

And one word more: everyone should read the legend of Nicholas Flamel and Pernelle his wife. It is not merely an important alchemical document; it is an enchanting romance.

Detective Stories and Real Life

It was in the Tremendous 'Nineties. I had just been introduced to Mr. Henry Harland, and had been expressing to him the very great pleasure with which I had been reading his exquisite story, *Mademoiselle Miss*—a much better book, as I think, than the more famous *Cardinal's Snuffbox*. My observation on this topic went very well; every fellow likes a hand, as Mr. Foker so justly observed to the young Pendennis. But a little later in the talk I blundered badly. I said I enjoyed "Sherlock Holmes". Mr. Harland looked incredulous and contemptuous. "Not really?" he said, with a very cold gaze in my direction. But I stood by my word, and thereby, I believe, lost all hope of being asked to write for the *Yellow Book*.

And I still stand by my word, both as to "Sherlock Holmes" and to all good detective and mystery stories. For all such tales are profoundly true to life, as true to life as the gossamer webs of psychology spun by Henry James and his school, and to me, at all events, of far more vivid interest. I know that there is an assumption that sitting in drawing-rooms and experiencing tenuous and subtle emotions which do not lead anywhere in particular is life, while obscure and mysterious crime is not life. But this is an assumption and nothing more; and it is demonstrably a false assumption. Mysterious crimes and enigmatic events abound in history and in the daily paper.

Take the Campden Wonder, of which Mr. Masefield made a play. A respectable land-agent goes for a stroll and disappears. His hat, his hands, and his comb are found by the roadside, and his hands are bloody. Whereupon his man-servant accuses himself, his brother, and his mother of murdering Mr. Harrison, the land-agent. No body is found, but the three are duly hanged. And in a little under two years Mr. Harrison came back and said he had been seized by unknown men, taken to Deal, and shipped as a slave to Smyrna.

Then there is the disappearance of Sir Benjamin Bathurst, Ambassador Extraordinary to Vienna, who vanished awfully in the twinkle of an eye from Perleberg in Prussia, in the year 1809, whose exact fate is uncertain to this day. And then, in low life, there is the mystery of Elizabeth Canning, the little servant-girl of the seventeen-fifties. She disappeared from the London streets, and reappeared in a month's time with a tale of adventures that nearly hanged an old gipsy-woman. Elizabeth's story was all lies; but nobody knows nor ever will know where Elizabeth spent that January of 1753. And, at the moment of writing, the papers are occupied with two strange and obscure murders in England, and a series of crimes, with no apparent motive, in Germany. All this is, evidently, life, and a proper subject for the writer.

In the broad sense, then, the detective story and the mystery story are true to life, so far as their subject matter is concerned. But I would not maintain that the methods of the detective of fiction are those by which actual crimes are usually detected. In actuality, I am told, the first thing that Scotland Yard does is to run over its list of criminals, to decide from the style and manner of the crime to whom it may probably be attributed, and then to ask A, B, C, and D to account for their movements on the night of the robbery or the murder. Here we have rather the methods of the art critic, pronouncing against a reputed Rembrandt or in favour of a questioned Vandyke than the chain of deduction and inference in which Dupin and Sherlock Holmes excelled.

But, it will be noted, this most sensible system only applies when the deed is the work of the habitual criminal. If the outsider, the mere lawful citizen, suddenly commits murder; if, again, there is no obvious motive for the crime; then the Yard is often baffled and sometimes, one may surmise, the murder is not accounted murder at all, but passes for death from natural causes.

But, considering Sherlock Holmes and his tribe from the viewpoint of actuality, the weakness of their method no doubt lies in this: that the criminal puzzle is like the crossword puzzle; it may have many possible solutions. Poe, who invented this literary mode, as he invented the mode of pirates and the mode of the cipher and the mode of terror, once tried his method of deduction on a case in real life. "The Mystery of Marie Roget" was, in fact, the mystery of Mary Rogers, a New York girl who was found murdered. Poe transferred the scene from New York to Paris, and with an exquisite chain of reasoning brought home the crime to a naval officer.

Nothing could be more convincing than his series of inferences; but the conclusion was false, and the naval officer innocent. And so we may say of the affair of the Rue Morgue: Dupin deduces an ape from the fact that all the persons who hear the murderer's voice declare that the words were in some tongue that was unknown to them. The Frenchman who knew no German thought the language was German, the Italian who knew no English thought it sounded like English, and so on. Hence, Dupin infers, the sounds heard were of no human speech, and thus he comes to his ape. Very well, indeed, in fiction; but in fact a Gaelic speaking Highlander or a big black man with an African idiom might well have been the criminal.

The method of the detective in fiction, therefore, is seldom that of actuality. But we gladly bear with this departure from fact for the sake of the pleasure that it gives us. Art must have its conventions. Nobody ever talked in hexameters or in blank verse—save Mrs. Siddons, who said at dinner: "I asked for water, boy, you give me beer"—yet we are very willing to bear with the rolling hexameters of Homer and Virgil, and with the blank verse of Hamlet and Macbeth. And so we may rejoice freely in the most intricate and elaborate chains of detective reasoning, and question them no more than we question *Infandum, regina, jubes renovare dolorem* or *To-morrow, and to-morrow, and to-morrow.*

But this admitted and allowed for, I am all for the rigour of the game. I am quite ready to admit that Sherlock Holmes had "written a little monograph on the ashes of 140 different varieties of pipe, cigar, and cigarette tobacco", and that he was thus enabled to identify the ash (in "The Boscombe Valley Mystery") as the product of an Indian cigar, "of the variety which are rolled in Rotterdam". This I accept; but I cannot accept Dr. Watson as a General Practitioner.

> "What do you think, Watson? Could your patients spare you for a few hours?"
>
> "I have nothing to do to-day. My practice is never very absorbing."
>
> "Have you a couple of days to spare?" . . .
>
> "I really don't know what to say. I have a fairly long list at present."
>
> "Oh, Anstruther would do your work for you."

And Watson rattles away to Paddington.

No practice would stand it, and Watson would be lucky if he did not get into grave trouble for gross neglect of his patients. I think I would have caused Watson to engage in research work, say, on "Some Varieties of Malaria peculiar to Afghanistan". Such a task might well be dropped for a couple of days without endangering human life.

And there is a serious offence and dereliction into which some detectives—never Sherlock—are apt to fall. They allow love to enter into their activities; they become maudlin over some young woman whom they have not known for more than half an hour. This is a deadly error. In a good detective story there should be no love interest, or at most, an entirely subordinate one.

I have no patience with the method of most American detective fiction. This consists in the casting of the strongest suspicion on the murdered man's wife, his brother, his uncle, his doctor, his solicitor, and his best friend; all in turn, one after another. Finally, it turns out that the deed was done by the boy who cleans the knives, or, perhaps, by the postman.

The good detective story and the good mystery story are always simple in their issues. There is one question in *The Moonstone:* "Who stole the jewel?" There is one question in Stevenson's great mystery tale: "What was the link between Dr. Jekyll and Mr. Hyde?" There is one question in the best of the Sherlock Holmes series: "What was the Speckled Band?"

The Line of Terror

On the Edge. By Walter de la Mare. Faber and Faber. 10s. 6d.

When the hour sounds from the belfry, the strokes sound clear, definite, and distinct in the air. Everyone can hear that it is one, or seven, or twelve, as it may be; and there the matter ends for most of us. But if we listen more curiously, and forget about dinner time and appointments kept or missed, we shall hear between the master strokes of the bell a melodious humming murmur, and this in its turn may be resolved into notes mounting the scale in a fixed and certain order, mounting and still mounting into worlds beyond our sense, into eternity. These sounds are the overtones, they have their analogies in the region of the arts, with a difference. For in the affair of the bell founders, the overtones are only of this importance, that the tuners have to take them into account if the bell is to be perfectly in tune; otherwise they are a mere by-product of the great stroke; incidental, not essential. But the arts exist for their overtones; it is by their presence or absence that we distinguish genius from talent. It is the main business, nay the only business, of the bell to tell us that it is twelve o'clock, but it is not the main business of Tennyson to tell us that Ulysses and his companions came into the land of the lotus eaters at some time after that hour. In the one case, the overtones are accidental; in the other, they are essential. It is the affair of the clock to tell us the time; it is the affair of the arts to take us out of time into eternity, into that region which is beyond the world of the logical understanding, beyond the power of direct utterance.

And yet, in the art of literature certainly, in the arts of painting and sculpture probably, the great stroke—to continue this bell analogy—must be clearly enunciated, with no doubtful sound. It is hard to believe that the Augustus John portrait of Madame Suggia suffers in any way from its being, quite evidently and undeniably, a picture of a woman playing the violoncello; it is hard to think it would have been a still greater masterpiece if it had looked rather like a tiger under a palm tree. But however this may be with painting and sculpture, it is certainly not true in prose literature: the finest work is defined. It need not be scientifically true. It is not scientifically true, as it happens, that human eyes and bones, when submerged at a depth of thirty feet, become pearls and coral; but the poet, though mistaken, is clear and definite in his statement. Poetry, it is true, has a larger licence in this matter than prose, since poetry is a near approach to that primitive incantation from which all literature proceeds. There is a certain confusion in the narrative of "Kubla Khan"; and the magic casements charmed by the song of the nightingale are misty. And it might be urged, perhaps, in some quarters that Mr. de la Mare has availed himself of his poet's licence in writing some of the curious and beautiful short stories in *On the Edge*. There is an everlasting question that besets not the minor but the major decisions of criticism. It is a simple thing to dismiss "Standing at the buffet in immaculate evening dress he selected a dozen of the succulent bivalves." It is more difficult to decide whether a clearer definition would have improved "A Recluse", one of the most singular of these singular studies.

In this tale the narrator, "Mr. Dash", is motoring one May evening along a country road, when he is strangely drawn by the appearance of a house seen through high gates of wrought iron. Mr. Dash, I say, was drawn to this house, but hardly by the attraction of love. It had about it those veils of mystery, that sense of *aliquid latet,* which haunt certain visible things: houses, trees, gardens, the shape of hills, secret and silent valleys:

> To all appearance it was vacant, but if so, it could not have been vacant long. The drive was sadly in need of weeding; though the lawns had been recently mown. High-grown forest trees towered round about it, overtopping its roof—chiefly chestnuts, their massive lower branches drooping so close to the turf they almost brushed its surface. They were festooned from crown to roof with branching candelabra—like spikes of blossom. Now it was daylight; but imagine them on a still, pitch-black night, their every twig upholding a tiny, phosphoric cluster of tapers.

Mr. Dash drives his car past the iron gates, and strolls by the terrace of the quiet red-brick Georgian house, with its singular hint of undefined mystery, and discovers that, after all, it is still tenanted. The owner, Mr. Bloom, a heavy, stooping, bearded man, is standing at the threshold; a bald man, with a domed brow. He greets Mr. Dash courteously, but that gentleman "wanted to shake him off, to go away. He was an empty-looking man . . . if his house had suggested vacancy, so did he; and yet, I wonder."

It is impossible to summarise Mr. de la Mare without committing outrage and injustice; but it must be said that Mr. Bloom lures Mr. Dash into his hall, strangely occupied with a hugger-mugger of fine old furniture, as if an antique dealer were about to flit. Mr. Bloom leaves his guest in the library for a moment, and when he returns Mr. Dash, distressed, uneasy, he knows not why, shakes hands, and in spite of protestations, makes his way to his car. The gear-key is missing; the nearest town is seven miles away; and Mr. Dash must be Mr. Bloom's guest for the night. The two dine together, simply and choicely; and Mr. Bloom speaks of his dead secretary who has been of great use to him in his "literary work"; and then the literary work becomes "little experiments", which yielded "the most curious and interesting results"; and the little experiments are at last defined as the processes of the séances of the spiritualists. Mr. Dash had dabbled a little in spiritualism and thought poorly enough of the results, and spoke of it all as a silly and dangerous waste of time; and his host grew grey with rage. The evening wears on; it becomes apparent that there was some hideous mystery about the death of Mr. Champneys, the secretary; and it is into the bedroom of the dead man that Mr. Dash is shewn. The servant who prepared the dinner is gone for the night: Mr. Dash and Mr. Bloom are the only tenants of the house. Mr. Dash falls asleep, and wakes suddenly with the dawn; and looking about him sees the room as it were drenched in terror: "this is how Mr. Champneys's room would appear to anyone who had become for some reason or another intensely afraid".

And then he heard voices speaking, echoing hollow in some distance of the house; one of the voices Mr. Bloom's, the other like it; and there was the sound of hurrying feet overhead. Mr. Dash goes into the study, and sees there a small bed, and on a table beside it the contents of Mr. Bloom's pocket, among them Mr. Dash's missing gear-key. And the bed:

> The lower part of it was all but entirely flat, the white coverlid having been drawn almost as neat and close from side to side of it as the carapace of a billiard table. But on the pillow—the grey-flecked brown beard protruding over the turned-down sheet—now shewed what appeared to be the head and face of Mr. Bloom . . . it was a flawless, facsimile, waxen, motionless; but it was not a real face and head. It was an hallucination. . . . it was inconceivably shocking.

Mr. Dash flees the abhorred, infested house.

I should have made it clear that Mr. Bloom detained Mr. Dash because he was human, because the horror that the necromancer had summoned from the depths pressed now so thick about him that even his foul soul was shaken and aghast. I should have mentioned also a faint hint that there was some tincture of corruption in the personality of Champneys, the dead secretary: medium, it is to be supposed, was his true title. Such, then, in crude outline, is the story of "A Recluse". Would it have been a better tale if it had been told more definitely? I leave that an open question.

Is the purely personal objection valid? I am not quite clear as to this; but I am bound to confess that I have such an objection to make against "A Recluse". It is this. The word of the enigma is, clearly, spiritualism; and no structure built on that basis can appal me, or enchant me, or make my breath come quickly, or, indeed, win the faintest interest from me. I take the word of the spiritualists themselves, that the seance is a homely, friendly, and helpful institution; that the spirits are as harmless and playful as kittens, and, sometimes, as helpful as big St. Bernards and Church Workers. No tale that begins with a planchette, a hidden slate, or a rapping table can make me quail. Whence another of the stories in the book, "Crewe"—. In that tale there is a scarecrow which is luminous, but not in the light of the sun—a hideous terror.

The Other Side

The Supernatural Omnibus. Edited by M. Summers. Gollanez. 5s.
The Place of the Lion. By Charles Williams. Mundanus. 3s.

The question may arise, of course, whether there is any other side; but I do not know that this doubt is of much consequence, so far as literature is concerned. It is certain that, even now, a vast number of people believe firmly in a region beyond the visible and material walls of the world. Many, again, believe vaguely in something that surpasses weight and measure; others are almost convinced that Hamlet was right and that we do not yet understand the whole scheme of the universe. The people who are sure that there is nothing but matter are negligible; and, indeed, the wall against which they lean is behaving in a strange way, and threatening to turn behind their backs first into energy, and then into mind. I think we may fairly assume that for the purposes of literature a ghost is every bit as good as a grocer. The one rule applies equally to both examples: our ghost must be made credible, and so must our grocer. I cannot recall any instance at the moment; but I am sure that the printed page must harbour many grocers who are quite incredible.

The credibility, naturally, must be the credibility of art, not of life. It is a very bad compliment to the writer of a good tale to profess that it must all be true, that he is a reporter of facts. This is the old story of Zeuxis, the grapes, and the birds in another form. We know that the clever effigies of the waxwork are not sculpture, and that the best of theatre backcloths are not paintings. These aim at delusion; the arts seek to produce illusion. If the scene in the play is well devised, the gallery feels that it could walk up the garden path; but the case of Turner would have to be weighed even more seriously if a man were seen attempting to climb one of his mountains at the National Gallery. Some years ago a good many people tried to climb up a hillock of mine, situate near Mons; and I have been unhappy about it ever since.

Mr. Montague Summers, editor of *The Supernatural Omnibus,* handling this question of credibility in his Introduction, quotes Dr. James. The reader of the story of the supernatural, says Dr. James, must be put into the position of saying to himself: "If I'm not very careful, something of this kind may happen to me!" Very good; but I would rather indicate the right frame of mind by the reflection: "Something like this may have happened a long time ago in England, or may be happening now in Finland or Lapland, or may have happened to that man the Smiths used to talk about." I think we like to keep ourselves out of our favourite ghost-stories, to regard them as possible, perhaps, but not likely to fall into our own experience. And, after all, the credibility of marvellous, ghostly, magical tales is according to another order altogether. In a sense we believe that the pointed splash of white and green and brown paint on the canvas is a mountain 10,000 feet high, though a footrule may assure us that it measures exactly 10¾ inches. And so we begin *The Turn of the Screw*—that masterpiece of the secret world—knowing, if you please, that it is all a pack of lies, and reading ever word of it, rapt out of actuality, only eager to know what happened next, what the end is to be. At the same moment, it seems, we firmly believe and firmly disbelieve; we are in a state of mind that is more mysterious than the most mysterious tale.

And this, I believe, is the state of mind which the artist in wonder should endeavour to induce in his subject, the reader. There are all sorts of ways and methods and means of doing this; and, as usual, all sorts of opinions as to the right way and the wrong way. Mr. Summers holds that amongst living artists in his kind the most successful are Dr. James and Vernon Lee; and, so far as Dr. James is concerned, at all events, I believe he has the great majority of readers with him. I differ profoundly from this judgment. Both these writers are scholarly in their knowledge and in their manner of using it, but their tales seem to me academic exercises in ghostly things. They say "Open barley," "Open oats," "Open wheat," with exact, measured, and melodious accents; but never "Open sesame": and the door into the wonderful cave remains closed. Dr. James is not represented in *The Supernatural Omnibus;* but there is a tale by Vernon Lee, called "Amour Dure". I had no sort of belief in the magic *idolino* or in the ghost, and read on without a shudder, but when all was done I felt mildly instructed in the ways of the Italian Renaissance. So far as living authors are concerned, I support with all enthusiasm the claims of Mr. Algernon Blackwood. There is a story in *John Silence,* a story of modern times, about certain evil brethren of a German teaching community, workers of all abomination in the flesh and in the spirit, long shamefully dead, but restored to a horrible life and to their nameless operations for a brief season. The apparition of Asmodelius, the Hauptbruder—his true name, as Mr. Blackwood knows, is Aschmoddai—is a terror that is worthy to be compared with the appearance of the young man with eyes of infinite sadness in "Aut Diabolus aut Nihil". And, again, there is the tale of "The Willows" by the same author. In this all the old rules, all the old technique, of the occult game are laid aside. "The Willows" grow in an undiscovered country, uncharted by any explorer before Mr. Blackwood. Two young men are camping on an island on the Danube. It seems one morning that there is a willow bush where there had only been bare sand the day before; and day by day the willows draw nearer and nearer to the camp. The terror is vague, inexplicable, without precedent in the science of the shadows: and all the more dreadful for its vagueness.

Without precedent; but I think it might well be made a precedent for future explorers of the world beyond the veil. Let them forget all they have learnt of the occult sciences, all the familiar formulæ which are too familiar to strike awe any longer. It is a doubtful speculation; but it is barely possible that the ghosts, the elementals, the familiar spirits, the possessing spirits, the fairies, all the mythology, as it were, of the other side are personifications, the best that could be found, it may be, of forces that veritably exist, though they can neither be named nor known. For example, I have never been able to make up my mind as to that too familiar spirit, the poltergeist. For all I know it may be nothing but trickery. It may be that adolescence all over the world—though that is mysterious enough—is irresistibly moved to fling things about, to smash, to bump, to break, to make itself extremely unpleasant and inconvenient. It may be also that this universal adolescence is gifted with the trick of doing this so secretly that the method is not found out. This may be the explanation: or possibly not. But at all events I prefer it, since, as I say, it is sufficiently mysterious, to the official talk of elementals, which explains nothing and pretends to explain everything; which assumes a science where there is, in fact, no science. Nothing is more irritating than the occultist who talks with the assurance of an analytical chemist. The true point of view, I would suggest, is to regard the human cosmos as a world with undiscovered, unconjectured regions, as the centre of powers of which we know nothing or next to nothing, of forces which are only manifested rarely, in one individual, let us say, out of a hundred thousand, or, if you like, out of a million. Spiritualism is a doctrine concerning the dead and a science of summoning the spirits of the dead. I believe no word either of the science or the doctrine; I have no doubt that a vast proportion of the spiritualistic phenomena are produced by deliberate fraud. But I am inclined to think that there is a certain remnant of manifestations with which fraud is not concerned; and behind the raps and apports of the séance and the bangs and the projections of the poltergeist I suspect there is a common cause. Here, I would submit, is the dim and shadowy and half-conjectured field most fit for the inventor of strange tales.

And so with the fairies; they have been photographed of recent years, and the camera has thoroughly confirmed the views of producers of pantomime as to gauzy wings, short skirts, and so forth. And the late Mr. Sinnett, the eminent theosophist, knew all about them. He explained that they were employed in flower-fertilisation, and were about intelligent as a Newfoundland dog. But, apart from these follies, there are, perhaps true fairy tales. There appeared in *Light* some months ago an account of the adventures of a party of six tourists who climbed Mount Nephim in County Mayo, in July, 1929. The story is too long to tell here; but it is an extraordinary one. The travellers were beguiled, illuded, led astray. They heard the sound of crying, as of a lost child. "Someone laughed"; but no laugher was to be seen. "She said it was as though there were *no time* for a moment, and some strange force were pulling her away: she does not know, cannot possibly imagine, what happened to her."

And I do not know, cannot possibly imagine, what happened to her. But I believe her story; and I would direct the teller of wonders to seek the heights of Mount Nephim—without a camera, without a manual of theosophy.

Here, at least, is one who has adventured into untrodden territory. I do not think that Mr. Charles Williams, in his *The Place of the Lion,* has succeeded in bringing down the archetypes, the creative Ideas, from their platonic heaven to the earth; but it is a brave adventure.

The Fair Folk

Fairies in Books and Fairies in Reality

I wonder whether Mrs. Murray, author of *The God of the Witches,* is right in maintaining that the "thumbnail fairies", the little people conceived sometimes almost as motes in the sun, sometimes as tall as two or three inches, were a pure Shakespearean fantasy and invention, without a history or a tradition before the writing of the *Midsummer Night's Dream* and *Romeo and Juliet.* It is a curious point, and perhaps we should await the results of further research before we come to a firm conclusion. But, pending the possible production of evidence on the other side, I should be inclined to think that Mrs. Murray is justified in holding that Pease Blossom and Mustard Seed and the rest of them are poetic inventions, not adapted and decorated figures from age-old legends. It will be noted that Shakespeare was not severely consistent in his delineation of the fairy realm: Oberon and Titania are conceived as of human height. And when Falstaff is to be tormented by fairies in Windsor Forest, it is the Windsor children who impersonate the Little People.

Mrs. Murray holds a view that has been advanced before. She thinks that the fairies of the genuine old tradition are really historical figures; the Stone Age people who inhabited these islands before the Celtic invasion of the Goidels and the Brythons. The existence of such a people is, of course, certain; indeed, their descendants survive to this day in Wales and Cornwall, Ireland and Scotland. They were a small people compared with the broad, big Celt. They were dark, with sallow skins and black hair. And they often lived underground. Not long ago a fairy rath, known as such by perpetual tradition, was excavated in Ireland. There was the deep place, hollowed out in the earth, where the little dark people had lived, and a shaft, once communicating with the hilltop above, confirmed the tales still told by the country people of those who had imprudently ventured near the place at night, and had seen flames leaping from the summit of the fairy fort. This stronghold, so the evidence shewed, had been raided by the Danes somewhere about the ninth century. Perhaps the dark folk returned to their secret castle later, and remained there for centuries. If not, the folk memory of wild Ireland must be long indeed, to remember those mysterious fires for nine hundred years.

It is not, then, a mere hypothesis, it is an ascertained fact, that a dark, short race dwelt in concealment, in wild and outland country, with their conquerors established in the more fertile plains. There was, to some extent, intercourse between the two races. Perhaps the tales of knights and poets and kings who sought the Queen of the Fairies in her hidden house may be gilded and ornate versions of actual, but less magical visits. It is likely enough; and it is highly probable that the Irish peasant and his wife who left their fair-headed baby fast asleep in the crib by the fire may have found on their return a little black, wizened creature in the lost child's place. On the whole, I am always inclined to believe in tradition, if it can be shewn to be undoubtedly ancient and of the soil. Traditions invented by idle men of letters about 1840 are a very different thing. But the people who said that fire had been seen at night above the fairy castle have been proved to be truth-tellers; it is probable, then, that these same people are also speaking the truth when they tell of changelings, and of men who imperilled their souls by living with the Fairy Queen.

And here we tome to a point which further and more emphatically differentiates the Daoine Sidhe (good folk) of Ireland and the Tylwith Têg (beautiful folk) of Wales from the literary inventions of Shakespeare and Herrick and their successors, even to the pretty, moral little fairy tales of yesterday, and the fairies of the Christmas Pantomime. The literary fairies are emphatically good little people. They are fantastic but their fantasy is kind and almost pious. In Shakespeare they are a little mischievous but never malignant. In the modern tales they may sometimes play tricks with children; but the tricks have always a good end in view. They tend to correct bad habits; they demonstrate in their odd fashion that the biting of nails and the leaving of rice pudding on the plate cannot lead to happiness. Indeed, one would almost suppose that the Good Fairy had conferred with Mamma and Nursey before putting her ingenious schemes into operation. Fairy Godmothers, it is true, have sometimes queer tempers, but they mean well, and generally do the handsome thing in the end.

There, roughly, you have your literary fairy. Now for the other side.

The year before the war I was being driven along a road leading from Belfast into hilly country by a good Belfast citizen, a solid man. I think he was an actuary, or he may have been an auditor: it was something very serious and practical at all events. His political colour was Orange. Like a good newspaper reporter, I took note of the sights by the way; of the general lack of flower gardens, for instance. But there was something considerably odder than all this.

"The people here," I said at length, "seem very fond of the mountain ash. Every house seems to have one in front of it."

"Well," said McAfee, "the fact is, they think the mountain ash keeps out the fairies." He smiled, and added: "And you'll see a good many of them round that little place of mine that I'm taking you to."

And I remembered how an old Monmouthshire farmer, talking of old days and old ways, had told me that people used to put boughs of May outside the door, "to keep out the fairies—a lot of silly old superstitious nonsense, no doubt", he added, fearing that I should think him a fool for even mentioning such absurdities.

Here, then, is the great distinction between the fairy of the printed book and the fairy of ancient popular tradition. The Daoine Sidhe and the Tylwith Têg were called "good" and "fair" and "beautiful" precisely because they were known to be evil, dark, and terrible; precisely as the prudent Greeks did not talk of the Furies, but of the Kind Ladies. The true fairies were beings to be shuddered at. Miss Œ. Somerville, the incomparable author (with the late Miss Martin) of *The Irish R.M.*, tells of an old family servant who once had his harness mended by two "quare" little men, and how he shook with dread at thought of the adventure.

Are we to conclude, then, that the genuine fairy tradition is a tradition of the dark, pre-Celtic people, who lived under the hills? Largely, perhaps; but I believe that there is something more. A party of tourists, who climbed Mount Nephim in county Mayo, about July 20, 1929, were strangely misled and bewildered by "small persons" who looked like children—but were not children.

Magic Still Flourishes

A magistrate from Rhodesia was once telling me a number of interesting things about the people he helped to govern. Among other matters, he imparted this odd bit of information. "There's no such thing," he said, "as natural death for the natives. On the face of it, a black man may seem to die of enteric, or small-pox, or heart disease. He may be crushed by an elephant, or torn by a lion, or bitten by a snake. You and I would think so, but the black man and his friends know better. There is only one cause of death; and that is witchcraft in one form or another. The snake and the elephant and the lion are simply wizards who have assumed animal forms; the various diseases are spells laid on the man by a magician."

Well, that is one way of looking at things; and perhaps this would be the right spirit in which to read Mr. Ahmed's book on *The Black Art.** You take Black Magic and Incantation as the background of the universe; and away you go into a world far removed from nature as we know it, or as we think we know it.

But there is another consideration before we plunge into this great chaos of necromancy and illusion, before we gaze into the witches' cauldron. The other day I was reading a masterly account of half-a-dozen English Messiahs, beginning with poor Nayler, the seventeenth-century Quaker, and ending with Smith-Pigott of the day before yesterday. And the point that struck me as extraordinary was not the craziness of the Messiahs, but the credulity of their disciples. It is a fact commonly and widely known that some men and women go raging mad; and we can only do the best we can for them, see that they do not harm themselves or others, and try to restore their sanity. But the true marvel is when these demented unfortunates find people to credit their wildest delusions.

**The Black Art.* By Rollo Ahmed. (John Long, 6s.)

When Brothers, formerly a lieutenant in the Navy, discovered his Messiahship, and proposed to take up his Kingdom at Jerusalem at the head of a great army, a member of Parliament, who had been Sheridan's close friend, and had been also an intelligent and valuable Indian Civil Servant, rose in his place in the House of Commons, and wished to know whether the Government intended to give Messiah Brothers proper support. Still more strange: a well-to-do Scotch lawyer, presumably a keen man of affairs, sold his practice, came down south, and spent the rest of his days and all his money in fighting for the cause of a hopeless and manifest lunatic. We have not changed: money, a great deal of money, is being spent to-day in the support of causes of much the same order.

"What is he prepared to swear?" Mr. Jaggers asked Mike.

"Well, Mas'r Daggers," said Mike, "in a general way, anythink."

And many of us are prepared to believe, in a general way, "anythink".

With this caution, let us plunge into Mr. Ahmed's cauldron. Everything of a magic kind is in it; the Black Art is exhibited in all its branches. Antediluvians, men of the East, ancient and modern, old Egyptians, Jews meditating Kabbalistic wonders in the darkness of the mediæval Ghetto, Greeks and Romans in their less austere moments—though I miss the story of the man who got hold of the wrong ointment and was turned into an ass instead of into an owl; the Satanists of the Middle Ages, and their weak or rascally imitators of to-day, alchemists and sorcerers in Europe, yogis and fakirs in India: the Evil Eye, the Vampire, the Werewolf, the Waxen Man that Sister Helen made, down to the mere Dowser, who is now sometimes paid a salary by the contractors—all are here. And there are some good recipes. Do you want a good, strong potion, such as Mr. John Wellington Wells supplied?

> For the most part such were composed of herbs like Artemisia, Hemp, Camphire, Flax, Coriander, Anise, Cardamour, Aloeswood, and Chicory. The purpose of the mixture was to make apparitions appear. A concoction founded on a basis of animal matter consisted of a Lapwing, Lion's Gall, Bull's Gall, the Fat of a White Hen, Eyes of a Black Cat, and Ants' Eggs all had to be boiled together according to the ancient manuscript in which the charm was found. Aromatics were used too, especially

> in necromancy, and an old recipe of that sort comprises Musk, Myrrh, Frankincense, Red Storax, Mastick, Olibaniun, Saffron, Benzoin and Labdanum. . . . Witches always anointed themselves with ointments before departing up the chimney to their Sabbaths. One such ointment was composed of Aconite, Belladonna, Water Parsley, Cinquefoil, and Babies' Fat.

And again; here is the fashion in which Paracelsus made his artificial men "called 'Homunculas'"—or, as I should prefer to call them, Homunculi.

> The necessary spagyric substances having been obtained, they were shut up in a glass phial and left to incubate in horse-dung for forty days. At the end of that time, something was found to be living in the phial, and that something was a man, but transparent and without a definite body. This creature consolidated and grew if fed with human blood consistently for forty weeks, by which time it would have developed into a child, but much smaller and needing more care than the usual human variety.

The magic of the Middle Ages was, as might be expected, richly ceremonial. Different days of the week were chosen for

> different magical performances, as exemplified in the writings of Abraham the Jew. White magic was to be enacted on Sunday, the magician wearing purple vestments ornamented with gold and jewels. The powers of the Moon were to be invoked on Monday, white vestments embroidered with silver being worn, and the head crowned with a tiara of twisted golden silk. Pearls and crystals, again, were the chosen ornaments, and an incense compound of camphor, aloes, amber, sandalwood, and cucumber seed was to be burnt. For evocations to acquire transcendental wisdom, the vestments had to be of a brilliant green, ornamented with pearls, white hollow glass beads were worn containing mercury.

The passage brings back an odd memory. I have a vivid recollection of a young friend of mine compounding what he called the Incense of the Moon in his chambers in Gray's Inn. Magic, as Mr. Ahmed reminds us, is still a going concern.

Here and there, I must differ from our author. With due respect, the Exorcists of the Church did not enter a circle at midnight, "wearing a new surplice and with a tall pointed cap on their heads on which appeared the ineffable name Tetragrammerton, written in the blood of a white dove. The circle itself was sprinkled with the blood of a black lamb and a white pigeon." Nor did the Exorcist go on "to abjure the spirits of Hell, in the name of Adonai, Eloahin, and Sabaioth". Neither the name Tetragrammerton—it is usually spelt "Tetragrammaton"—nor the blood of lambs or pigeons, nor the names Adonai, Elohim, or Sabaoth are used in the Church Ritual of Exorcism. The object of that Rite is to cast out an evil spirit, and neither the Rite nor the Ceremony is modelled on magical incantations. The Ritual consists in the main of a marshalling of the Hosts of Heaven against the powers of evil.

And I believe that Mr. Ahmed includes too much under his definition of Elementals. Of these he says:—

> First, there are the strange quasi-intelligent thought creations, usually of an evil and malevolent character, that dwell upon the lower regions of the astral plane. Secondly, there are the so-called Nature Spirits. Thirdly, there are the "Shells" or astral simulacra of those whose actual spirits have become sunk in evil to the extinction of the ego.

As I say, the definition is too broad. Elementals are the spirits of the four elements of the old science: Earth, Water, Air, and Fire, which were governed by the Gnomes, Undines, Sylphs, and Salamanders. With these, the modern Thought Forms—a Theosophic invention?—and the Kabbalistic Shells, or Cortices, have nothing to do.

Of these last, Lilith, whom Mr. Ahmed calls "Lilas", is the most illustrious example:—

> Not a drop of her blood was human,
> But she was made like a soft, sweet woman.

Introduction to *Witches and Warlocks*

A few weeks ago, some serious and responsible personage writing to the paper about delusions past and present, dwelt with especial fervour on the witchcraft prosecutions of the seventeenth century. He was horrified at the iniquity of such proceedings, at the wickedness of executing these poor women for crimes which, as he said, they could not possibly have committed.

He meant, I take it, that there was no such thing as witchcraft, that there never had been such a thing, that in the nature of things there never could be any such thing. He meant that when the seventeenth century accused people of witchcraft it might just as well have accused them of breeding Wyverns and Gorgons.

Very well. But I would remark, in the frequent phrase of an old Yorkshire friend of mine: "A don't know about that."

Let me go again to the newspaper, and to the issue of this very day of writing. Here I read:

"A nerve specialist told a representative of the *Daily Telegraph* yesterday that an unusual number of people were going to him for treatment, and there was a big demand for tonics. . . .

"'My experience is' (said the doctor) 'that busy people do not need tonics. They are demanded by people with a good deal of leisure, and no satisfactory way of filling it. I have told some of my patients that a visit to a cinema would probably do them more good than a bottle of medicine.'"

One can imagine the symptoms of the sort of patient that the consulting physician had in mind. They are very distinctly physical. The sufferer feels that his joints have turned to a weak jelly. His head is heavy, as if a weight rested on it. It aches a little. There is a lack of appetite, a general and a most depressing *malaise,* a sense of utter unfitness. So the unfortunate individual consults Harley Street, in the expectation of being given certain vegetable or mineral substances—

quinine, perhaps, or iron, or strychnine—which will remove these distressing physical symptoms, and make him as fit as a fiddle.

And the doctor says: "Go to the pictures." Or, in other words: "There's nothing really the matter with your joints, or your head, or your stomach. The trouble is in your mind. Apply a mental remedy and your physical ailments will disappear."

The mind, that is, has dominion over the body. But the essence of this alleged offence of witchcraft is that certain persons were said to have the power of exercising, and did exercise, an injurious and sometimes fatal mental dominion over the bodies of others. And I suppose there are still parts of Africa where at this very moment black Ngamba and Nbamba are being told by the witch that their days are numbered. Whereupon, the said Ngamba and Nbamba know that doom is upon them and—it may safely be prophesied—will soon be dead. And it is not necessary to go so far as Africa. I was talking a week or two ago to a Portuguese friend. He was telling me about the methods of witchcraft in his country. One of these, he said, was the concoction of certain foul matters made slab and thick with pitch. A portion of this abomination was placed at night on the doorstep of the person attacked by the witch, as a sign that he was "overlooked". And quite recently, my friend proceeded, a wealthy business man of Lisbon, setting forth for his office in the morning, saw the black horror on the step before him as he opened the door. I think the poor man was stout and middle-aged; but he leapt into the air, as if he contended for the High Jump at the Olympic Games. The story went no farther; but it seems to me probable that this Lisbon merchant had little appetite for lunch that day, and that his dinner disagreed with him. And, for all I know, the consequences of this mental shock may have had yet more serious results.

But I have a better instance than this. The story was told me about forty years ago by a friend of mine, a solicitor, a sober man and no dabbler in occult things. The scene is laid in Drury Lane, between the corn-dealer's and the chemist's. In those days, it must be remembered, the horse was still abroad, and I daresay that there were many stables poked away among the purlieus and dark passages about the Lane. By consequence, there was a corn-dealer, who set out his various stores in small bins before his shop window. And the small and villainous boys of Drury Lane delighted to rush past this good man's shop, howling derisively and grabbing handfuls of grain from the bins as they dashed by. The corn merchant was vexed and irritated by these outrages. He set an ambush and caught one of the young ruffians. He threatened the boy with a terrible punishment, and forthwith dragged him to the chemist's shop, which, I think I remember as being at the entrance of Broad Court, leading into Bow Street. Here, holding the criminal tightly the while, he whispered a few words in the ear of his friend the chemist. He gave the boy, already white with terror, an awful glance and went busily to work—or seemed to go to work—with his dreadful Latin bottles on the shelves. Holding a vessel inscribed with unknown characters in his hand, he appeared to the lad to measure terror and destruction into it. He went into the hidden place at the back of the shop and glass was heard clinking. Then he emerged with his hieroglyphic vessel filled with a clear, colourless fluid, and held it to the boy's lips, with the words: "Drink that, you young scoundrel, and you'll remember it to the last day of your life."

The boy staggered away to his home, more dead than alive already. The next morning his foaming mother, accompanied by an officer from Bow Street Police Station, appeared at the chemist's shop. She charged the chemist with having administered to her son a dose so vile and so virulent that he had all but died in the night. She described the symptoms, which were, indeed, severe. For a detailed account of them, read in *Don Quixote* of the state of Sancho Panza, after he had partaken of the Balsam of Fierabras.

The chemist summoned his young man, and between them they were able to convince the constable that the wretched boy had drunk pure distilled water and nothing else. But it is difficult to distinguish this matter of threat and event from many cases of witchcraft, ancient and modern.

But my last example is, perhaps, the strangest of all. The account of it appeared fifty years ago or more in a textbook of medical psychology, and has often been quoted.

A lady was sitting in her garden on a fine summer morning, watching her little girl playing at the open drawing-room window, inside the room. The child—five or six years old, if I remember—presently stopped her play, and leaned forward to speak to her mother, one of her small hands resting on the sill of the window. At that moment, there was the crack of a breaking cord, and to her horror, the mother saw the heavy window frame flash down like the guillotine blade on her child's hand. She fainted forthwith. In the turmoil of the house that followed, the child was found crying but unharmed. She had been quicker than the descending window, and had drawn back her hand in time. Her mother was still insensible, and the doctor was summoned. He soon brought the patient back to consciousness, and she told him the story of the shock she had suffered. She complained that the fingers of one of her hands were painful. The doctor examined the hand and found the fingers red and swollen. In due course the skin broke, and in the exact though unpleasant language of the surgeon: "purulent sloughing set in". In common English: the poor woman's fingers became dreadful sores, reproducing in her (physically) untouched, uninjured member what would have been the state of her child's hand—if the little girl had allowed the heavy window to fall on it.

Of course, I might urge in addition the phenomenon of the stigmata, which a few years ago was regarded as perhaps a mere lie, perhaps a swindling trick, but most certainly not as a plain fact in the natural order. Now the stigmata are accepted by all men of science; as Mr. Gerald Heard said recently, we know that the mind can raise blisters on the body. Still, it has perhaps not yet filtered down into the general consciousness that a passing thought, the emotion of a moment, can do as much harm, and the same sort of harm to the physical human frame as a coal-hammer or the kitchen poker. And let us note this: in theory, at all events, this stroke of thought or emotion must be capable of almost any degree of intensification. It would not have been incredible, or even improbable, if the story of the young guttersnipe of Drury Lane had ended with his agonising death. And supposing that it had been the head, and not the fingers of the little girl that had been under the falling window: would the mother have escaped so lightly? Probably not. The emotion or thought, "my child's hand is terribly hurt" produced in the mother a hand that was terribly hurt. The emotion or thought, "my child is killed" would, it seems probable, have stricken the mother with death.

So far, we are on solid ground. Given certain circumstances, a certain degree of belief, and a certain sensitive habit, it is clear that mind can alter body, as Mr. Heard puts it. Sometimes the result of this mental process may be a mere blister, sometimes, it seems likely, it may be death. And there are cases amongst those recorded by Mr. Sergeant wherein the witch has intimated by a threatening word or look her potent displeasure to the person who presently finds himself bewitched. In such cases as these, the necessary condition or circumstance is the general belief, shared by learned and ignorant, of the malefic powers of the witch. In the seventeenth century, Mr. Sergeant's chief hunting ground, the belief in witchcraft was firm and general. If a woman, whom you held to be a witch, intimated to you that you were under her displeasure and would suffer for it, the high probability was that you did suffer. The Drury Lane boy knew very well that terrible doses sometimes came out of the learned jars and bottles of the chemist at the corner of Broad Court. The lady in the garden knew that a heavy window falling on her child's hand would hurt it most grievously: in all of these cases, old and new, you have that necessary substratum or ground of belief.

So much is firmly established: now we enter on more dubious ground. The next question is: can one person communicate a thought, an emotion, a message, or an image to another, without the use of the ordinary physical means of communication? We are agreed, I take it, that the curse, the threat, the scowl, the menacing gesture of the reputed witch would, probably, result in unpleasant consequences for the person cursed, denounced, or menaced; these consequences ranging from a bad toothache down to death. But could the witch produce the like results without making use of any of the sensible channels of communication? And, put in other words, that question is: are we to regard the theory of telepathy as established? To the best of my belief, that question is to be answered in the affirmative. The matter is too ample and intricate to be argued here, but I do think that there is a large body of solid evidence in favour of the existence of telepathy—the faculty of communicating impressions from one mind to another without using the medium of the senses.

And if that proposition is granted, then the whole ground of witchcraft is accepted. We must be prepared to affirm that it is entirely possible for one human being grievously to afflict the mind and body of another human being by the telepathic transmission of mental impressions. And that is witchcraft.

So much for the theory. Here comes Mr. Sergeant with his account of the practice.

Bibliography

"American Letter." *Literature* 2 (12 March 1898): 292–93 (unsigned).

"An Ancient Mystery." *Bookman* (London) 70 (September 1926): 281–82.

"Aristotle and Art." *Literature* 2 (2 April 1898): 367–68 (unsigned).

"The Black Art." *Academy and Literature* 80 (20 May 1911): 609–10.

"Books of To-day." *Evening News* (London) (12 February 1916): 1.

"Can We Trust Tradition?" *John o'London's Weekly* 35 (12 September 1936): 821–22.

"Detective Stories and Real Life." *John o'London's Weekly* 22 (8 February 1930): 731.

"The Fair Folk." *Independent* 2 (10 February 1934): 21 (as by "Our Literary Critic").

"Farewell to Materialism." *American Mercury* 36 (September 1935): 43–51.

"Folklore and Legends of the North." *Literature* 3 (24 September 1898): 238–39.

"God's Beasts." *Academy and Literature* 82 (20 January 1912): 70–71.

"Has Spiritualism Come to Stay?" *John o'London's Weekly* 1 (18 April 1919): 4.

Hieroglyphics. London: Grant Richards, 1902. London: Martin Secker, 1910, 1912, 1923, 1926 (New Adelphi Library). New York: Mitchell Kennerley, 1913. New York: Alfred A. Knopf, 1923.

"The 'Inhumanity' of Art." *Literature* 2 (4 June 1898): 631–33.

"Introduction to *A Handy Dickens.*" In *A Handy Dickens: Selections from the Works of Dickens.* London: Constable, 1941. vii–xviii.

"Introduction to *Witches and Warlocks.*" In Philip W. Sergeant. *Witches and Warlocks.* London: Hutchinson, 1936. 5–10.

"Jack London the Man." *Evening News* (London) (21 October 1921): 6.

"The Line of Terror." *New Statesman* 36 (11 October 1930): vi, viii.

"The Literature of Occultism." *Literature* 4 (18 February 1899): 181–82.

"Magic Still Flourishes." *John o'London's Weekly* 35 (27 June 1936): 460.

"Man, the Mad Mammal." *John o'London's Weekly* 26 (19 December 1931): 489.

"The Matter of Romance." *Academy* 73 (30 November 1907): 182–84 (unsigned).

"Mr. Algernon Blackwood: Some Brilliant Short Stories," *Daily Mail* (London) (18 June 1910): 10.

"*Le Morte d'Arthur.*" *Observer* (17 December 1933): 6; (4 February 1934): 8 (as "Le Morte Darthur").

"A New War Poet." *Evening News* (London) (9 October 1915): 2.

"The Other Side." *New Statesman* 38 (14 November 1931): xii, xiv.

"The Paradox of Literature." *Literature* 2 (27 August 1898): 180–81.

"Poe the Enchanter." *T.P.'s Weekly* 16 (28 October 1910): 553.

"Poet—and Cockney." *Evening News* (London) (23 February 1921): 4.

"Preface to *Afterglow.*" In Mitchell S. Buck. *Afterglow: Pastels of Greek Egypt, 69 B.C.* New York: Nicholas L. Brown, 1924. 7–19.

"Realism and Symbol." *Academy* 75 (1 August 1908): 109–10.

[Review of *The War of the Worlds* by H. G. Wells.] *Literature* 2 (5 February 1898): 145–6.

"Romance and Reality: An Introduction." In W. J. T. Collins. *The Romance of the Echoing Wood.* Newport, Wales: R. H. Johns, 1937. 1–6.

"Science and Art." *Academy and Literature* 82 (6 January 1912): 8–9.

"Science and the Ghost Story." *Literature* 3 (17 September 1898): 250–52.

"True Comfort." *Academy and Literature* 82 (25 May 1912): 646–47.

"A Vision." *Evening News* (London) (10 October 1916): 2.

"The Wonder from Wales." *Bookman* (London) 87 (November 1934): 90, 92.

www.ingramcontent.com/pod-product-compliance
Lightning Source LLC
LaVergne TN
LVHW020536100826
845148LV00010B/1492

* 9 7 8 1 6 1 4 9 8 3 5 9 0 *